SPEAKING TRUTH TO EVIL

THE MYTHS AND FACTS SURROUNDING TODAY'S SERIAL KILLERS

PHIL CHALMERS

WILD BLUE
P R E S S

WildBluePress.com

SPEAKING TRUTH TO EVIL published by:
WILDBLUE PRESS
P.O. Box 102440
Denver, Colorado 80250

Publisher Disclaimer: Any opinions, statements of fact or fiction, descriptions, dialogue, and citations found in this book were provided by the author, and are solely those of the author. The publisher makes no claim as to their veracity or accuracy, and assumes no liability for the content.

WILDBLUE PRESS is registered at the U.S. Patent and Trademark Offices.

ISBN 978-1-964730-54-7 Hardcover
ISBN 978-1-964730-52-3 Trade Paperback
ISBN 978-1-964730-53-0 eBook

Cover design © 2025 WildBlue Press. All rights reserved.

Interior Formatting and Book Cover Design by Elijah Toten
www.totencreative.com

SPEAKING TRUTH TO EVIL

This book is dedicated to my amazing wife Wendi, who is always there to support me and allow me to do what God has called me to do. Besides my two sons, Phillip and Jacob, Wendi is without a doubt the best thing that has ever happened to me. I am blessed and honored to share my life with her, my partner in crime, Bonnie and Clyde, until death do us part.

I also want to thank my parents for teaching me a hard work ethic and for raising me with the best of their abilities. My mom and dad have been there for me when nobody else was, and I will forever be grateful to them.

The statistics, data, and research information in this book come from three main areas, and when possible, I will add a notation of the resource. Most of the data and research in this book is from my forty years of researching, studying, and interviewing these violent offenders. I have personally spoken to hundreds and hundreds of these dangerous killers.

I also glean some statistics from our government agencies, mainly the Federal Bureau of Investigation, Homeland Security, and the Secret Service. Lastly, much of my stats and serial killer data comes from an amazing resource at Radford University in Virginia, and their Serial Killer Research Project. This project is known as The Serial Killer Information Center, and it is led by the brilliant Dr. Mike Aamodt. These college students have been studying these killers and providing important data and information for decades, and it is time this information makes its way to the general public.

CONTENTS

INTRODUCTION   **11**
How it all Began

CHAPTER ONE   **19**
Charles Manson and David Berkowitz: The Early Years

CHAPTER TWO   **27**
Serial Killers 101: Who Are They, and Why Do They Kill?

CHAPTER THREE   **38**
The Most Shocking Cases I Have Studied in my Career

CHAPTER FOUR   **41**
The Modus Operandi and Signatures of Serial Killers

CHAPTER FIVE   **55**
*Mutilation, Dismemberment, Cannibalism, Necrophilia, and
Other Paraphilias*

CHAPTER SIX   **64**
The Myths and Truths of Today's Serial Killers

CHAPTER SEVEN   **89**
The Creepy Predator Van: Truth or Urban Legend?

CHAPTER EIGHT   **94**
The Unsolved Case I Want to Solve

CHAPTER NINE   100
My Most Interesting Case to Study: The Taco Bell Strangler

CHAPTER TEN   107
Raising Killers in America: Where Are Our Leaders?

CHAPTER ELEVEN   128
Don't Be a Victim: A Crime Prevention Plan

SELECTED PHOTOS   139
Speaking Truth To Evil

APPENDIX A   145
The Longest List of Black Serial Killers Ever Published

WANT MORE PHIL CHALMERS?   292

ABOUT THE AUTHOR   294
Who Is Phil Chalmers?

INTRODUCTION

HOW IT ALL BEGAN

I grew up in the inner city of Cleveland, Ohio, surrounded by crime, poverty, violence, and dysfunction. I know what it feels like to live in fear, not knowing if the bad guys might break into your home. We lived above a greasy motor repair shop at 8873 Broadway Avenue, with rats in the basement and a gravel parking lot for a back yard. I was robbed at knifepoint on the way to school, and violent crimes took place right outside our front door. My parents would hammer 2x4 boards inside the exterior doors at night to keep potential intruders out.

At the same time, my parents tried to give my brother and me a normal upbringing, with birthday cakes, camping trips, and Christmas celebrations. My mother had been raised by foster parents, and my father was raised by an abusive and odd father. My father struggled with alcoholism when I was growing up, but my parents did the best they could with what they were given and how they were raised. Even with these efforts, our home and family was a far cry from a *Leave it to Beaver* family, and it had its share of dysfunction.

I don't talk about my upbringing to embarrass my family or to gain some sort of credibility. I only share it because it is a big part of who I am today, and why I do the work I do.

If I am being honest, I would rather tell you a story about growing up in the suburbs and living with a healthy, stable family, but unfortunately, that isn't my story.

My father spent quite a bit of time at the local bars, sometimes with me in tow, and the weekends were usually spent with my parents' friends, many whom were alcoholics and drug addicts themselves. Early memories include being tripped by a cousin and splitting my forehead wide open, being forced by my dad to fight another kid as a youngster, and "shifting" a family friend's penis as a party game. Mixed in with these not-so-happy memories were some good memories of going hunting, fishing, camping, and spending time at our camp in Cook Forest State Park near Clarion, Pennsylvania.

In 1974, when I was ten years old, my life changed for the better as we were able to move out of the city and into the suburbs, inheriting a building lot. I would live a more normal childhood, spending time around traditional families and growing up in a safe community. My parents and us kids built a home ourselves in Aurora, Ohio, an idyllic Hallmark-style town. Not only did I no longer have to fear for my safety every day, but we had grass to play on, and I was able to participate in activities that normal kids took part in, like summer baseball, weightlifting, wrestling, football, and riding bikes around town. I was also able to observe healthy, loving families and I decided that when I grew up and had my own family, this was the kind of family I would have. This was the life I had always dreamed of, and I enjoyed every minute of it. My middle school and high school years were what every inner city kid dreams about and should experience.

My family relationships improved when my father quit drinking, and things seemed to get better for everyone. It was never perfect, but better, for sure. I graduated from high school in 1983, and after deciding that college wasn't for me, I left college in 1985 and began the work that I am doing today. My passion was to reach and to save wayward kids, and my gifts were speaking and writing. I began working with church youth groups, speaking at youth conferences, and spending all of my time trying to help kids who were growing up like I had. I enjoyed using my gifts and talents to positively affect the lives of young people, and it was very rewarding, way more rewarding than the accounting job I thought I would land after I completed my college degree. I am so glad I made that move, and instead, I pursued my passion and used my gifts and talents to foster change in young people.

I had experienced a spiritual breakthrough myself after high school, and I was now living a faith-based life filled with mission, purpose, and a calling. I eventually began working with incarcerated juveniles at a correctional center in Cleveland, and I absolutely loved it. Many of these young men were juvenile rapists and juvenile killers, and I could connect with them because of my life experiences and upbringing. I could look those kids directly in their eyes, and they knew that I knew. It allowed me to make an impact at an early age, which was very rewarding.

I began the quest of finding out how kids grow up to be killers and rapists, in hopes that I might help prevent some of these violent crimes. It led to me interviewing those who had already committed murder, been convicted, and were willing to talk about their lives and crimes. This helped me understand what makes someone victimize and murder their parents, siblings, or classmates. At the same time I was speaking to teens and studying crime, I was also involved in business, selling residential real estate and other types of sales jobs. My day job helped provide the income I needed to continue to follow my passion and my quest to find out why teens killed, and how we could stop them.

Eventually, I would be married to my first wife in 1987 at the age of twenty-three, and I rose to the top of the youth speaking game, landing on the "Acquire the Fire" tour with Ron Luce, alongside other acts like singer Katy Perry and actor Stephen Baldwin. I was speaking in coliseums to thousands of teens every weekend, and it was super exciting. I eventually transitioned to school assemblies, talking to the students about bullying, suicide, substance abuse, and school violence. That work was fulfilling, and I did that until my major book release in 2009, *Inside the Mind of a Teen Killer,* after which I transitioned to speaking and training professionals like law enforcement officers, school counselors, teachers, probation officers, and school administrators.

In 1990, I began interviewing convicted killers in person, since many of these offenders don't speak at their trials, nor do they give interviews. You also can't trust the media reports, which are mostly inaccurate. I began my quest to interview more convicted killers than anyone in history, and I believe I have accomplished that goal, having interviewed hundreds and hundreds of dangerous killers, including serial killers, school shooters, mass murderers, spree killers, and juvenile killers.

My first face-to-face prison visit was to Oklahoma's death row in 1990, to interview Sean Sellers, a Satanist and triple murderer who killed a store clerk and both of his parents, shooting them all to death. The victims were sacrificed to the devil, and it landed Sellers on death row. He was eventually executed and became the only modern-day killer who was executed for crimes that he committed under the age of seventeen.

The interview was a great learning experience, and one that would set the trajectory for my future life and career. I even brought a film crew with me for this interview, and a movie would be made to help thousands of other troubled teens, titled *Stuck in a Nightmare.*

A life-changing moment for me took place on April 20, 1999, when I, along with the rest of the world, watched the Columbine High School massacre unfold on national television. It was at that moment that I decided it was time for me to step it up and discover why these juveniles were committing heinous, adult-like crimes. That is the day I embarked on my ten-year research project and study of juvenile killers and school shooters, interviewing hundreds of them in person, over the phone, and through the mail. I was on a mission to discover the causes of these violent incidents, the warning signs that were missed, and the triggers that turned regular kids into cold-blooded killers.

I accomplished that goal and in 2009, I released a landmark book with Thomas Nelson Publishers, titled *Inside the Mind of a Teen Killer.* I followed up that book with an updated book on juvenile homicide in 2019, titled *The Teen Killer Whisperer,* and I am proud to say that after my book was released, the FBI, Secret Service, and Homeland Security released their studies on juvenile violence and school shootings, and none of their research contradicted anything that I had been teaching for decades. I had discovered why teens kill, and I used that knowledge to do my best to stop school shootings, mass shootings, family murders, and teen suicides. It was rewarding work, for sure.

After adopting two boys, my marriage was slowly unraveling, and unfortunately I came to the realization that I had married the wrong person. I should have divorced this woman many years earlier, but I stayed married to her for twenty-five years for the sake of my children, finally divorcing her in 2013. Our relationship became super unhealthy, and my home had become dysfunctional. She loved to fight and argue, especially in front of my boys, and she always dared me to divorce her. She was also hard on my boys, and there was no peace in our home whatsoever. I hate divorce, and I always recommend staying married if possible, but this marriage had become toxic and unhealthy for my kids. After trying marriage counseling and dealing with years of her negative behaviors, it eventually led to her physically assaulting me, slapping me and pulling my hair in front of my young son. I found myself with no other choice but to end this toxic marriage and protect my two sons from any further harm.

My ex-wife refused to co-parent with me, weaponized the family court system against me, took everything I owned, and also won a $5000 per month child support and alimony payment. She also did her best to turn my sons against me, and she almost succeeded. She has been able to keep my youngest son from me for thirteen years, and I will not be able to contact him until he is eighteen years old. It is a very sad situation, but I knew the kind of person I was divorcing, and I knew the potential of her evil ways. She would go on to tell the story of how I cheated on her, and it was all my fault. She did her best to turn our friends against me, and she even has attempted to turn some of my family members against me. It is amazing how dark and vengeful people can become, even though they claim to be religious.

While I was going through my divorce, I continued to tour the country speaking, and to be honest, I was looking for a soulmate, one who would complement me. The mistake I made is I should have waited until I was officially divorced, but I didn't, and that's something God and I have dealt with. But while going through my divorce, I met my life partner and my best friend in the middle of a cornfield in

Paris, Missouri. She was the principal of the school I was speaking at, and I was the school assembly speaker. And as they say, the rest is history. We were married on October 10 of 2013, and we have enjoyed a beautiful life together, filled with peace, love, joy, and lots of happiness.

As I write this book, I want you to know that life is good. At sixty years old, I have had many ups and downs in my life, with way more ups than downs. I have been doing this important work with convicted killers since 1985, and at the writing of this book, I am celebrating the forty-year anniversary of launching this company. And because of the work I do, I have had the wonderful opportunity to be a part of stopping many teen suicides, many juvenile homicides, and many school shootings. I am also hoping that since I began working exclusively with serial killers, that I can solve many cold cases and hopefully locate many victims' bodies for their families.

Wendi and I live a quiet life, and we have a very small circle of friends. I feel I have accomplished all of my goals and dreams in life, and my work is nearing its end. I have one final task to accomplish, and that is to discover how people become serial killers and how we can stop them before they take innocent lives. This book is about serial killers, their shocking crimes, and what I have discovered talking to hundreds of these offenders. I hope you learn something valuable as you turn the pages of this book, and should you ever need to contact me, you can message me directly on my website, www.philchalmers.com. I always want to be approachable and reachable, and to be there when someone needs me. Lastly, I want to share with you my life verse, which is tattooed on my chest, that inspires me to keep moving and keep working. The verse reads, "I can do all things through Christ who gives me strength." The verse is Philippians 4:13, and with Christ, you can accomplish all of your goals and dreams. My wife and I love you all, and we thank you so much for your love and support over all of these years. Stay safe, friends.

CHAPTER ONE

CHARLES MANSON AND DAVID BERKOWITZ: THE EARLY YEARS

Imagine getting a Christmas card from Charles Manson in the mail, complete with a swastika. I'm not sure how many people can say that, but this strange occurrence became a regular part of my life, beginning in the early 1990s. As a middle schooler, I watched the television movie *Helter Skelter* in 1976, and at twelve years old, I will never forget just how scared I was watching this horrific crime. This was a movie about a real-life boogeyman, and I was so shaken that I slept on the floor of my parents' bedroom for several nights. It would be surreal that two decades later I would be communicating with that scary man from the movie, Charles Milles Manson. As I began communicating with serial killers, Manson stood out as one of the more interesting, for sure, although he was more of a cult leader than a serial killer. I can't really remember what we discussed, but I do remember that he wanted books of stamps, and in return, he would send me letters, postcards, and greeting cards.

Manson influenced a group of young people to do his killing for him, three women and one man, Charles "Tex" Watson, who was the leader of this killing crew. These horrific murders occurred on two consecutive nights in

August of 1969, when I was just four years old. The group murdered seven people during those two nights, including eighteen-year-old Steven Parent, pregnant actress Sharon Tate, and a coffee heiress named Abigail Folger. The way these murders were carried out would make them one of the crimes of the century, as the method of murder included stabbing, slashing, shooting, and hanging the victims. The crime scenes were bloody and outright shocking, with words written in the victims' blood on the walls, silverware sticking out of the victims' bodies, and slurs carved into their bodies. Manson coached the four killers, demanding that they leave "something witchy." Later, I would meet his grandson Jason Freeman and get an entirely new view of Charles Manson from his grandson's eyes.

A short time later, I was communicating with the lead killer from the Manson murders, Charles "Tex" Watson, who over the years has become very religious. He has always been cordial with me but would never speak about his crimes. The same could be said for David "Son of Sam" Berkowitz, whom I not only communicated with, but visited face-to-face. Instead of seeing an infamous serial killer, Berkowitz seemed gentle in person, like someone's grandfather and, quite frankly, he was probably nicer and kinder than my own father. He would pray for me and encourage me, and we have remained in contact for twenty years. You would never know by looking at Berkowitz that he was once a serial killer who terrorized all of New York City. He told me that he acted alone, that he was motivated by Satan, and that there was no such thing as a barking dog sending messages, which was made up by his legal team. During his crime spree, he would shoot and stab seventeen people, killing six. Berkowitz and I have had a very cordial relationship over the years. He has even allowed me to interview him for my podcast, which he rarely does.

The more I met with and talked to these so-called monsters, the more normal they became. And the more I got to know them, the more I was further emboldened to discover why they had committed the crimes that they were responsible for. That quest continued with several big name serial killers, including Lawrence Bittaker. He and his partner Roy Norris were known as "The Toolbox Killers." Those two killers carried out one of the most heinous crime sprees in California history, picking up unsuspecting young girls and torturing them for hours before raping and killing them. Some of their crimes were recorded on a tape recorder so they could listen to them later. Bittaker was very bossy and demanding at times when I communicated with him, and he was kind of an ass, if I'm being honest. Even though I began the process of setting up a visit and an interview with him, I decided to move on to other subjects, someone who would be easier for me to work with.

I also briefly corresponded with Kenneth Bianchi, known as "The Hillside Strangler," but he would plead his innocence and there wasn't really a reason for me to continue on with him, since I don't work with innocent people. I talk to guilty people who are open to discussing the motivations of their crimes and willing to share that with the public.

Another killer who claimed he was innocent was the infamous serial killer known as "The Want Ad Killer," whom I had several conversations with. Harvey Carignan began killing in Alaska, meeting his victims in want ads before killing them. He was also called "Harv the Hammer" due to his MO of paying women for sex, and while they were giving him oral sex, he would bash them in the head with a hammer, killing them. It was always my goal to gain a confession from Carignan, but he never budged on his innocence. Unfortunately, he died in 2023, taking his confessions with him to the grave.

I spoke to two inmates at length who were facing execution, and both would eventually die by lethal injection in Florida's death house. Both Danny Rolling, known as "The Gainesville Ripper," and Gary Ray Bowles, known as "The I-95 Killer," were afraid to die, talking to me at length about their upcoming fate. Rolling committed some very violent and shocking crimes in Gainesville, Florida, murdering five college students and inspiring the slasher film series, *Scream*. He would stage the crime scenes to shock first responders, including removing the victim's head and placing it on a shelf. Bowles was responsible for the murders of six men along the I-95 corridor, beating and strangling them to death. His victims had objects jammed down their throats to suffocate them, including rags, leaves, and dirt. He was working as a male prostitute when he carried out his crime spree.

Another movie that I watched in 1979, at the age of fifteen, was *The Amityville Horror*, about a haunted house in Long Island, New York, and it scared the living shit out of me. Oddly enough, two decades later, I would be speaking to the killer who inspired that entire series, Ronald Defeo Jr., who murdered his entire family in that house in 1974. Even though I believe that book and movie are both a hoax, it was probably one of the scariest movies ever made, along with *The Exorcist*. It is always surreal when you have watched these scary movies on your living room couch and later find yourself talking to the very people who inspired those films. I guess it just became part of my job, in my quest to get answers to questions that seemingly had no answers or explanation.

At the same time I was interacting with serial killers, I was continuing to interview school shooters, juvenile killers, and Satanic killers, many of whom killed their own parents. That list is endless and covered twenty-five years of my work and research, but it contains hundreds of names like Sean Sellers, Luke Woodham, Michael Carneal, Mitchell Johnson, Evan Ramsey, Charles Williams, John Jason McLaughlin, and Jamie Rouse, who were all school shooters. It was quite an interesting start to my career, and at the time, I didn't know how special it was to be able to talk to the very people who made headlines all over the world. Years later, as I look back, I realize I was in a very small group of people talking to these offenders. What I gleaned from those conversations would propel me into my career decades later and give me an insight into these crimes that very few people had.

Later years would have me speaking to many well-known serial killers, along with hundreds of unknown serial killers. My interview list contains names like Keith Jesperson, who would kill eight female victims and write a confession on a bathroom wall with a drawn smiley face. When nobody believed him, he began writing letters to the media, always including a smiley face. This would lead the media to call him "The Happy Face Killer." He is very full of himself, thinking he is a celebrity, and quite frankly, I didn't enjoy interacting with him. He also is a very talented artist, and his art is always for sale on serial killer websites.

My wife and I spent many hours on the phone with Dennis Rader, known as "The BTK Strangler," who again was very normal and was never inappropriate with my wife or me. He would talk about his Lutheran faith and his life inside prison walls. I wanted to do a book project with him, but the only book he wanted to write was a book about the Lutheran Church, which was something I wasn't interested in. I offended him once by asking him if he ever had sex with any of his victims, and he responded in a bewildered tone that he "was married, so of course not." Eventually, others who talked to Rader made up some story about me to get him to stop talking to me, and it worked. At times, Rader was a narcissistic asshole, so I really don't miss talking to him.

Another serial killer I spend a lot of time talking to is Heriberto Seda, known as "The Copycat Zodiac," who impersonated "The Zodiac" killer from California and walked around New York City shooting unsuspecting victims to death. He would send letters to the media and police claiming he was the Zodiac, even using symbols like the California Zodiac did. Seda, who goes by Eddie, asks me to look up information weekly on the web and send him photos and descriptions. His main interests seem to be religious and military history. Often he will ask me to email him a photo of some temple in Bethlehem, or an atomic bomb or warplane used in World War Two. He has always been very cordial with me.

Seda explained to me that when he was rejected by the US Army, his life spun out of control, and while watching a serial killer show on television, he decided that doing a serial killer crime spree would give him some meaning and purpose in life. He wanted to show the government that he would have been a good soldier, so he actually made his own zip guns, began shooting unsuspecting victims in New York City, and got away with murder for several years.

Another case that was important to me was the Anthony Sowell case, which took place not far from where I grew up. Known as "The Cleveland Strangler," Sowell lured eleven drug-addicted women to his home, where he would rape them, strangle them, and keep their bodies in his house. His house of horrors had nude, decapitated bodies in his bedroom, his basement, his attic, and buried in his back yard. He was caught when he allowed one of his victims, Latundra Billups, to escape. Billups explained that while they were smoking crack together, he attacked her, raped her, and choked her unconscious.

When she came to, she knew her life was in danger. She asked him if she could use the bathroom before he killed her, and while walking to the bathroom, she looked into his bedroom and saw two nude, headless corpses. While in the bathroom, she jumped out his second-story window, getting the attention of someone passing by. This not only saved her life, but it brought an end to the Cleveland Strangler murders. I talked to Sowell on the phone and corresponded with him by mail, but he was very full of himself and had no interest in working with me. Like some of the serial killers do, he envisioned himself as a celebrity and felt he was too good to speak to someone like me.

Another serial killer who is very similar to Anthony Sowell is Harrison Graham, known as "The Corpse Collector." He would lure women to his apartment in Philadelphia, Pennsylvania, then rape and strangle them to death. He kept their bodies in his apartment closet, and in the end, authorities found seven decaying corpses when they arrested him. One of the victims was killed when she discovered another body in his apartment. It is always wild when I talk to people who kept their victims' bodies in their homes, similar to John Wayne Gacy.

I have also had the privilege of getting to work with two historical serial killers: the deadliest serial killer in American history, and the youngest serial killer in American history. Sam Little, known as "The Choke and Stroke Killer," killed ninety-three victims, and possibly has more victims than Ted Bundy, John Wayne Gacy, and Jeffrey Dahmer combined. He is America's deadliest serial killer, and when I first started talking to him, he told me he was innocent. He eventually would admit his guilt, and he had a photogenic memory, drawing pictures of his victims for law enforcement investigators. He had such a good memory that they took him on a US tour, and with the help of his drawings, he was able to help the authorities close fifty cold cases. He would eventually die of natural causes, but he is alive in my live shows as I display one of his historical victim drawings with my artifacts.

Craig Chandler Price is America's youngest modern-day serial killer. He killed a neighbor when he was thirteen years old, stabbing her fifty times. He took a two-year cooling off period, and at the age of fifteen, stabbed three more females to death, one adult and two children. He was arrested at the age of fifteen and dubbed "The Warwick Slasher." Due to the law at that time, Price would only serve six years for his crimes and be released back into society at the age of twenty-one. During the course of his incarceration, he broke some rules and the Department of Corrections has kept him incarcerated even until today, at the age of fifty-one. He may have a parole date coming up soon and could possibly obtain freedom. He has been cordial and friendly. He explained that at that time of the murders he was experiencing racism in his community, and he also had an unstable family. He told me that his anger got the best of him, but today, he regrets his actions during those years in his life and is remorseful for his crimes.

So, that is a little recap of my early years in my career of profiling dangerous killers, and the basis for what I am doing today. The knowledge I have gained from all of those interviews and interactions has helped me become a seasoned profiler, interviewer, and law enforcement trainer, helping law enforcement and other professionals spot dangerous killers before they strike, saving countless lives in the process. It is rewarding to know that you can use your knowledge to help others and maybe make a difference in keeping our children and citizens safe.

CHAPTER TWO

SERIAL KILLERS 101: WHO ARE THEY, AND WHY DO THEY KILL?

Let's take a look at today's serial killers and lay the ground work for who they are, and why they do the things they do. The most surprising thing for me about serial killers, after having looked into the eyes of hundreds of them, is that they don't look like killers. They also don't act like dangerous killers. This must be how they are so good at avoiding detection, and how they are able to continue on with their crimes, sometimes for years, even shocking the very people who know them best.

Today's killers also don't fear death or prison, so there really is no deterrent for these dangerous individuals. Most of them have accepted death, and they have also accepted the fact that they might end up in prison for the rest of their lives. In all reality, many have already been to jail or prison, so they know exactly what to expect. They are willing to risk death or incarceration to satisfy their wants, needs, desires, and addictions. This is why I treat everyone as a possible killer and never look for trouble. You won't catch me beefing with my neighbors, causing drama on social media, or getting involved in road rage incidents. I pretty much keep to myself, maintain a small circle of friends, and spend most of my time with my beautiful wife. I recommend you do the same.

So, what exactly is a serial killer? According to the FBI's new definition, a serial killer must kill at least two victims with a cooling off period, which could be a week, a month, or a year. I usually don't include bank robbers, gang members, or hit men, but the FBI is beginning to include them in the definition. A serial killer differs from other killers because of their cooling off period, allowing them to satisfy their need, take a break from killing, and allow the desire to build up again. How does a serial killer differ from a mass murderer or a spree killer? According to the FBI, a mass murderer must kill at least four people at one time and in one location, and a spree killer must kill at least two victims in separate locations in a short period of time, with no cooling off period. The spree killer's crime spree usually lasts between two days and a week.

Let's answer a hotly debated question in the serial killer world: Are serial killers born or made? Is it nature or nurture? Many people think serial killers are born, which they call nature. Others believe serial killers are made, which they call nurture. I believe unless someone is born mentally ill, serial killers are made. I believe they are born just like any other baby, but something happens to them to propel them toward murder. It could be some sort of strong sexual incident, an unstable family, sexual or physical abuse, or unloving parents. Most serial killers never bonded with their parents, were unloved by their family, and were unwanted. This plays hell on one's mental state growing up, and I see it often with serial killers.

So, how would you describe a serial killer today? What is your profile? Are they mostly men or women? Are they White, Black, Hispanic, or Asian? Are they in their twenties, thirties, forties, or fifties? Come up with your profile, and

I will tell you who they really are in the upcoming pages. After reading this book, you will know more about serial killers than most police officers and FBI agents. How do I know? Because I train them and, as a group, they answer my questions incorrectly just like civilians do. This book is part entertainment, so I hope you enjoy it. It is part my life story, so now you know. But it is also a learning tool, like going to college, so I hope you learn a lot as you turn the upcoming pages or listen to the next few hours on audiobook.

Who is the youngest serial killer in modern US history? As I mentioned earlier, that would be Craig Chandler Price, known as "The Warwick Slasher." Angry about experiencing racism and only thirteen years old, Price killed an adult female neighbor, stabbing her to death with fifty stab wounds. He took a two-year cooling off period and then, at the age of fifteen, stabbed three more females to death in his neighborhood, an adult female and two young girls. They were all stabbed dozens of times. Price is housed in Florida today, and we talk often. He is the only Florida inmate I visit at the time of this writing.

Another young serial killer would be Robert Dale Segee, who at nine years old set fire to a Hartford, Connecticut circus tent on July 6, 1944, killing 168 people. He then admitted to killing four others in separate incidents, including Barbara Driscoll, nine years old. Born in 1929, his first murder would have been at the age of nine, in 1938, of the nine-year-old female, whom he beat to death with a rock. He then killed an adult and strangled a twelve-year-old boy in 1943, at the age of fourteen. The circus fire mass murder occurred in 1944, when he would have been fifteen years old. He confessed and was arrested in 1950, at the age of twenty-one, and was sentenced to four to forty years in prison. He was paroled in 1959 at the age of thirty and died in 1997 at the age of seventy-two.

Another young serial killer was Jesse Pomeroy, known as "The Boston Boy Fiend," who was born in 1859 and killed at least two victims. He tortured many more, beginning his crimes in 1871, when he was twelve years old. He was arrested for his crimes and sent to a boys' reform school, but he was paroled a short time later. In March of 1874, at the age of fourteen, his murder spree began. He first killed a ten-year-old female, Katie Curran, and then a month later, on April 22 of 1874, the mutilated body of four-year-old Horace Millen was found in the Dorchester Bay marsh. They finally found Katie Curran's body in the basement of Pomeroy's mother's dress shop, and Pomeroy was sent to prison for life for his crimes.

The oldest serial killer in US history was a cattle farmer Ray Copeland from Missouri. In 1986, at the age of seventy-two, he began killing drifters and farmhands and burying them on his property. He is responsible for at least five murders and is suspected of a dozen. He was arrested and became the oldest person ever sentenced to death in the US, at the age of seventy-six. His wife was also arrested, but she claimed that he had forced her to participate in his crimes. Ray Copeland died of natural causes on death row at the age of seventy-eight.

America's deadliest serial killer is a Black male named Sam Little, known as "The Choke and Stroke Killer." Little killed ninety-three victims, probably more than Gacy, Dahmer, and Bundy combined. He had a photogenic memory and drew pictures of his victims for investigators. Because of his great memory, members of law enforcement took him on a US tour to meet with detectives across the country, and he was able to close fifty cases, making him America's deadliest serial killer.

Prior to Sam Little, the deadliest US serial killer was Gary Ridgway, "The Green River Killer," who had forty-nine closed cases. I had the opportunity to talk with Little many times, and I even own one of his rare victim drawings. He was very cordial and easy to talk to, and a person would never know he was a dangerous killer when interacting with him. Many of his victims approached him and asked for a ride.

How many serial killers have there been in the United States so far? The research done by Radford University states that there have been 4743 serial killers so far worldwide that we know of. Although the United States doesn't lead the world in violent crime rate, suicide, deadliest mass shootings, or deadliest school shootings, we do have the most serial killers in the world. Norway has the deadliest mass shooting, Germany and Russia have the deadliest school shootings, and China and Japan have the highest suicide rate. Here are the top five countries with the number of serial killers and the percentage of serial killers worldwide.

Worldwide serial killers: 4743
United States: 3204 (68%)
England: 166 (4%)
South Africa: 117 (3%)
Canada: 106 (2%)
Italy: 97 (2%)

And although we lead the world in the number of serial killers, we don't have the deadliest serial killer. Luis Garavito, known as "The Beast of Columbia," leads the world in serial killer victims with 221 mostly young male victims. He was actually about to be paroled in Columbia when he thankfully died of natural causes.

What are the causes and warning signs of serial killers? The causes can be similar to the causes of juvenile killers and school shooters in my earlier books, but I believe the causes of serial killers include unstable homes, physical abuse, sexual abuse, emotional abuse, physical ailments like seizures, and head trauma. Many serial killers have experienced head trauma growing up, including David Berkowitz, who was hit with a metal pipe; Richard Ramirez, who had a dresser fall on his head; Dennis Rader, who was dropped on his head as an infant; Albert Fish, who fell out of a tree; and John Wayne Gacy, who was hit with a swing at the age of eleven. Even more important and more impactful than those causes are the rejection from one's parents, the lack of bonding, love, and connection with parents, and parents telling their children they were unwanted and should have never been born.

There are very few warning signs to be recognized in potential serial killers, which makes them very hard to apprehend. It is much easier to spot a school shooter or a mass murderer using my warning signs in my other books, but serial killers are tough. Growing up, a serial killer might display one of the behaviors of the FBI's Homicidal Triad, also known as the MacDonald Triad. These behaviors include the killing and torturing of animals, wetting the bed as an adolescent, and setting fires. I would include voyeurism as a warning sign as well, since many serial killers like Ted Bundy talk about peeping into people's windows as young people.

Killing and torturing animals is a rehearsal for people, setting fires causes fear in the community, and bedwetting is an emotional behavior that cannot be controlled. I then add voyeurism and pornography, especially peeping Tom activities, because someone who moves from their pornography to real people is alarming and a very dangerous step.

Some of these peeping Toms even sneak into the homes of people and steal their underwear, which is also troubling behavior. These behaviors seem to be the first red flags we see before someone takes the giant leap to rape and homicide. Please report these activities when you see them in your community.

The signature and modus operandi of serial killers is a good way to track them, identify them, and arrest them. The signature of a serial killer is their calling card, and they rarely change their signature. Remember the movie *Home Alone*? The "Wet Bandits" had a signature, flooding the sinks of the homes they burglarized. Marv called it their "calling card," and that is exactly what a signature is. The signature of Jack Spillman, known as "The Werewolf Butcher," was to cut his victims open from their sternum to their pelvic bone. Richard Cottingham, known as "The Times Square Killer" and "The Torso Killer," would meet women for sex in hotel rooms in New York City, then rape and murder them, dismember them, and finally set the hotel room on fire. He would then place their head and hands into his duffel bag and take them with him as trophies.

Dennis Rader, known as "BTK," wouldn't only bind the hands and feet of his victims, but he would also bind their knees, making him the only killer I have ever observed doing that. He also exclusively used the clove hitch knot when tying up his victims. Jeffrey Dahmer, known as "The Milwaukee Cannibal," would decapitate his victims and arrange the body into a strange pose, preparing it for sex. Ed Gein, known as "The Plainfield Ghoul," would hang his victims up in his barn and dress them out like a deer, keeping their entire body as a trophy. He would make bowls, masks, and chairs out of their body parts. Albert DeSalvo, known as "The Boston Strangler," would rape and strangle his victims, and then remove their pants and underwear. He would spread their legs toward the door of the home to shock first responders. Before he left the scene, he would always tie a bow around the victim's neck with a pair of their own pantyhose.

The most shocking signature I have seen to date has been the murders and the staging of victims' bodies by George Russell Jr., known as "The Eastside Killer." His first victim was strangled and laid behind a dumpster, with her hands and feet crossed, a pinecone in her hand, and a coffee lid on her eye. When he didn't get the response he wanted from the community, he upped his game and decided to go into the homes of average women and violently kill them, staging the scene like a horror movie. The second victim was bludgeoned with a plastic bag over her head, high heels on her feet, was nude, and had a rifle inserted into her vagina. The third victim was stabbed all over her body and was nude with her legs spread. She had a sex toy sticking out of her mouth and a sex book lying by her head. Russell also enjoyed having sex with his victims' corpses, as well as inflicting damage post mortem.

Some of the telltale behaviors of serial killers that differentiates them from other killers include cannibalism, dismemberment, torture, necrophilia, and the posing and staging of dead bodies. We will get into these behaviors in a later chapter, but what the killers tell me when explaining why they include these shocking acts is simply that they wanted to try something new, or that they wanted to live out a fantasy. And when asked why they prefer sex with their victims after death, they explain that their victims don't scream, they don't fight back and resist, and the killer can take their time with their victims.

When it comes to the types of serial killers, I don't like to rehash the research done by the early profilers, like John Douglas and Robert Ressler. Some of it still applies, but most of it is out of date. In my research, there are only a few types of serial killers today. I have them classified as the following:

Lust killers, who kill for sexual reasons.

Anger and retaliatory killers, who kill because they are angry and want to get back at society.

Racist and cult killers, who are driven by a cause.

Financial gain killers, who enjoy killing while they are committing crimes like robbery and burglaries.

Serial killers seem to speed up their frequency as they continue on with their killings, sometimes killing someone every six months and speeding up to every three months, then every month, every week, and sometimes only days, as in the case of the Taco Bell Strangler, who ended his spree by killing three victims in three days. Serial killers also get careless and overconfident as time goes on, many times leading to their arrest. Arresting a serial killer can be very challenging, as they are difficult to apprehend. It usually takes something like a DNA hit or the killer making a mistake, allowing the investigators to identify them.

As an example, John Wayne Gacy decided to kill a young man he met at his local drugstore, where people not only knew him, but had seen Robert Piest and him together. Jeffrey Dahmer got careless, and his final victim was able to escape from Dahmer's apartment with one arm in a handcuff and alert the authorities. Ironically, Tracy Edwards, the surviving victim, was later himself sentenced to prison for murder. And Dennis Rader, "BTK," trusted the police when he asked them if they could track a floppy disk and they told him they couldn't. When he sent the floppy disk, it was tracked to his church within twenty-four hours, and he was quickly apprehended. Later, during the interrogation, he confronted the investigators in the interview room, telling them that he couldn't believe they had lied to him.

Two more random thoughts and facts about serial killers. Has any serial killer been murdered in prison? The answer is yes, many serial killers have been murdered in prison. The most infamous are Jeffrey Dahmer, known as "The

Milwaukee Cannibal"; Gerard Schaefer, known as "Killer Cop" and "The Butcher of Blind Creek"; Roger Kibbe, known as "The I-5 Strangler"; and Billy Chemirmir. Interestingly, I speak to all of the men responsible for those deaths: Christopher Scarver (Dahmer), Vincent Rivera (Schaefer), Jason Budrow (Kibbe), and Wyatt Busby (Chemirmir).

Has any serial killer gone to prison and continued their lust murders in prison? The answer is yes, although the only one I know of is New York's Lemuel Warren Smith, whom I have talked to many times. In prison for five murders, with an MO of kidnapping, raping, shooting, stabbing, strangling, mutilating, and biting his victims, he killed his sixth victim in prison, a female corrections officer named Donna Payant. She was kidnapped in an office, raped, bitten, tortured, and finally strangled to death. Her body was wheeled out of the prison in a cart and dropped into a dumpster. The trash company took the dumpster to the garbage dump, and Smith got away with a sixth murder. He was eventually charged with the murder when they matched his dental records to the victim's bite mark. He denied committing the murder but was eventually charged for the crime.

SINGULAR SERIAL KILLER

One last thing I want to do before I end this chapter is to create a new type of killer definition, one that many feel is necessary. The FBI's Robert Ressler coined the term "serial killer," and I have created six types of teen killers in my previous books. But I want to introduce and create a new term that is necessary today in the true crime world, which I am calling a "singular serial killer."

The definition of this term is a serial killer who only kills one person, but who kills and operates just like a serial killer. I study so many crazy cases where I think that this person is really a serial killer although they have only killed one victim, because they act and operate just like a serial killer. But we can't call them a serial killer, so we need a new term. This killer enjoys his violent acts, is fulfilling his fantasies, but unfortunately for him, he was arrested after only one murder. We know that due to his fantasy life and his method of murder, he would have killed again, making him a serial killer. But he isn't just a killer or a murderer; there is more to him than the average killer.

For example, when Pennsylvania's Gregory Graf had a sexual desire for his stepdaughter Jessica Padgett, and his fantasy was to murder her and have sex with her corpse, this behavior is very serial killer-like. Graf waited until Jessica's mother was out of town, then he shot his stepdaughter in the head, set up a camera to record, and had sex with his victim's corpse. That is serial killer behavior. When a guy breaks into an elderly woman's house, nails her hands to a wooden chair, sexually assaults her, and then sets her on fire, that is serial killer behavior. So, I believe we need a name for that, and I'm now calling that person a "singular serial killer," a serial killer who has only killed one person. Help me spread the word.

CHAPTER THREE

THE MOST SHOCKING CASES I
HAVE STUDIED IN MY CAREER

When I am out doing my thing, speaking and training, I always get the same question, asked in a few different ways: Who is your favorite serial killer? What is your favorite case? Who was the scariest person you ever interviewed? What case shocked you the most? I will answer those questions in this chapter.

The worst crime scenes I have ever viewed are the crime scenes of Spokane, Washington's Jack Owen Spillman III, known as "The Werewolf Butcher," as well as Bellevue, Washington's George Russell Jr., known as "The Eastside Killer." Spillman committed his crimes in 1994 and 1995, killing a nine-year-old female, a fifteen-year-old female, and an adult female. The crime scenes were horrendous and included the removal of breasts and vaginas, and cutting the victims open from sternum to pelvic bone. The fifteen-year-old victim had an aluminum baseball bat inserted into her vagina.

George Waterfield Russell Jr. carried out his murders in 1990, and not only did he enjoy sex with his victims after death, but he enjoyed the postmortem attack. After killing his victims, he would take the time to pose and position their bodies in grotesque and shocking positions. One victim was laid behind a restaurant with her hands and feet crossed, and a pinecone in her hand. The second victim had a plastic bag over her head, her legs were spread, and she had a rifle inserted into her vagina. The third victim was stabbed on every part of her body, and she had a sex toy sticking out of her mouth and a sex book laid by her head.

The stories that William Clyde Gibson, a Southern Indiana serial killer, told me, if they are true, are about as shocking as I have ever heard. His talk about having sex with the victims as they were dying, eating parts of their sexual organs while the victims were still alive, and his dismemberment and necrophilia activities are as shocking as I have ever heard personally from a killer. Another case that shocked me early in my career occurred in 1987, when seventeen-year-old Daniel LaPlante killed a mother and her two young children. The crime occurred in Townsend, Massachusetts, when a pregnant mother was found face down on her bed, raped, and shot multiple times. Her seven-year-old daughter was found drowned in one bathtub, and her five-year-old son was drowned in another bathtub. LaPlante continues to serve his life sentence at the age of fifty-four.

The most disturbing serial killer crimes usually involve kidnapping, rape, sodomy, torture, dismemberment, and decapitation. The crimes of "The Toolbox Killers," Lawrence Bittaker and Roy Norris, are about as bad as it gets. They would rape, torture, and murder their young female victims, grabbing their nipples with pliers and inserting an ice pick into their ears, and would record these evil activities to listen to later. Leonard Lake and Charles Ng carried out a similar crime spree, killing and torturing between eleven and possibly thirty victims in the mid-1980s. David Parker Ray from New Mexico was also into extreme torture, and he had a metal trailer he used to torture his female victims in, which he called his "toy box." Although he was never charged with murder, he was suspected of dozens of murders in that area.

I would also have to include the Houston mass murders carried out by Dean Corll and the crimes of John Wayne Gacy, "The Killer Clown," who both carried out long and deadly crime sprees, responsible for sixty-one murders between them. Their victims consisted of boys and young men, whom they tortured, raped, sodomized, and violently murdered.

One last case that I need to include is Philadelphia's Gary Heidnik, who kidnapped six victims, keeping them as sex slaves in his basement, and killing two. He would use electric shock as a form of torture on his captives, and when one of his victims died, he would dismember her and ground her up to feed her to his other victims. It is absolutely unbelievable what human beings are capable of doing to one another, and I will never understand this part of my job. I personally could never hurt an animal, let alone a human being. The evil that I have seen and heard firsthand is something you never forget, and it changes the way you think about life and humanity.

One last thing. When people ask me who my favorite serial killer is, I usually respond, "Favorite?" I don't have a favorite killer; this is not the NFL. They are all monsters, and there is no way I could have a favorite or be a fan of any of them. I am interested and intrigued by some of their cases, but I don't have a favorite, and I won't be sporting their images on my T-shirts. They are all evil, and they have hurt many people. Once proven guilty, they deserve the worst punishment possible that could be given to them in our current society. And thankfully, most of them do get that kind of punishment.

CHAPTER FOUR

THE MODUS OPERANDI AND SIGNATURES OF SERIAL KILLERS

There are two ways to track and profile serial killers, and to connect them to multiple homicides and crime scenes. The FBI calls them the modus operandi, more commonly known as the MO, and the signature. I want to teach you exactly what these two identifiers and behaviors are, and how they differ. In short, the MO is how a killer operates, kind of like the "mode of operation," and the MO often changes. The signature is the killer's "calling card," and it rarely changes.

If you have ever watched the movie *Home Alone*, which is one of my favorite Christmas movies, you will see the work of two criminals known as "The Wet Bandits." Although they aren't killers, they are well-known criminals who will help you understand the difference between signature and MO. For reference's sake, Harry is the brains of the crime duo and Marv is the brawn, and probably not the sharpest tool in the shed. Their MO is to burglarize homes when people are out of town, and they love to steal televisions, VCRs, and jewelry, using their favorite burglary tool, the crowbar.

Their signature is to always leave the water running, flooding the homes when they leave. When Harry asks Marv why he always leaves the water running, and that it is stupid to do that, Marv explains, "It's our calling card. All the great ones leave their mark. We are the Wet Bandits." He was referring to their signature which, when they are arrested, allowed the authorities to tie them to all of the local burglaries. While they are being taken into custody, the arresting police officer says, "Nice. Always leave the water running. Now I know each and every house that you hit." He would use their signature to connect them to multiple crime scenes, just as an investigator might do with a serial killer.

The Modus Operandi, or MO, actually means "method of operation," or how a serial killer operates. The MO can change for a couple of reasons. One, the killer gets better at killing and learns from his or her mistakes. Or two, things always don't go as planned, so the killer makes adjustments at the murder scene. The MO could be that a killer targets elderly white females who live alone, and he might enter their homes at night. He also might prefer strangulation as his method of murder, or maybe stabbing the victim with a knife from inside the home. How could his MO change? Maybe as he improves his skill of getting into the house or apartment quickly, undetected, killing quickly, and escaping the scene leaving little evidence. And things can change as he encounters his victims, maybe getting more resistance than usual, maybe being confronted by a dog or being surprised by other people in the house who weren't supposed to be there. The MO can include bindings, stab wound patterns, the weapon used, the type of strangulation, where the crime occurs, when the crime occurs, and the targeted victim's race.

The Modus Operandi can include actions like home invasion, rape, torture, sodomy, picking up hitchhikers, doing business with sex workers, kidnapping, abducting, meeting for sex in hotel rooms, ligature strangulation, stabbing, dumping bodies, shooting victims in the head, bludgeoning victims, taking home bar customers, killing prostitution customers, and the storage of bodies inside a home or apartment.

The signature is an act that isn't necessary for the murder to take place but is something that has meaning to the killer. The signature is the killer's calling card, and it rarely changes. They will use their signature to either sexually stimulate themselves, to degrade their victims, or to shock those who discover the body, be it family members or police officers. As an example, the killer might pose the body when they are done, spreading the legs of the victim toward the door, and then tie a makeshift bow around their neck. These are the actions of "The Boston Strangler," and these would be signature behaviors. They will try to leave that same signature at every crime scene if possible, which does help investigators connect the crime scenes. Other signatures could be bindings, knots, ligatures, blunt objects, posing, staging, trophies, writing on walls, as well as notes and messages left at the murder scene.

Let's take a quick look at a few serial killers and break down their signatures and MOs.

David Berkowitz, known as "The Son of Sam," would prowl the streets of New York hunting for victims, and when he found a couple parked in a car, he would open fire on the vehicle with a .44 handgun. One of his signatures was to send taunting notes to the media.

The Manson family would change their MO over the course of two nights of murder and mayhem, shooting, stabbing, slashing, strangling, and hanging their victims. But their signature was the same at both crime scenes, which was writing haunting messages on the walls and doors in the victims' blood, doing exactly what Charles Manson had asked them to do, to "leave something witchy."

Ted Bundy's MO was to hunt for pretty young women who might fall for his deceptive ruses (for example, having an arm in a sling), targeting either hitchhikers or trusting souls. He would use a ruse to get them into his car and, once inside, he would attack them with a crow bar-type weapon and handcuff them inside his vehicle. His signature was to use bludgeoning as his preferred killing method, and he would prefer to have sex with his victims after they were dead. Many times, he would decapitate the victim and take their head with him as a trophy, to be used for sexual purposes later.

Other MOs would be Jeffrey Dahmer luring men to his apartment to be photographed, only to drug them, handcuff them, and strangle them to death. His signature would be to decapitate the victim, pose them, and then have sex with their corpse.

Richard Cottingham, known as "The Times Square Killer," would meet his victims at hotel rooms for sex, first raping them and finally strangling them to death. His signature would be to decapitate his dead victims and to dismember them, removing their arms, legs, feet, hands, and breasts. He would then set the hotel room on fire, place his victim's head and hands into a duffel bag to take with him, and walk right out of the hotel.

Albert DeSalvo's MO would be to talk his way into women's homes to measure them for a possible modeling job, then rape them and strangle them to death. His signature would be to remove their pants and underwear, pose the body, and tie a bow around their neck out of their nylons. Because of this MO, DeSalvo was originally known as "The Measuring

Man," but later, he gained a much scarier moniker, "The Boston Strangler."

Dennis Rader, known as "The BTK Strangler," would sneak into women's homes when they were at work and attack them when they arrived home, using a gun and a ruse that he was from California and that he just needed to use their vehicle. He would only attack women who lived alone, with no men in the home and no dogs. He would bind their hands and feet before announcing that he was BTK, and that they were going to die today.

After seven murders, Rader's MO would drastically change. After leaving the first seven victims dead inside their homes, his last three victims' bodies were placed in plastic bags and taken away from the crime scene. Rader would take the bodies to the basement of his church, pose and photograph them, and then dump them along busy roadways. This change of his MO completely confused local law enforcement, as they believed that serial killers don't change their MO. What that meant to them was there must now be two serial killers stalking Wichita, Kansas. In all honestly, I don't think they could have connected all ten homicides together without Rader's confession, since the crimes scenes were very different. Some victims were men, some were children, some were elderly women, some were left inside the home, and some were taken. This is the danger of believing that the MO never changes.

Dennis Rader's signature was unique, and I have never seen it used by any other killer in history. Along with binding his victims' hands and feet, he also placed a binding around their knees. And he always used the clove hitch knot when binding his victims. When he wasn't actively killing victims, he would bind and torture himself, and when he did, he would also use the clove hitch knot, and he would always bind his arms, legs, and his knees as well. I talked to

Rader many times over the years, and most of the time he was pretty friendly and cordial.

Other signatures of well-known killers include:

John Wayne Gacy, known as "The Killer Clown," who would use the rope trick and the handcuff trick to subdue his victims, then sodomize their corpses, and finally stuff their underwear down their throats before disposing of them in the river or his crawlspace.

Charles Albright, known as "The Eyeball Killer," would always remove his victims' eyeballs after shooting them to death, taking the eyeballs with him as a trophy. I talked to Albright many times before he died, and he tried to tell me he was innocent. When he was in school, it is alleged that he had cut out the eyes out of every female in his yearbook. There were several stories of Albright being obsessed with eyes his entire life.

Jerome Brudos, known as "The Shoe Fetish Slayer" and featured on the Netflix show *Mindhunter*, would remove the foot of his victim with a hacksaw, place it into a high heel shoe, and keep this trophy in his basement freezer for masturbatory purposes. He would pose and photograph the corpse of his victim, and he also kept their shoes and underwear as trophies.

Danny Rolling, known as "The Gainesville Ripper," would pose his victims, decapitate them, and place the head facing the door to shock first responders. I talked to Rolling many times before his execution, and he would always tell me that he was afraid to die. How ironic!

Richard Rogers would leave the bar with his victims, and once he killed them, would dismember their bodies and place the body parts into black garbage bags, disposing of them along the freeways. He was known as "The Last

Call Killer" because he left with men he met at bars, and he usually left late at night with them.

Rober Kibbe, known as "The I-5 Strangler," wouldn't only abduct and kidnap his victims along the I-5 freeway, but he would always cut their clothing off in bizarre patterns with scissors before killing them. I talked to Kibbe many times before he was killed in prison, and now I talk to his killer, Jason Budrow. Budrow's description of how he groomed Kibbe to become his cellmate, with the intention of killing him, is very interesting. In his first night with Kibbe, he wrapped a ligature around his neck and began strangling him in the same fashion that Kibbe had killed his victims. He cut his clothing and then carved a pentagram into his chest. It is an unbelievable story, for sure.

Gary Ray Bowles, known as "The I-95 Killer," would work as a male prostitute, and once alone with his customers, he would bludgeon them to death and force a rag, dirt, or leaves down the throats of his victims. His crimes scenes were usually very bloody and violent. I talked to Bowles at length, and just like Rolling, he was afraid to die and always wanted to talk to me.

Rodney Alcala, known as "The Dating Game Killer," would abduct, torture, rape, and strangle his victims to death. His signature was an odd one, as after he killed them, he would pose his victims' bodies, sometimes leaving them kneeling. He always took their jewelry as trophies, as well as taking their picture. This guy was so charming and polished that he entered *The Dating Game* television gameshow and actually won the show. To win the show, the female contestant would choose who she wanted to go on a date with, and of course, she chose the sexually sadistic serial killer. Thankfully, later she explained that he creeped her out, so she decided not to go on a date with him after all.

Angel Maturino Resendiz, known as "The Railroad Killer," would use trains to travel from place to place and attack people who mostly lived near railroad tracks. He would invade the victims' homes and quickly bludgeon them to death, leaving their bodies amid a very bloody crime scene. The last thing he would do was lay their driver's license on the pillow next to their dead body and then help himself to some food before he fled the crime scene.

Steven Pennell, known as "The Route 40 Killer," would kidnap and abduct his victims using his blue predator van. Once he had the victim in his grasp, instead of raping them, he preferred torture. He enjoyed using tools like pliers to torture his victims, many times removing their nipples while they were still alive.

Andre Crawford, known as "The Englewood Killer," would use drugs to lure prostitutes into his lair, exchanging drugs for sex. Once he had the victims in his grasp, he would bludgeon them to death with a 2x4 piece of wood, cover their faces, and always take their shoes with him as trophies. I talked to Crawford a few times before he died.

Derrick Todd Lee, known as "The Baton Rouge Serial Killer," would use home invasion to gain access to his victims. Once under his control, he would violently overkill his victims and leave them in a pool of blood. After killing his victims, he always took their car keys with him as trophies. When police initially began working this case, they were after a White male with a pickup truck, even having a drawing of him. This happens too much when the offender is Black, allowing them more time to fly under the radar and kill many more victims.

Paul Stefani, known as "The Weepy Voice Killer," was a dangerous predator who would abduct young girls, and then rape and torture them for hours. He enjoyed killing them with an ice pick and a screwdriver. His signature would be a phone call he would make to the police department, sometimes letting them know where the victim's body could be found. His voice on the 911 call was strange and weepy sounding, leading to his nickname.

Salvatore Perrone, known as "The Son of Sal," would kill shopkeepers in Brooklyn by shooting them to death. He was angry because they were interfering with his business. He would attack Middle Eastern store owners, and his signature was that after killing them, he would cover their bodies with their merchandise. I talked to Sal a few times, and he wasn't the easiest guy to work with.

Heriberto Seda, also known as "The Zodiac Copycat," stalked the streets of New York City at night, shooting his unsuspecting victims to death. He would then send letters with Zodiac signs to the media, pretending to be the original Zodiac. His signature was to use his homemade zip gun to shoot his victims. I talk to Seda a lot, as we are in constant communication. In exchange for helping me, he asks me to look up religious images or military images online, and to email him the images so he can study them.

Robert Hansen, known as "The Butcher Baker," would abduct prostitutes and sex workers in Anchorage, Alaska, take them to his house, and keep them chained up in his basement as a sex slave. He earned his nickname because of his line of work, working as a butcher and operating the Hansen bakery. When he was done with his victims, he would strip them naked, load them up in his airplane, and release them in remote areas, finally hunting them down like prey and shooting them to death. Investigators found a map with many X's on the map, probably marking where he killed his many victims. I talked to Hansen a few times before his death and he was pretty cordial, telling me that he was old, and I should work with the younger guys.

Bobby Joe Long, known as "The Classified Ad Rapist" would use classified ads to lure women in the Tampa Bay, Florida area to their death, and enjoyed raping, binding, and strangling his victims. He would then pose their bodies after he killed them, and his signature was using a noose to control them and strangle them to death. He also committed over 100 rapes, leading to his nickname. I had the opportunity to talk to Long a few times before he was executed, and I really didn't enjoy talking to him.

Randall Woodfield, known as "The I-5 Killer," operated like many serial killers do, abducting his victims, raping them, and shooting them to death. His signature was to always use athletic tape to bind them, which probably turned him on. The reason Woodfield preferred athletic tape was because he was a former athlete and NFL football player, and he was probably around athletic tape most of his life. He is the only serial killer I have ever come across to use that kind of binding.

Paul Runge, known as "The Classified Killer," was a very good looking and well-spoken serial killer who used classified ads and homes for sale by owner ads as his way to contact his victims. He would visit the home or apartment to scout the scene, then come back again to kill his victims. He would bind, rape, strangle, and then slit the throats of his victims, some of whom were children. He would use a pay phone to make the phone calls to his victims, so the calls couldn't be traced. After killing his victims, he would always set the house and the victim on fire, destroying much of the evidence. Many of his victims were killed in pairs. I have talked to Runge many times, and he has always been cordial and very easy to work with.

Larry Eyler, known as "The Highway Killer," would abduct, kidnap, rape, and murder young men and boys in Indiana and Illinois, many times dumping their bodies near highways. The victims were usually stabbed to death, and they always had their pants pulled down when their bodies were found, which was his signature.

Lonnie Franklin, known as "The Grim Sleeper," was one of the most prolific serial killers in California history. He would kidnap, rape, and photograph his victims, and when he was done, he would shoot them to death with a .25 caliber handgun. He took a very long break from killing, earning him his nickname, a take on "The Grim Reaper."

Anthony Allen Shore, known as "The Tourniquet Killer," abducted his victims, mostly young girls, using a van, and would rape them and violently murder them. His signature would be to always ligature strangle his victims to death. He at first only used a cord, but when he hurt his hands, he shifted to using a tourniquet with a piece of wood, earning him his nickname. The tourniquet was his signature, and another signature of his was to lay his victims on their backs when he dumped their bodies.

Richard Ramirez, known as "The Night Stalker," would kill his victims in many different ways, including stabbing, cutting, and shooting. His signature was a unique one, as he made his victims pray to Satan before he killed them, and before he fled the crime scenes, he drew pentagrams on the walls, mirrors, and sometimes the victims' bodies.

David Leonard Wood, known as "The Desert Killer," would abduct his victims in the El Paso area of Texas, rape and murder them, and bury their bodies in shallow graves in the desert. The burying part was his signature.

Mark Godeau, known as "The Baseline Killer" and "The Baseline Rapist," would attack his victims in Arizona, rape them, then shoot them at close range with a handgun. After he killed his victims, and before he left their bodies, he would pull their shirts up, unzip their pants, and pull their pants down.

William Heirens, known as "The Lipstick Killer," would sneak into women's apartments in Chicago and violently stab them to death, sometimes leaving the knife still stuck in their bodies. He may have also abducted a child from her home and killed her. Although he proclaimed his innocence, many do believe that he is the Lipstick Killer. His signature is what gained him infamy, as he wrote in lipstick on the wall of one of his victims, "For heaven's sake catch me before I kill more. I cannot control myself."

Sean Vincent Gillis, known as "The Other Baton Rouge Killer," would kidnap, rape, and strangle his victims to death with zip ties, but what he did to them after their deaths makes his signature very unique. He would remove their nipples, parts of their flesh, and eyelids, and he would stab and cut their bodies numerous times post mortem. He sometimes cut their hands off as well.

Ronald Dominique, known as "The Bayou Strangler," would talk Black men in Louisiana into either having sex with him, or with his fictional wife. He would convince them to allow him to bind them and tie them up, because either he enjoyed it, or his wife did. Once tied up, he attacked his victims, raping them and ligature strangling them to death. The victims had no defensive wounds, which is how they knew he tied them up and incapacitated them before attacking them.

Matthew Steven Johnson, known as "The Skull Crusher," would rape and attack his victims in a violent fashion, usually stomping them to death and crushing their skulls. Before he left the scene, he would pull the victim's pants down, which was his signature.

John Allen Muhammad and Lee Boyd Malvo, known as "The DC Snipers," would rig up a vehicle to allow them to shoot unsuspecting victims to death in Maryland, Virginia, and Washington, DC. These were random, sniper-type shootings, and they went undetected because they were shooting from the trunk of a vehicle. They caused fear and panic for weeks in a major metropolitan area before they were arrested. Their signature was to send letters to the police calling themselves "God," and they also left the Death Tarot card at many of the crime scenes with messages written on the Tarot card to police.

One of the most shocking signatures was the staged crime scenes of Washington's George Russell Jr., known as "The Eastside Killer." His first victim, a twenty-seven-year-old White female, was found laid out behind a dumpster, posed like she was in a coffin. She was nude, her hands and feet were crossed, and she had a pinecone in her hand. She also had a coffee lid covering one of her eyes. The second and third victims were found inside their homes, and the crime scenes resembled horror movie scenes. Not only was posing his victims part of his signature, but he also enjoyed post mortem attacks, as well as sex with his victims after death.

The second victim, a thirty-five-year-old White female, had her skull crushed and had a plastic bag wrapped around her head. She was nude in her bed, had bite marks on her arms, and her legs were spread open. She was wearing high heel shoes on her feet, and had a rifle shoved into her vagina. The third victim was a twenty-four-year-old White female, also found nude in her bed, who also had her skull crushed. She was stabbed on every part of her body, had her legs spread open, and had a sex toy inserted into her mouth. She also had a sex book placed by her head.

Serial killers like George Russell Jr. really get off on staging and posing their victims, not only turning themselves on, but knowing it will shock whoever finds the body. Thankfully, Russell was arrested after his third murder and will spend the rest of his life behind bars.

CHAPTER FIVE

MUTILATION, DISMEMBERMENT, CANNIBALISM, NECROPHILIA, AND OTHER PARAPHILIAS

A paraphilia is an object or behavior that provides sexual arousal to a person, usually outside the bounds of what most people consider "normal," and it usually relates to sexual arousal. "Paraphilia" actually means "other" or "outside of" and "loving." There are supposedly over 500 paraphilias, and they can get very strange as you scroll down the long list. This includes necrophilia, foot or shoe fetishes, pedophilia, voyeurism, sadomasochism, sexual sadism, zoophilia, exhibitionism, and hybristophilia. Other behaviors that are common with serial killers might include the posing and staging of dead bodies, the hanging of victims, cannibalism, dismemberment, and decapitation. Let me give you a quick definition of a few of these interesting behaviors:

Necrophilia: The real definition is the love of corpses or dead bodies, but most define it as the sexual attraction to corpses.

Foot or shoe fetishism: The sexual attraction to shoes or feet.

Pedophilia: The sexual attraction to children.

Voyeurism: Being sexually aroused by watching others who are either nude or involved in sexual activities. Some just enjoy watching unsuspecting people living their daily lives.

Sadomasochism: Also known as S&M, the sexual arousal of giving or receiving physical pain.

Sadism or sexual sadism: Inflicting pain on non-consenting victims.

Zoophilia or bestiality: The sexual arousal toward animals or the act of having sex with animals.

Exhibitionism: The sexual arousal of exposing your genitals to non-consenting individuals.

Hybristophila: The sexual interest and attraction to those who kill or commit crimes. This could also show itself as being attracted to serial killers, killers, and other inmates. I see this all the time, as most of the serial killers I speak with have girlfriends or wives.

Cannibalism: The act of consuming or eating another human being.

Dismemberment: The act of cutting apart or tearing apart a human body, including the legs, arms, hands, feet, breasts, or genitals.

Decapitation: Removing the head from the human body.

As we apply these paraphilias to serial killers, we have to ask the question: Do serial killers have paraphilias, and why? The answer isn't as easy as it seems, but in short, many of the lust killers do have some sort of paraphilia, because many are sexually driven. The non-lust killers, those who kill for reasons like anger, retaliation, or racism usually don't have paraphilias, but rather, fantasies about their crimes. All serial killers are different, so we can't lump them all into the same category. I also think serial killers can get bored with just killing victims over and over, and they want to experiment with more deviant behaviors. This would be why they begin to explore some of these paraphilias and the strange behaviors that we see them doing.

Two of the most disturbing lust killers in history are Roger Kibbe, "The I-5 Strangler," and Germany's Peter Kurten, known as "The Vampire of Dusseldorf." Kibbe was a California serial killer responsible for eight or more murders of young women, raping and strangling them to death. As a child, Kibbe would steal clothing off of clotheslines and cut it into little pieces. When he began killing young women, he would also cut their clothing into pieces with a pair of scissors and remove it.

Peter Kurten was responsible for nine or more murders of young women in Dusseldorf, Germany. He had an early fascination with blood and was sexually aroused by blood spurting from his victims' bodies. He would experiment with different types of weapons to see which caused the most bleeding, and his weapons included a hammer, a pair of scissors, and different types of knives. For this book, I wanted to focus on three paraphilias that I see often when interviewing and studying serial killers: necrophilia, cannibalism, and the combination of mutilation, dismemberment, and decapitation.

I think most lust killers perform the act of necrophilia, whether they admit it or not. Some will talk about this act, but most are embarrassed and won't tell me about it. In some cases, investigators can tell by looking at the evidence that the killer may have had sex with their victims post-mortem, even if the offender won't admit to it. Well-known serial killers like Dennis Rader, Jeffrey Dahmer, Ted Bundy, Gary Ridgway, John Wayne Gacy, Earle Nelson, and Edmond Kemper admitted to taking part in sexual activities with their victims after death.

Dennis Rader, known as "The BTK Strangler," told me he would never have sex with his victims because he was married, and he would never cheat on his wife. But he did remove the clothing from his victims, and after he killed them, he would masturbate onto their corpses, leaving semen at some of his crime scenes. Jeffrey Dahmer also enjoyed having sex with his victims after death, sometimes having intercourse with their corpses. Gary Ridgway, known as "The Green River Killer," was also known to have sex with his victims after they were deceased.

Ted Bundy admitted that he would return to his victims' bodies to have sex with them a day or two after their death, and many times he would remove the head and take it home as a trophy, to use for sexual activity later. Imagine the depravity of having sex with a deceased woman's head? Ed Kemper was also known to have sex with his victims after death, and we know he decapitated his victims to have sex with just their heads. Earl Nelson, known as "The Gorilla Man" due to his large hands, and the first "Ted Bundy" admitted that he preferred sex with his victims after death. Nelson was the first lust killer to roam the country targeting unsuspecting women, similar to many of today's lust killers. Thor Christiansen, known as "The Hitchhiker Slayer," would pick up hitchhikers, shoot them in the head with his .22 caliber handgun, and have sex with their corpses.

A recently arrested serial killer in Georgia, Dennis Lane, was sentenced to life in prison for killing two women, having sex with one of their corpses, then dumping their bodies behind a grocery store. It is also suspected that he recorded the act on his cell phone. Lane had been released from prison after serving seventeen years for sexually assaulting a ten-year-old female, allowing him to begin his serial killing spree.

An Indiana serial killer whom I have spent a considerable amount of time with, William "Clyde" Gibson, told me that he preferred sex with his victims after he killed them because he could take his time with them, and they didn't resist him. He also told me his favorite thing ever was to kill his victims while he was having sex with them, strangling them to death while having intercourse. He told me this act really turned him on and "made him cum." Gibson was convicted of three murders, with one of his victims buried in his back yard, and was sent to Indiana's death row.

When I think about necrophilia, I always think about Illinois serial killer Lorenzo Fayne. Fayne killed an adult female in Wisconsin, then moved to Illinois to live with his grandmother. It is then he began a string of child murders near St. Louis. His MO would be to strangle and stab his victims to death, and once they were dead, he enjoyed sodomizing their corpses. Fayne was sexually assaulted many times growing up, and I am sure this is part of why he committed these violent and sexual murders.

Fayne's Illinois victims included a six-year-old male, a nine-year-old female, and four teen girls ranging in age from fourteen to seventeen years old. He explained to me that he preferred sex with his victims after death because they didn't scream, they didn't resist, and he could do the things he really wanted to do, mainly sodomy.

Cannibalism is another common paraphilia among serial killers, and when most people hear that word, they think of Jeffrey Dahmer. Quite a few serial killers have taken part in cannibalism, including Joe Metheny, "The Cannibal"; Albert Fish, "The Brooklyn Vampire"; Richard Chase,

"The Vampire of Sacramento"; and Arthur Shawcross, "The Genesee River Killer." Dahmer would dismember his victims' bodies, keeping some of the body parts in his freezer to be eaten later, and he would cook those body parts to consume. He explained that he preferred their thighs, calves, and buttocks.

Joe "The Cannibal" Metheny would kill his victims and combine their human flesh with animal meat, which he would then serve at his roadside barbecue stand in Maryland. He is suspected of five murders but admitted to killing up to thirteen mostly female victims. I talked to Metheny a few times, and he seemed pretty normal to me.

Arthur Shawcross, known as "The Genesee River Killer," talked about eating parts of his victims, including the vulva and genitals of his female victims and the penis of his young male victim. Shawcross was suspected of killing fourteen people, his first two victims being children, and after spending fourteen years in prison for those two child murders, he was released to kill again. I attempted to interview Shawcross, but he refused since I had already been talking to David Berkowitz, known as "The Son of Sam," whom he despised. Shawcross took a swipe at me personally when he was interviewed for the book titled *The Serial Killer Whisperer*, which of course I took as a compliment.

Richard Chase and Albert Fish are two of the most disturbing cannibals in US history. Chase, known as "The Vampire of Sacramento," killed six victims in Sacramento, California, had sex with his victims' dead bodies, and then ate parts of their remains. He also enjoyed drinking their blood, and when he arrived home, he would use a blender to mix together their blood and organs, creating a human remains smoothie. Chase suffered from mental illness and began his cannibalistic activities by first killing animals.

He would shoot animals in the head and eat their remains. When he began hunting and killing humans, his MO was to walk up to the front door of a house, and if the door was locked, it was a sign to leave. If the door was unlocked, he would enter the home and kill whoever was inside.

Albert Fish, known as "The Brooklyn Vampire," "The Werewolf of Wysteria," and "The Gray Man" was a rapist, a child molester, a cannibal, and a serial killer who was active in the 1920s. He is suspected of killing at least three children, but there could be many more as he claimed to have had 100 child victims. He was arrested after kidnapping, killing, and cannibalizing ten-year-old Grace Budd. He used the ruse of taking Grace to a child's birthday party to get her away from her family. Once alone, he strangled her to death, dismembered her, and ate her remains.

This case became infamous because of the letter Fish sent Grace Budd's mother, which in part read, "First I stripped her naked, how she did bite and scratch. I choked her to death, then cut her up in small pieces... How sweet and tender her little ass was roasted in the oven. It took me 9 days to eat her entire body. I did not fuck her tho I could of had I wished. She died a virgin." Fish was into sadism, and an X-ray taken of his body after death showed he had shoved pins and needles into his pelvic area for years, and dozens still remained. He was sentenced to death and finally executed in New York's electric chair in 1936.

Many serial killers also take part in mutilation, dismemberment, and decapitation, as we talked about earlier. This usually goes hand in hand with necrophilia and cannibalism. Along with Ted Bundy and Jeffrey Dahmer, many others use these paraphilias as part of their MO. Names like William "Clyde" Gibson, Richard "The Times Square Killer" Cottingham, Jack "The Werewolf Butcher"

Spillman, Charles "The Eyeball Killer" Albright, and Jerome "The Show Fetish Slayer" Brudos come to mind.

When William "Clyde" Gibson was arrested, he had one of his victim's breasts on the console of his vehicle. He told me that just prior to his arrest he was eating lunch at Hooters, fondling the human breast in his pocket, eating chicken wings and watching the Hooters girls. Richard Cottingham, "The Times Square Killer," would meet his victims at hotels in New York City, first raping and strangling them, then dismembering and decapitating their bodies. Sometimes he would take the head and hands with him before he set the hotel rooms on fire.

In a separate chapter in this book, I talked about some of the most disturbing cases I have examined, along with some of the most disturbing killers I have interviewed. Jack Owen Spillman, known as "The Werewolf Butcher," is one of them. He would cut his victims' breasts off and place them on the kitchen table, cut their vaginas off and place them in their mouths, and he would cut his victims wide open from breastbone to pelvic bone. He would also enjoy drinking their blood.

Two of the most famous cases of dismemberment are the crimes of serial killers Charles Albright and Jerome Brudos. Charles Albright, known as "The Eyeball Killer" and "The Dallas Ripper," operated in the Dallas, Texas area, and is suspected of killing at least three female victims. His MO was to target sex workers, rape them, then shoot or stab them to death. He would then remove their eyeballs and dump their bodies on busy roadways. I talked to Albright a few times, but unfortunately, he would never admit to committing his crimes to me.

The story goes that Jerome Brudos, known as "The Shoe Fetish Slayer," found a pair of women's high heel shoes at the city dump. When he took them home and wore them around the house, his mother caught him, beat him, and threw the shoes away. Since that day, Brudos talked about how he formed a foot and shoe fetish, which he had until his death. Brudos would end up killing four victims, all while being married and having two children. Growing up, he would steal women's lingerie and women's shoes, and as a minor, he sexually assaulted a neighbor girl, luring her to his home. He was sent to prison for that assault but was released to continue his violent crimes.

In 1968 and 1969, Brudos would abduct and kill four women and attempt to abduct two others. Three of the victims were killed inside his home, and a fourth victim was killed inside his vehicle. After killing his victims, he would pose their bodies in sexual poses and dress them in lingerie and high heel shoes. He also had sex with their corpses and dismembered some of their body parts. He would keep their underwear and shoes in his home as trophies, and he removed the foot of his first victim with a hacksaw. He kept her foot inside a high heel shoe in his basement freezer, to be used for masturbation. Sadly, his first victim was a nineteen-year-old female going door to door selling encyclopedias, and he was able to lure her into his home and accompany her to his basement, where he bludgeoned her to death with a piece of wood. She would become his first murder victim. When Brudos died of natural causes in prison, he had photos of women's feet and high heels hanging in his prison cell.

CHAPTER SIX

THE MYTHS AND TRUTHS OF TODAY'S SERIAL KILLERS

In 1985, I began my quest to discover why killers commit the crimes they commit. Why would juveniles kill their parents? Why would students murder their classmates? And why would someone want to kill innocent victims over and over again? I'm pleased to know that I discovered why teens kill, and why students shoot up their schools. You can read my research and discovery in my two previous books about juvenile killers, titled *Inside the Mind of a Teen Killer* and *The Teen Killer Whisperer.* This last step is to discover how one becomes a serial killer, what old research about serial killers is still true, and what has changed since the early research on serial killers done by John Douglas, Roy Hazelwood, and Robert Ressler.

Most of what the public believes and thinks about serial killers today is learned from movies, television shows, and media reports. Many of those beliefs are no longer true or are grossly inaccurate. In this chapter, I want to set the record straight about today's serial killers, exposing the myths and teaching you the truths. I want you to know what is fact and what is fiction, and after studying what people really think about today's serial killers, I have come up with twelve myths that most people believe to be true. Not only do many fans of true crime believe these myths, but so do many of our law enforcement professionals who are working these cases and chasing these dangerous killers. Those twelve myths are:

1. To be a serial killer, you must kill at least three, five, or ten victims.

2. Serial killers are mostly White males.

3. Serial killers kill mostly victims of their own race.

4. Serial killers kill up close and personal, like strangulation.

5. Serial killers kill for sexual reasons.

6. Serial killers are male.

7. Because serial killers are mostly male, their victims are predominantly females.

8. Serial killers only operate in populated areas and large cities.

9. Serial killers never change their modus operandi (MO).

10. There are very few active serial killers today because of DNA and technology.

11. Serial killers are never released from prison.

12. The 1970s were the Golden Age of serial killers, with the most active serial killers operating at that time.

The problem with people's knowledge and understanding of today's serial killers is that they are stuck in the 1970s and the 1980s, reading the initial research done by John Douglas, Robert Ressler, and the early FBI profilers. A lot has changed in fifty years, and because of those changes, we must change the way we study these offenders, and we must update this research. This book will not only update this research, bringing it into the 2000s, but it will update many of the conclusions that were made in the initial profiling work. I want to bring you up to speed with the serial killers of the 2020s and beyond.

To begin, we must understand one very important fact: We cannot place all of these serial killers into neat little boxes, because it doesn't work anymore. The old titles like "organized" and "disorganized" no longer apply, in my opinion. And we have to stop classifying them like they are Bundy, Dahmer, and Gacy. The one thing these serial killers have in common is that they are all different, and until we get that, we will never understand them.

I see so many people today, even so-called "experts," still quoting the research from 1970, and it tells me one thing: They haven't spoken to any recent serial killers and are simply regurgitating old and outdated research. If you talked to the killers I talk to and studied the latest serial killer cases, you would be more aware of the idiosyncrasies of today's offenders. I hear these myths quoted daily by so-called "experts," "criminologists," and "profilers," and it really surprises me. I often hear quotes like "most serial killers are White," "serial killers kill mostly within their own race," and "serial killers all have had bad childhoods" from experts on all kinds of television shows and documentaries. So, let me make my contribution to this research, and hopefully you will learn something new in this book, and then apply it and test it with your own research and investigation.

I would be remiss if I didn't give credit where credit is due, as to where I get my information. First, I have spent forty years interviewing hundreds and hundreds of violent killers and studying thousands and thousands of cases. A lot of my basic stats and research come from trustworthy resources like our government organizations, including the FBI and their Uniform Crime Report, the Secret Service, and Homeland Security. But the majority of this new research on today's serial killers is done by Radford University in Virginia, and their Serial Killer Information Center. The students and professors at Radford University have done an amazing job of studying serial killers since 1992, compiling over thirty years of data and research. They have studied 4743 US and international serial killers and broken them down like nobody has in history. This project is led by Dr. Mike Aamodt, and it is a brilliant piece of research. I want to thank Dr. Aamodt and all of his students over the years for their tireless efforts in helping us track and understand today's serial killers.

And before we dive into these truths and myths, when I am asked what shocks me the most about interviewing all of these serial killers, my answer is always that they seem so normal. When I say normal, I mean like regular people. You would never know these people are serial killers if you met them at a bar or talked to them online. They blend in to society, which is why they are so dangerous. Ted Bundy said it best when he explained, "I was essentially a normal person. I had good friends, I led a normal life, except for this one small, but very potent and very destructive segment." So, join me as we dispel these commonly believed myths and uncover the truth about today's serial killers.

Myth Number One: To be a serial killer, you must kill at least three, five, or ten victims.

Fact: The FBI has just adjusted their definition of a serial killer, and now it is defined as "the unlawful killing of two or more victims by the same offender, in separate events, with a cooling off period."

Notice that the motivation of the killer wasn't included, like killing for financial gain. I have always wondered why the FBI included in their definition of a serial killer as someone who had to kill three victims with a cooling off period. This never made sense to me, because I always wondered why not two? Why is three the magic number? I always thought if you killed someone, took a cooling off period, and killed again, you were a serial killer. You killed people in a series of murders. Today, I interview some killers who have only killed one victim, but in a serial killer kind of way, meaning if they hadn't been caught after this one murder, they surely would have killed again. I see it so much that I have coined a new term. I call them a "singular serial killer," a serial killer who only kills one person. What I really mean is that I have seen people kill one victim, but they have a serial killer mindset, and they operate just like a serial killer. For what it is worth…

Myth Number Two: Serial killers are mostly White males.

Fact: Most serial killers are Black.

The latest numbers from the last decade has the racial breakdown of serial killers today as follows, and I slightly rounded the numbers to make them easier to study.

Black: 60%
White: 31%
Hispanic: 8%
Asian: 1%

When I begin my live training, I always ask my audience to raise their hand and name a serial killer, and I also ask them to help me profile today's serial killers. It's a way for me to gauge the knowledge of the room. The serial killers usually mentioned include John Wayne Gacy, Ted Bundy, Jeffrey Dahmer, Charles Manson, Ed Gein, Richard Ramirez, Dennis Rader, Gary Ridgway, and The Zodiac. I then joke with the audience that they didn't mention any Black serial killers, so I ask them to name a Black serial killer. They usually respond with "That Atlanta guy" and "The DC Snipers." I then ask them what the actual names are of the Atlanta Child Killer and The DC Snipers, but they can't answer that question. It's almost like Black serial killers don't exist or rarely exist. There is a reason why the public isn't familiar with Black serial killers, so let me explain.

The American news media, out of fear of being labeled racist, will not report on cases involving a Black serial killer, so in people's defense, they rarely hear about these cases. Also, when you watch serial killer movies, the killer is almost always White. In the midst of my decades-long research, I began stumbling across Black male serial killers in every state. And I have been speaking to many of them for years.

My hunch was confirmed when I discovered the Radford University study. It is one thing if the general public doesn't know about this, but it is a problem when law enforcement and investigators don't know about it, which could result in many more deaths. This is why I continue to train law enforcement and the FBI, and why I am writing this book. We all need to know the true facts, so we can apprehend these dangerous killers before they kill again.

The biggest obstacle we face in getting this information out to the public is that the American news media is very racist—one of the most racist organizations in the world. For example, when it comes to missing children or females, usually only the White suburban females get the attention of the news media. The same goes for high profile murder case victims. Think Caylee Anthony, JonBenet Ramsey, Laci Peterson, Natalee Holloway, Martha Moxley, Jessica Marie Lunsford, Sharon Tate, Nicole Brown Simpson, Gabby Petito, Rebecca Schaeffer, Shanann Watts and her two daughters, Abigail Williams and Liberty German, known as "the Delphi girls," and the quadruple Idaho stabbing deaths of young blonde girls. I could go on and on, but you get the point. Can you name a Black child or Black female who made headlines, either missing or murdered, and is still ingrained in our memories? I know, don't feel bad. I can't either.

The media is also racist when it comes to victims of homicide. Only some victims get the attention they deserve, and in case you haven't guessed it yet, non-White victims aren't that important to the media. When a serial killer is killing White victims, especially pretty female White victims, they are going to get all kinds of attention. Think Ted Bundy and David Berkowitz. The serial killers who kill mostly Black victims are pretty much unknown. Think Henry Louis Wallace and Anthony Sowell. A third way the media is racist is in the way they handle offenders. When a White perpetrator attacks or kills a Black victim, it is big news. But when a Black perpetrator attacks or kills a Black victim, or even a White victim, it rarely makes the news. And if it does make the news, they never mention the race of the attacker or the victims. When it is a White perpetrator, they always mention the race, that a White suspect killed a Black victim, for example. So the media's racism comes in all shapes and sizes, and they report it only when it fits their agenda.

In my company and in my work, I value all victims. Period. It doesn't matter if they are Black, White, or Brown, and it doesn't matter if they might have been addicted to drugs or worked in the sex industry. Nobody deserves to be murdered, and all victims deserve our effort and attention. This is why I am practically the only person out here talking about Black serial killers, because I value the victims and their families more than I fear being called a racist. When people get to know me, they can quickly tell that I despise racism. But more importantly, the families of the victims thank me for talking about their loved ones' cases, since everyone else out there has ignored them.

Even though Black serial killers are mostly unknown, when you study their cases, you will see that their crimes are just as crazy as their White counterparts' crimes. If you have no knowledge of Black serial killers, you have missed over 1000 cases of serial homicide and some of the most interesting cases that I have ever studied. With 3200 known serial killers in US history, you have missed almost a third of US serial killers, so you have some work to do to catch up. At the end of this book, I have the longest list of Black serial killers ever published, with a short description of each. I will list some of the more interesting cases below.

Joshua Julius Anderson, 5 victims

Jake Bird, The Tacoma Axe Killer, 46 victims

Henry Brisbon, The I-57 Murderer, 3+ victims, stabbed John Wayne Gacy

Wesley Brownlee, The Stockton Serial Killer, 6 victims

Rufus Cantrell, King of Ghouls, Grave Robber, Black HH Holmes

Jarvis Roosevelt Catoe, DC Strangler, 8-11 victims

Billy Chemirmir, 24-30 victims

Nathaniel Robert Code Jr., The Cedar Grove Killer, The Shreveport Serial Killer, 8-12 victims

Alton Coleman and Debra Brown, 8 victims

Dellmus Colvin, The Interstate Strangler, 40-50 victims

Paul Durousseau, The Jacksonville Strangler, 9 victims

Roberta Elder, Atlanta's Mrs. Bluebeard, 13 victims

Lorenzo Fayne, 6 victims

Kendall Francois, The Poughkeepsie Killer, 8-10+ victims

Lonnie Franklin, The Grim Sleeper, 10-68 victims

Carlton Gary, The Stocking Strangler, 4-9 victims

Alfred Gaynor, Big Al, 9-10 victims

Lorenzo Gilyard, The Kansas City Strangler, 6-13+ victims

Fred Glover, 15 victims

Mark Godeau, The Baseline Killer, The Baseline Rapist, 9 victims

Harrison Graham, The Corpse Collector, 7 victims

Vaughn Greenwood, The Skid Row Slasher, 11 victims

Geoffrey Griffin, The Roseland Killer, 7-8 victims

Robert Hayes, The Daytona Beach Killer, 4+ victims

Ivan Hill, The 60 Freeway Killer, The Southside Slayer, 9+ victims

Calvin Jackson, Manhattan's West Side Killer, 9 victims

Charles Jackson Jr., The East Bay Slayer, 8+ victims

Elton Manning Jackson, The Hampton Roads Killer, 12 victims

Pearl Jackson, Odelle Jackson, Peyton Johnson, The Axeman of Birmingham, 14-15 victims

Ray Shawn Jackson, The Gillham Park Strangler, 6 victims

Wilbur Lee Jennings, The Ditchbank Murderer, 6+ victims

Milton Johnson, The Weekend Murderer, 5-17 victims

Vincent Johnson, The Brooklyn Strangler, 5-6 victims

Andre Jones and Freddie Tiller, 8 victims

Anthony Joyner, The Elderly House of Horrors, 6-18 victims

Posteal Laskey Jr., The Cincinnati Strangler, 7 victims

Derrick Todd Lee, The Baton Rouge Serial Killer, 7+ victims

Samuel Little, The Choke and Stroke Killer, 93 victims

Franklin Lynch, The Day Stalker, 3-13 victims

Jerry Marcus, The Tuskegee Strangler, 7 victims

Hulon Mitchell Jr., Yahweh ben Yahweh, 15 victims

Eddie Lee Mosley, The Rape Man, 8-16+ victims

Gerald Parker, The Bedroom Basher, 6 victims

Craig Chandler Price, The Warwick Slasher, Youngest US Serial Killer, 4 victims

Cleophus Prince, The Clairemont Killer, 6 victims

Anthony Robinson, The Shopping Cart Killer, 6 victims

Marc Sappington, The Kansas City Vampire, 4 victims

Morris Solomon, The Sacramento Slayer, 7 victims

Erno Soto, Charlie Chop-Off, 4-5 victims

Anthony Sowell, The Cleveland Strangler, 11 victims

Lonnie V. Spells, The Trucker Murderer, 12 victims

Timothy Wilson Spencer, The Southside Strangler, 5 victims

Edward Surratt, The Shotgun Killer, 11-18+ victims

Brandon Tholmer, The West Side Rapist, 12-34 victims

John Floyd Thomas, The Westside Rapist, The Southland Strangler, 7-15+ victims

Maury Troy Travis, The Bi-State Strangler, 12-17+ victims

Chester Turner, The Southside Slayer, 16+ victims

Henry Louis Wallace, The Taco Bell Strangler, 11 victims

Carl Eugene Watts, The Sunday Morning Slasher, 15-100+ victims

Nathaniel White, 6 victims

Nicholas Lee Wiley, The Syracuse Serial Killer, 3-7 victims

Wayne Williams, The Atlanta Child Killer, 24-30 victims

The Zebra Murderers (Manuel Moore, Larry Green Jessie Lee Cooks, and J.C.X. Simon), 73 victims

The danger of not educating the public about this new crime wave is that they might be caught off guard, believing that serial killers are White males. A perfect example is the case of Khalil Wheeler-Weaver, a good-looking and well-spoken Black man from New Jersey. Weaver is very much a modern day Ted Bundy, and his victim count is at four. He also attempted to kill a fifth victim, who escaped, leading to his arrest. He would meet his victims on dating apps, set up a rendezvous in a hotel room for sex and, once in the hotel room, he would rape and strangle them to death, then dump their bodies in vacant lots.

When he connected with Sarah Butler, a beautiful college student, on a dating app, they set up a date at a local hotel, and he offered her $500 for sex. Being a broke college student, the deal sounded good to her, because she really could use the money. She was nervous and may have not ever done this before, but he assured her that everything would be fine. While she was on her way to getting strangled, raped, and murdered by Weaver, she sent her last text message that she would ever send, to her killer. She texted him the message: "You're not a serial killer, right?" Well, he was, and had she known that most serial killers are Black males, she may have been much more careful. This is why I am sharing this valuable information, for victims like Sarah, may she rest in peace. All of Wheeler-Weaver's victims were raped and strangled, and one was set on fire.

Myth Number Three: Serial killers kill mostly victims of their own race.

Fact: 95% of White serial killer victims are White, 42% of Black serial killer victims are Black.

So. the statistics state that White serial killers kill mostly White victims, and Black serial killers also kill mostly White victims. White females are the most targeted victims of serial killers, as 37% of all serial killer victims are White females, while 31% of all serial killer victims are White males. In comparison, 12% of all serial killer victims are Black males, and 12% of all serial killer victims are Black females. White serial killers basically stay within their own race, killing mostly White victims. Black serial killers do kill a lot of Black victims, but they also murder victims of other races.

The exception would be a serial killer like Gary Ridgway, known as "The Green River Killer," who wanted to wipe out all of the prostitutes in Seattle, and who killed victims of multiple races. Jeffrey Dahmer is another example of a White serial killer who killed outside of his race, as he preferred Black males. This is the reason why I am one of the very few people you will see talking about Black serial killers, because I care about Black victims. I care about Black women. And I care about Black children.

A serial killer was stalking the city of Baton Rouge, Louisiana, killing women of all races. His mostly White victims, along with Hispanic and Black victims, were beaten and killed violently. The police were looking for a White male with a pickup truck, and they had a drawing of both. Someone suggested that they take a look at Derrick Todd Lee, but the Baton Rouge police felt like they had the correct suspect. After a few more murders, they decided to take a look at Lee, who was Black. Upon getting his DNA and entering it into the system, they discovered a match with the DNA that had been left at the Baton Rouge crime scenes.

Why is this story important? Because some of the victims weren't White, and this should have alerted investigators to expand their suspect list to Black males. The easiest way to explain this is if you have Black victims, you are probably hunting a Black serial killer. If you have White victims, you must have White suspects, as well as Black and Hispanic suspects. I am asking investigators to expand their suspect lists, in hopes they will apprehend the killer quicker, saving innocent lives.

Myth Number Four: Serial killers kill up close and personal, like strangulation.

Fact: 43% of serial killers prefer killing by shooting, 22% prefer to kill by strangulation, 15% prefer to kill by stabbing, 9% prefer to kill by bludgeoning, and 7% of serial killers prefer to poison their victims.

An example of this new way of killing occurred in Florida when two serial killers were stalking large cities in Florida, shooting their random victims to death. Nathaniel Petgrave was targeting homeless men in Fort Lauderdale, shooting four victims, killing three of them. He used a hatchet and a machete on one of the victims, and once he killed his victims, he would write a message to the police on the sidewalk using the victims' blood. In Tampa, Howell Donaldson was shooting victims as they exited the city bus, killing four innocent victims. They included three Black males and one White female. He was a good kid from a good family, which shocked those who knew him.

Everyone knows the DC Snipers, but there are quite a few who do this, including Atlanta's Aeman Presley, Stockton's Wesley Brownlee, and "The Daytona Beach Serial Killer," Robert Hayes.

Myth Number Five: Serial killers kill for sexual reasons.

Fact: Only 60% of serial killers are lust killers, with the other 40% being anger killers, retaliation killers, racist killers, or profit-driven serial killers.

An example of a serial killer who was an anger retaliation killer was long haul trucker Dellmus Colvin, known as "The Interstate Strangler." Colvin killed upward of fifty victims as he drove his long haul semi-truck across the country. He would strangle his victims to death, wrap a plastic bag around their head with duct tape in case they woke up, strip them naked, and dump their bodies two or three states away from where he killed them. He would then drop their clothing and ID in a dumpster wherever his final destination was, usually two to three states away from the body dumpsite.

Using this MO, Colvin was able to get away with murder for twenty-four years, even being stopped by the police with a body in the truck on multiple occasions. One thing Colvin didn't do was have any sexual contact with his victims. Why was he so angry? His father had remarried, and his stepmother didn't love Dellmus and his brothers and sisters, which angered Colvin. He explained that the first time he thought about killing someone was when he was fourteen years old, and it was his stepmother. He told me what stopped him was that he had no place to bury her body.

Another serial killer, Craig Chandler Price, known as "The Warwick Slasher," was America's youngest modern-day serial killer, with four victims under his belt at the age of fifteen. His victims were White, and he was angry about the racism he experienced growing up in his Rhode Island neighborhood and school. He never had sexual contact with any of his victims, which is surprising, because as a young teen, you would think he might have wanted to explore that part of these crimes, but he didn't.

Another serial killer, Heriberto Seda, known as "The Copycat Zodiac," went on a shooting spree in downtown New York City, shooting unsuspecting victims with a homemade zip gun, proving to the government that he could have been a soldier in the US Army. He had been rejected by the Army and was very angry about it. He had watched a serial killer show on TV, and he decided to pretend he was the Zodiac killer, since he was never caught. Seda never had sexual contact with any of his victims, instead shooting them at point blank range and running home to watch the media coverage of his crimes.

Myth Number Six: Serial killers are male.

Fact: 93% of serial killers are male, but 7% of serial killers are female, meaning that there have been 220 female serial killers in US history.

When it comes to regular homicide, 10% of US killers are females. In regular homicide, females typically kill their spouses or their children, as well as patients at hospitals and nursing homes. When I mention female serial killers, just about every person in the crowd yells out Aileen Wuornos, who was made famous because of the movie *Monster*.

Although her case is very interesting and she is far from a typical serial killer, she isn't the deadliest female serial killer in US history. She would kill seven men, a similar victim count as "Son of Sam" David Berkowitz. The deadliest female serial killers in US history are:

Roberta Elder, Atlanta Mrs. Bluebeard, 13 victims

Nannie Doss, The Giggling Granny, 11 victims

Dorothea Puente, Death House Landlady, 9 victims

Marybeth Tinning, 9 victims

Roberta Elder, known as "Atlanta's Mrs. Bluebeard," was a Black female who killed thirteen victims in Georgia, including many family members, relatives, and friends. Nannie Doss, "The Giggling Granny," killed eleven victims from the 1920s to the 1950s, in Alabama, North Carolina, Kansas, and Oklahoma. She killed four husbands, two children, one sister, one mother, two grandsons, and one mother-in-law. Other deadly female serial killers include Dorothea Puente, "The Death House Landlady," who killed nine victims, and Marybeth Tinning, who murdered eight victims.

Myth Number Seven: Because serial killers are mostly male, their victims are predominantly females.

Fact: 51% of serial killer victims are female, and 49% are male.

Although most serial killers are men, and female victims are the most portrayed in the movies, the fact is that only 51% of serial killer victims are women and girls, and 49% are men and boys. Many male serial killers, including William

Bonin, Jeffrey Dahmer, Dean Corll, and John Wayne Gacy, prefer to kill only men and boys. And many male serial killers target both men and women.

William Bonin, known as "The Freeway Killer," murdered between fourteen and thirty-six young men and boys in California, picking them up with his predator van, torturing and killing them, and dumping their bodies along California freeways. Bonin was assisted by one or two accomplices who helped him with his devious crimes. His typical MO was to lure his victims into his van, rape and strangle them to death, and dump their bodies alongside California freeways.

Well-known serial killers Jeffrey Dahmer and John Wayne Gacy killed only males, Dahmer killing seventeen and Gacy killing thirty-three. At the time of Gacy's arrest, he was the deadliest serial killer in US history. Just prior to Gacy, Dean Corll shocked the world with his Houston Mass Murders crimes, where he killed twenty-eight boys and young men in Houston. Corll, known as "The Candy Man," used two accomplices to help him lure young men to his home, where he would torture them, rape them, and finally kill them. Corll was shot dead by one of his accomplices, Bonin was executed in California, Dahmer was killed in prison, and Gacy was executed in Illinois.

Myth Number Eight: Serial killers only operate in populated areas and large cities.

Fact: Serial killers don't have to operate in large cities, as many operate in small towns, rural areas, and the suburbs.

For every serial killer who operates in a large city like Chicago, Los Angeles, or New York, there are just as many operating in smaller towns like Park City, Kansas and New Albany, Indiana. Here are the top fifteen states that have the most serial killer victims:

1. California
2. Texas
3. Florida
4. Illinois
5. New York
6. Ohio
7. Pennsylvania
8. Washington
9. Michigan
10. Georgia
11. Indiana
12. Missouri
13. Louisiana
14. North Carolina
15. Virginia

Myth Number Nine: Serial killers never change their Modus Operandi (MO).

Fact: Serial killers often change their MO, but they rarely change their signature.

I covered this at length in an earlier chapter, but serial killers do change their MO. As I explained, there are two main reasons for this: One, they get better at killing, and two, things don't always go as planned. Serial killers will improve on their killing skills, use better techniques, and learn from their mistakes. Three examples of serial killers who changed their MO are Dennis Rader, known as "BTK," Richard Ramirez, known as "The Night Stalker," and Henry Louis Wallace, known as "The Taco Bell Strangler."

Dennis Rader killed his victims mostly by strangulation, but at times he had to shoot and attempt to stab those who weren't cooperating with his demands. Then after killing seven victims, he completely changed his MO. The first seven victims were killed and left inside their homes, while the last three victims were killed and taken away from the scene. Rader placed the last three victims' bodies into plastic bags and loaded them up in his vehicle, taking them with him. He would take the bodies to his church basement, pose the victims, then photograph them. Later he would dump their bodies along roadways. He completely fooled the local investigators, as they were hunting for two serial killers: the one who killed seven victims, and the one who killed three victims. They actually believed that there were two serial killers actively killing elderly white females in Wichita, which would be a rare event for sure.

Richard Ramirez killed in many ways, and he was all over the place when it came to his MO. His first victim was a nine-year-old female, who was beaten, raped, and strangled to death. His next victim was stabbed to death in her bed and had her throat slashed. Most of his victims were couples who were shot in the head, and most of the women were raped. One woman had a large inverted cross carved into her chest, and another was beaten with a hammer, bound, and raped. Two of the female victims were shocked with an electrical cord, another was beaten with a crow bar, and another was strangled with an electrical cord. Some of the victims had pentagrams drawn on the walls of their homes with lipstick, and some were made to pray to Satan. Another victim was told to go tell everyone that the Night Stalker was here.

Henry Louis Wallace, known as "The Taco Bell Strangler," changed his MO several times as he killed eleven woman in Charlotte, North Carolina, all the while managing the local Taco Bell. One woman was found floating in a local lake, and another was found floating in her Charlotte bathtub. Many were strangled, some were stabbed, and one was set on fire. Some were found in their homes, while others were missing because he took their bodies with him and dumped them. One had her car stolen, and another had her baby strangled after he killed her. This is the ultimate example of a changing MO, and because many law enforcement professionals believe that the MO never changes, some killers evade detection for much longer. Wallace was killing everyone he knew, including two of his own Taco Bell employees. Thankfully, he left a palm print on the stolen car, and when confronted, he confessed to all eleven murders, landing him on North Carolina's death row.

Myth Ten: There are very few active serial killers today because of DNA and technology.

Fact: The FBI predicts that there are at least fifty active serial killers operating in the US at any given time.

I actually disagree with the FBI on this number, believing that there are at least 100 or more active serial killers at any given time. And I also believe that there is at least one active serial killer at any given time in most large cities, like Chicago, Dallas, New York, Memphis, Houston, and Cleveland. With the new definition of only two or more victims, and the thousands of urban homicides we have every year, coupled with the 4000 unsolved murder cases every year, I feel pretty sure that there are more than 100 active serial killers at any given time.

There are also a lot of long haul trucker serial killers active now, making it nearly impossible to catch them. These long haul truckers kill prostitutes and drug addicts who usually aren't missed, and are what I call "less dead," meaning that probably nobody will be looking for them. It is very sad, but unfortunately, it is true. These long haul truckers have a moving crime scene, and they abduct and kill their victim in one state, dump their body in another state, and dispose of their belongings in a third state, making it very difficult for investigators to connect the dots.

Myth Eleven: Serial killers are never released from prison.

Fact: Believe it or not, many serial killers have been released from prison. Twenty former death row inmates have been released from prison, and hundreds of killers have been released to kill again.

Regular killers get released from prison all the time. They are what I call "released to kill again." There are many reasons for this, but our justice system is broken, for sure. There are people serving life sentences for drug offenses, and there are those who kill multiple people getting released from prison. It doesn't make sense, but with our broken justice system, I don't see it changing. Here are a few names out of the hundreds who have been released to kill again:

Randy Alana
Caruthers Alexander
Tyrone Arnold
Malcolm Berard Benson
Clifford Bolden
Arthur Jerome Bomar

Willie Bonner
Michael Joe Boyd
James Opelton Bradley
Robert Joe Butler
Xavier Demark Chase
James Edward Daniels
Daron Duane Davis
Zollie E. Dumas
Andrew Raymond Engram
Lavell Frierson
Andre Cleveland Gay
Gregory Vicente Green
Richard Grissom Jr.
Arthur Bomar
John Coleman Hardaway Jr.
Paul Harrington
Arthur Bomar
James Donald King
Anthony Kirkland
Edward Lewis Lagrone
John Henry
Walter Hill
Douglas Hines Jr.
Anthony Jerome Hipps
Earl Howard
Frank Hubbard
Richard Hilliard Jackson
Steven Jefferson
John Cornelius Jenkins
Jonathan Lynn Jenkins
Andrew Jett
Eddie James Johnson
Peter Gerard Jones
Robert Charles Ladd
Travis Lewis
Curtis Lee Kyles

Harry Little Sr.
Arthur James Martin
James David Martin
Glenford J. Martinez
Eric L. McDade
Gregory B. McKnight
William Gerald Michael
Joseph Eli Moss
Michael Wayne Norris
Geno Paget
Reginald Wendell Perkins
Charles Henry Rector
Robert Rembert
Marlon D. Ricks
Alexander Robinson
Theodore Rodgers
Marcus Antonio Royal
Nathaniel J. Smith
Tommy Lee Stewart
Alex Dale Thomas
Troy Tyrone Thomas
Scottie L. Thompson
James William Tolbert
John Thomas Trevillion
Emerson Tucker
Richard Tucker
Clarence Victor
Tony Lee Walker
Tyrone Walker
Charles Edward Washington
Dameon Lareese Wesley
Connie J. Williams
Donald Williams
Ronnie Keith Williams
Samuel Carlton Wright

Myth Twelve: The 1970s were the Golden Age of serial killers, with the most active serial killers operating at that time.

Fact: The decade with the highest number of active US serial killers was the 1980s, with 768 known serial killers.

The next highest decade was the 1990s, with 669 known serial killers. The 1970s were actually third with 605 known active serial killers. So, the heyday and the Golden Age of serial killers was really the 1980s and the 1990s, with 1437 known serial killers in those twenty years.

CHAPTER SEVEN

THE CREEPY PREDATOR VAN: TRUTH OR URBAN LEGEND?

With the new show on Amazon Prime called *The Man in the White Van*, I wondered if people believe the predator van or the serial killer van is real or a myth? I wondered if people really believe that predators use a creepy van to abduct unsuspecting victims, or do they think it is an urban legend? Often on social media I see a picture of a creepy van with the words "Free Candy" emblazoned on the side. It is a funny meme, but is it true? Let's set the record straight.

The story of a sexual predator or serial killer using a creepy van to abduct their victims is true, and the legend is actually based on real cases. I believe three major predators are responsible for this scary piece of American culture, and these crimes took place in the 1980s and the 1990s.

Using a creepy predator van, and also recruiting accomplices, William Bonin, known as "The Freeway Killer," stalked young men and boys in California between 1968 and 1980, killing upward of thirty-six victims. Bonin was born in Connecticut, where he was abused growing up. As a teen, he was tied up and sexually assaulted by an older boy in a reform school. He was in and out of juvenile detention centers, and he would later admit that he began molesting young boys as well. He would eventually join the US Air Force and marry a woman, and he was sent to Vietnam for active duty combat. He spent three years in the military, was discharged, and moved to California.

Bonin's first violent crime took place in 1968, at the age of twenty-one, when he picked up a fourteen-year-old boy, raped and beat him, and dropped him off at a park. Nine days later, he did it again to a seventeen-year-old male. Two months later, he picked up two more boys and molested them. He was finally arrested for these rapes and attacks and was sent to a mental hospital, where he continued to have sex with other inmates. After serving three years, he was released from custody, the experts thinking he was no longer a threat. After bouncing in and out of prison, he moved into an apartment in 1978, when he began his freeway killing spree.

His MO was targeting hitchhikers, school children, or male prostitutes, and his victims ranged in age from twelve years old to nineteen years old. He usually lured them into his Ford van, overpowered them, and bound them, usually with handcuffs. They were then sexually assaulted, beaten, tortured, and strangled to death. They were unable to escape his van because he had removed the interior door handles, a trick also used by Ted Bundy. He would torture his victims with instruments like coat hangers, pliers, and knives, and after he killed them, he would discard their bodies along California's freeways, earning him the nicknames "The Freeway Killer" and "The Freeway Strangler." Bonin had up to four accomplices, including James Munro, Gregory Miley, William Pugh, and Vernon Butts. He was eventually arrested, convicted, and executed in California by lethal injection in 1996.

Another serial killer duo who used a creepy predator van to abduct their victims were Lawrence Bittaker and Roy Norris. Bittaker and Norris killed five young girls in California in 1979, kidnapping, raping, torturing, and finally killing them. Their bodies were disposed of in the San Gabriel Mountains, and most of their victims were never found. They actually had a name for their predator van, which they called "Murder Mac." The FBI's John Douglas has described these killers as the most disturbing case he has ever profiled. I had the opportunity to speak to Lawrence Bittaker many times, and I found him difficult to work with.

Bittaker and Norris would begin their crime spree by picking up dozens of female hitchhikers and releasing them without harm, as they practiced and honed their skills. Their first murder victim was a sixteen-year-old female walking home from church, whom they abducted. The young girl was bound, raped, and strangled to death with a wire coat hanger, and she asked if she could pray before they killed her. Her naked body was dumped in an isolated canyon, and she was never seen again. Their second victim was abducted, raped, photographed nude, had an ice pick jammed into her ear, and was strangled to death. Some of the girls were tortured by the duo using a pair of pliers to squeeze their nipples until they passed out. They also recorded one of their murders on a cassette tape, which eventually led to their arrest.

Some of their victims were picked up hitchhiking, which at the time was deemed safe and something everyone did. Bittaker would usually tighten a wire coat hanger around the victim's throat with a pair of pliers, giving him the nickname "Pliers." They used tools from their toolbox to torture their victims, which gave them the nickname "The Toolbox Killers." They were finally arrested after five murders and sent to prison for the rest of their natural lives.

They eventually both died of natural causes in San Quentin State Prison.

Two Florida cousins also used a predator van to abduct and kill six young girls between 1981 and 1983, earning them the nickname "The Killing Cousins." David Alan Gore and Fred Waterfield began their crime spree in 1976, when they raped a female at gunpoint. Unfortunately, they were never charged with that crime, claiming the sex was consensual. They attempted to kill four others who escaped with their lives, but in 1981, their killing spree began. Their first victims were an Asian mother and her daughter, whom Gore lured into his van using a fake police badge. They took these two women to a remote area, tied the mother to a tree, took turns raping the teenaged daughter, and eventually killed them both. Their bodies were dismembered and placed into barrels, which were then buried.

The killing would continue with five more murders, and their next victim would eventually be abducted after they disabled her vehicle at the beach. They offered the victim a ride, raped her, strangled her, and dumped her body into a swamp. Their next victims were two fourteen-year-old female hitchhikers, who were raped, murdered, and dismembered. Their last two victims were a fourteen-year-old female and a seventeen-year-old female hitchhiking together. The two young girls were taken to a house owned by Gore's family, and they were both bound, placed in separate rooms, and raped. One of those girls was shot in the head trying to escape, and the other was rescued alive from the attic.

Gore would eventually confess to all of his murders and lead police to the remains of his victims. He was sentenced to death and executed by lethal injection in Florida, while Waterfield was sentenced to life in prison and continues to serve his life sentence. I have spoken to Waterfield a couple of times, and he continues to claim he is innocent, which I don't believe. He was definitely involved in at least two murders, and those are the two murders he was convicted of.

So now you know—the predator van is real, and the truth behind it is even scarier than the urban legend itself. Moral of the story: Never hitchhike, never take a ride from a stranger, and never ever climb into a creepy predator van!

CHAPTER EIGHT

THE UNSOLVED CASE I WANT TO SOLVE

The case that I want to see solved before I die is the JonBenet Ramsey murder case. I, like many, are stumped by this case, and I can't wait to see who committed this crime. The Boulder Police immediately thought the perpetrator was the family, and they have never looked away from them as suspects. After examining the evidence, I truly believe it wasn't the family but instead, a child predator, a sexual sadist, or a serial killer who committed this unspeakable crime.

I had the great opportunity to speak with one of the investigators working the case, John Anderson, and I believe he is on the right path to solving this murder. John has just released a book titled *Lou and JonBenet*, and it is a must-read if you are interested in this case. I already had my thoughts on this case, and when I learned of John's theory, I was in full agreement with him. Here is how he believes this crime went down, and how we might finally catch the killer. I am going to describe this crime like I see it occurring, because I really believe this is how it happened.

The Ramseys went to a Christmas party, spending three hours that night eating and visiting with friends. I believe a bad guy had locked onto the young girl and had been watching her. I believe he is a sexually deviant predator and possible multiple killer. He decided to target JonBenet that night, of all nights, on Christmas Day in 1996. He watched the entire family leave and felt this was his chance to get into the house and carry out his evil plan.

JonBenet Ramsey was an innocent six-year-old girl who enjoyed dancing, singing, acting, and competing in beauty pageants. The killer may have first seen her at one of those pageants, but he also may have just crossed paths with her in day-to-day activities in the safe Colorado town of Boulder. While the Ramseys were away at their dinner party, I believe the killer snuck into the Ramsey home through a basement window, evading detection. I believe he spent those three hours they were away scouting the inside of the home, familiarizing himself with its layout. He also spent some time in John Ramsey's office, discovering his work bonus of $118,000. It was then that he could have written the ransom note, taking his time to write the suspicious and odd three-page note. This is the one piece of evidence that pointed the finger at the family in many people's eyes, because it made no sense. But understanding my take on what happened, the note seems to make more sense.

In preparing for the family to come home, this killer located JonBenet's room and hid under the bed in the bedroom next to hers. There was proof that not only was he under the bed, but he left a bag that he had brought with him in that room. Once the family fell asleep, he put his plan in motion, which was to abduct the little girl for ransom money, and the amount he stated was the exact amount that John Ramsey had been awarded in his bonus. I am sure that once he had her in his custody, he would also enjoy sexually assaulting the little girl. I can tell you one thing for sure, with my vast experience in homicide, that this killer had done this before, and he probably did it again, as long as he didn't die or go to prison.

He snuck into little JonBenet's room, slapped duct tape over her mouth, and may have stunned her with a stun gun. I am not sure when she was stunned, but he stunned her at least two times, leaving stun gun marks on her back and face. He picked her up and took her down to the basement, where he attempted to place her into a suitcase, along with some of her toys. She resisted and wouldn't cooperate with his plan. So, he was forced to move to a backup plan, which was a brutal sexual assault and a violent murder. Her father John explained that his daughter wouldn't have cooperated with her abductor, and he is sure she fought, unfortunately leading to her death.

Once he realized that he wouldn't be leaving with the little girl, the killer probably then dragged her into the wine cellar room, where he bound her hands behind her back and tied a ligature around her neck with a garrote, tightening it with a broken paint brush handle. At some point, he hit her over the head with a baseball bat, causing a large skull fracture. Although the skull fracture was a very bad injury, authorities believe she died from asphyxia due to ligature strangulation because of the garrote. Once he had her tied up, he removed her pajama bottoms and underwear and sexually assaulted her with the broken paint brush handle, jamming it into her vagina. He ejaculated onto her underwear due to the sheer excitement of the attack, then strangled her to death, making sure she was dead. He covered her body with a blanket and made his escape out the same basement window he had entered through. And I am sure, to his amazement, not only did he get away with this shocking crime, but immediately the investigators focused on the family, practically guaranteeing that he would get away with murder.

When the parents woke, they found the ransom note and believed, like every parent would, that their daughter had been abducted. They immediately called the police, and neither the family nor the investigators found the little girl's body in the basement, which was the first major mistake the police made. The second was allowing dozens of people into the home, contaminating the crime scene. John Ramsey finally found his little girl in the wine cellar and carried her body upstairs. From that moment on, the authorities believed that the family committed this crime, and they have never looked at any other suspects. Also, their inaccurate media releases further convinced the general public that the family had something to do with this murder, or that they may have been solely responsible. The most popular theory was that the brother killed the little girl and the parents covered up the crime, staging it to look like an abduction for ransom case.

It doesn't take much crime knowledge to look at this crime scene and conclude that there is no way a nine-year-old boy could have committed this sexually deviant murder, nor could a nine-year-old boy have the criminal sophistication to create the bindings and the garrote used in this horrific murder. The torture and sexual assault that this little girl endured wasn't an average homicide, and I also don't think the parents could commit this heinous crime. Whoever did this had done this before and was an experienced sex killer. Not to mention that the DNA left at the scene in the form of semen and touch DNA didn't match any of the family members.

The one thing that causes people to suspect the family and the parents is the bizarre three-page ransom note. If you know anything about kidnappers and ransom notes, nobody leaves a ransom note behind that is that long and that detailed—it just doesn't happen that way. When you break down the ransom note, you see that this kidnapper knew exactly what John Ramsey's work bonus was, so that was the amount he asked for. And you can also tell that the killer had watched several kidnapping and ransom movies prior to this crime, to learn as much as he could from those movies. Gleaning ideas from those movies, he used several lines from them in his ransom note. As we look at this ransom note, you can search the image of the note online and follow along with me.

On page one, the note begins with "Listen carefully!" This is taken from the kidnapping movie *Ruthless People*, which was released in 1986, ten years before this crime. The note continues with "We are a group of individuals." That line is taken from a 1995 kidnapping movie called *Nick of Time*. And of course, the $118,000 ransom demand, which was the exact amount of John's bonus. When the kidnapper demands "You withdraw $118,000 from your account, $100,000 will be in $100 bills and the remaining $18,000 in $20 bills," this is also taken directly from a movie, the 1996 kidnapping film *Ransom*.

The second page of the ransom note makes the threat of "… will result in your daughter being beheaded." This is taken from *Seven*, a serial killer movie released in 1995. And the strangest line in the ransom note, on page three, is when the kidnapper tells John Ramsey "Don't try to grow a brain, John." This is a direct quote from the 1994 movie *Speed*, which also has a type of kidnapping and ransom, taking place on a city bus.

With Netflix starting in 1997, and Amazon Prime much later, in those days you had to either go to the theater to watch a film or rent the VHS tape or DVD from a video store. There is no record or history of the Ramseys ever watching any of those films, but whoever did this was a big fan of those types of movies, and he probably watched them many times, memorizing lines. The killer studied and learned from those movies, and he used them to get ideas for his own kidnapping crime.

It is our hope that with the help of the investigation team led by John Anderson, and the large amount of DNA evidence collected at the crime scene, this suspect will someday be apprehended. I will continue to work with my inmate contacts in Colorado to do my best to get any information from them and the Colorado prison system, hoping someone may have been talking to another inmate while in custody. It would be my dream to help the authorities solve this crime and finally get justice for JonBenet. May that little angel and her mother, who passed away in 2006, rest in peace.

CHAPTER NINE

MY MOST INTERESTING CASE TO STUDY: THE TACO BELL STRANGLER

One of my most interesting cases to study is the serial killing case of Henry Louis Wallace, a Taco Bell manager from Charlotte, North Carolina. The reason I find it so interesting is that it boggles my mind that someone could kill so many young women in one town, especially people who were associated with him, and somehow get away with these murders and dodge arrest. We must learn from this case, and from my research in this book, so this type of crime spree never happens again. I have been talking about this case for years and most, if not all, of the attendees at my live conferences have never heard of it, even those who live in North Carolina. So, in honor of the beautiful young ladies who fell victim to Henry Wallace, I will continue to talk about this very sad case.

Henry Louis Wallace was born in 1965 in South Carolina. He grew up in what looked like a normal family, as he enjoyed playing summer baseball, being a male cheerleader for his high school sports team, and even spending time as a DJ. He eventually graduated from high school. But behind that normal facade was a rage that was building in Henry since he was a little boy, one that he eventually couldn't control.

Henry was beaten and abused by his mother growing up, and he was bullied at school because of his race and also because he was a cheerleader. He was rejected by women most of his life, and because of these numerous rejections, I believe he turned his anger and rage toward the women he knew in Charlotte. When he strangled and stabbed these innocent women to death, he was killing his mother, his bullies, and the women who rejected him.

In 1985, at the age of twenty, Wallace joined the Navy, proudly serving his country, and married his high school sweetheart. In 1987, he was honorably discharged and moved back to Barnwell, South Carolina. While in the Navy, Wallace had begun using drugs, and he had his first brush with the law in 1988, being arrested for breaking into a hardware store. In 1990, at twenty-five years old, Wallace killed his first victim in his hometown, an eighteen-year-old high school student. Tashanda Bethea was strangled to death, and her body was found floating in a lake. He was a suspect in that homicide but was never charged. At the same time as this murder, Wallace was fired from his job at a chemical plant, and his wife also filed for divorce, so his world came crashing down. In 1991, he broke into the school's radio station and stole some electronic equipment, which he would later attempt to pawn for drug money. Suspected of the murder, and with police investigating him for the school's break in, he left town and moved to Charlotte, North Carolina in 1991.

Wallace began working at several fast food restaurants before landing a job as manager at the Taco Bell restaurant in Charlotte, which was near the now closed Eastland Mall. In May of 1992, Wallace picked up a sex worker and drug addict named Sharon Nance. He had sex with her, and when she asked for payment, he exploded with rage, beating her in the head with a rock and killing her. He placed her body near the railroad tracks, where it was discovered a few days later. Nance liked to draw, write poetry, and she loved her son greatly.

One month later, on June 14, 1992, Wallace began what would be known as "The Taco Bell Stranglings," killing nine females with whom he had a connection. He entered the home of Caroline Love, twenty, and raped her before strangling her to death. He then loaded up her body and dumped it in a remote area, which went undiscovered for two years. Love was friends with Wallace's girlfriend, working with her at Bojangles restaurant, and living with her as her roommate. Wallace and his girlfriend went to the police station together to file a missing person's report. Eight months later, Wallace would kill again.

In February of 1993, Wallace entered the home of twenty-year-old college student Shawna Hawk, raping and strangling her to death. He then placed her body in the bathtub, which is where her family members found her. Hawk had worked at Taco Bell for Wallace, and Wallace would attend her funeral and hug her grieving mother. Four months later, on June 22, 1993, Wallace would strike again, raping and strangling another one of his Taco Bell employees, twenty-four-year-old Audrey Spain. Her body was also dumped and was found three days later. Her parents called her "Baby," and she wanted to work with computers someday.

Two months later, on August 10, 1993, Wallace struck again, killing his sixth victim, as he raped and strangled twenty-one-year-old Valencia Jumper, who was friends with Wallace's sister. After killing Jumper, Wallace opened up a can of food, placed a pan on the stove, turned a burner on, and set the victim on fire. He made it look like Jumper died in a cooking fire, and the murder was ruled an accident by investigators. A few days later, Wallace and his sister would attend Jumper's funeral, hug her mother, and send the family their condolences. Jumper was a computer science major in college.

One month later, on September 14, 1993, Wallace killed again, his next victim being twenty-year-old Michelle Stinson, who was a friend of his from Taco Bell. He raped Stinson and brutally strangled her and stabbed her to death in front of her oldest son.

Five months later, Wallace was arrested for shoplifting, but the police didn't make the connection between this crime and the murders that were happening in Charlotte. Two weeks after getting picked up for shoplifting, on February 20, 1994, Wallace killed again, this time raping and strangling twenty-five-year-old Vanessa Mack. Mack's sister worked for Wallace at Taco Bell, and after killing Mack, he left her four-month-old daughter alone in the apartment on a couch, where she remained for hours.

On March 9, 1994, three weeks after his last murder, he robbed, raped, and strangled twenty-four-year-old Betty Baucom, a co-worker of his girlfriend at Bojangles. He took several valuables from her apartment and left in her vehicle, making it look like a robbery. He would then pawn her valuables and abandon her stolen car in a parking lot not far from the murder scene. Stealing her car would eventually be his undoing and would lead to his arrest and apprehension.

On the same day as the Baucom murder, in the same apartment complex, Wallace struck again, this time killing his friend's girlfriend, eighteen-year-old Brandi Henderson. Brandi was watching her ten-month-old baby when he entered her apartment, and he raped her while she was holding her baby. When he was done raping her, he strangled her to death, and when the baby fell to the floor, he strangled the baby as well. Miraculously, the baby survived.

Killing a third person in three days, on March 12, 1994, Wallace robbed, raped, and strangled to death his girlfriend's co-worker, thirty-five-year-old Debra Ann Slaughter. He also stabbed Slaughter thirty-eight times in the chest and stomach because she fought back, angering him. After eleven murders, with most of the victims having a personal connection to him, Wallace was never a suspect. The investigators hadn't tied these murders together, and they had no idea who was killing pretty, young Black women in Charlotte until Betty Baurom's friend came forward to break the case.

Betty's friend called police and told them that the only man Betty would have allowed into her apartment would have been Henry Wallace. When police started looking at Wallace, they did another dusting of Baucom's vehicle and found a palm print on the trunk lid. Amazingly, the palm print matched Henry Louis Wallace. So, on March 13, 1994, Wallace was brought in for questioning.

While being interrogated, investigators tried to get Wallace to confess to the four victims they suspected him of killing, but he would not confess. One of the investigators then grabbed Wallace's hand and prayed with him, asking God to help him do the right thing. After that prayer, Wallace asked for a piece of paper, and wrote the following nine names, exactly as shown below:

Caroline Love
Shawna Hawk
Audrey Spain
Valencia Jumper
Michelle Stinton (sp)
Betty B
Brandy
Vanessa Mack
Debra Slaughter

The investigators were stumped, as they had no idea he had killed nine victims, let alone the eleven that he actually killed. He eventually confessed to all eleven murders, but he was only charged for the last nine murders he committed in Charlotte. Wallace was convicted of nine counts of murder and sentenced to death. He was sent to Central Prison in Raleigh, North Carolina, where death row is located. While in prison, in 1998, he married the prison nurse.

At the writing of this book, I have begun speaking with Wallace, and he has been very cordial and friendly. If you want more information on his case, check out the documentary on Amazon Prime called *Bad Henry*.

What can we learn from the Wallace case to make sure it never happens again? How did he get away with killing everyone he knew for so long? How can you kill that many people associated with you and not be a suspect? Some claim it was racism on the part of the Charlotte Police Department. Some say the victims weren't that important because they were Black. The Charlotte Police Department explained that they had over 100 homicides that year and didn't have enough detectives to work all of those homicides. So basically, they were understaffed and couldn't keep up with the multiple murders that occurred. But I have a different idea.

Yes, I do believe that in our society today, people of color don't get the same treatment sometimes as White victims. I am not saying all the time, or that every detective feels this way, but as a general rule, there is some truth to that. But what I believe the biggest mistake the Charlotte Police Department made is that they believed that the MO of offenders doesn't change. And when Wallace continued to change his MO, strangling some victims, stabbing some, drowning some, dumping the bodies of some, this threw the police off. And that is one of my missions of this book.

This is the reason why I do these trainings at law enforcement conferences and FBI conferences, doing my best to train our law enforcement professionals on the intricacies of serial killers today. I hope that my efforts change the way investigators look at crimes, and serial killer cases. Facts like "most serial killers are Black" and "serial killers often change their MO" are very important for these professionals to learn.

The victims' families were outraged over their loved ones' murders, and rightly so. Wallace should have been apprehended after three or four murders, especially after killing his girlfriend's roommate and two of his own Taco Bell employees. Most of these victims should still be alive today, raising families and living life to the fullest. I feel very bad for the victims and their families, and I want to promise them that I will continue to do everything I can to prevent this kind of crime spree from happening again. I also want to continue to keep the victims' memories alive. May these beautiful and bright young ladies rest in peace.

CHAPTER TEN

RAISING KILLERS IN AMERICA: WHERE ARE OUR LEADERS?

Back in the day, our government and our appointed leaders protected children, and they cared about protecting the innocence of children. Back in the day, they put morals, character, and the safety of our children before financial gain. Today, it seems to be exactly the opposite, where financial gain comes first. Our leaders and action groups today are so biased and agenda-driven that they have forgotten about protecting our most valuable assets—the next generation. We need to get back to protecting morality and character and place that before the almighty dollar.

Another problem I see in the US is that our elected leaders are able to stay in power for decades, somehow amassing millions of dollars in the process. Their number one goal becomes reelection, and what is best for the people comes second. Instead of supporting parents in helping raise these children, when a tragedy does happen, many times they actually blame law-abiding citizens and the parents themselves. I rarely see political leaders take any responsibility for the tragedies that do occur.

I believe today the United States is literally raising killers and manufacturing school shooters, along with mass murderers, gang killers, and serial killers. In this chapter, I will show you how I believe this is happening, and what we can do to both stop it and change the course of history.

The number one cause of most killers in my books and research is the fatherless component, and most of the killers I study either didn't have a father or had an abusive or dysfunctional father. Just as damaging as fatherlessness would be growing up in an unstable home, including one with physical abuse, sexual abuse, mental abuse, emotional abuse, dysfunction, drug use, divorce, and abandonment. There has been a major breakdown in families in the US, and our government in some way has encouraged it, rewarding single mothers with housing, child support, and welfare. It seems our government encourages women to not only not get married to the child's father, but even worse, disconnect completely from the father. This is causing complete chaos in our society, and it needs to change.

This isn't only the government's fault, and you can't just blame the mother, as many men have abandoned their role as father and daddy, leaving the important responsibility of raising children solely to the mother. As much as mothers think they can raise a child without a father, saying things like "they don't need a man," actually, this is very damaging and detrimental to the child. According to recent studies, children without fathers are twice as likely to have mental health issues, as well as struggle with depression and personality disorders. Children from fatherless homes are ten times more likely to be addicted to drugs. Children without fathers are twenty times more likely to end up in prison, and much more likely to be homeless. On the flip side, children with engaged fathers are 43% more likely to get A's in school.

In a 2022 study, eighteen million children were found to be living without a father in the home, about one in four US children. Most of the single parent homes, 80%, are being led by single mothers. Children from single-parent homes are twice as likely to suffer from mental health issues and behavioral problems as those living with married parents. In one study, 70% of youth in State-operated facilities, like detention centers, were from single-parent homes.

Female children are seven times more likely to become pregnant teenagers if they come from a fatherless home. Kids without a father are four times more likely to live in poverty, and two times more likely to drop out of school. They are also more likely to abuse alcohol and drugs, more likely to commit crimes, and more likely to go to prison. Lastly, in a 2022 study of fifty-five school shootings, only ten of the school shooters, 18%, were raised in a home with both biological parents. Eighty-two percent grew up in an unstable family or a single parent home.

The saddest thing about these statistics and studies is that our government and our political leaders know this information but choose to do nothing about it. Our leaders need to start enacting programs that reward mothers and fathers who stay together, providing our children with a more stable home life. It would be an easy fix, so I am hoping something changes in the near future. Let's do everything we can to encourage fathers and mothers to stay together for the health of their children.

Another problem facing today's children is bullying at school, which is the number one cause for school shootings. And with the rise in popularity of social media and cell phones, and apps like Snapchat and TikTok, these kids have many more opportunities to bully their classmates. Schools must have a very strict and enforceable bullying policy, and they must enact very serious consequences for those who bully and abuse other students. This bullying takes place at school, as well as after school, at places like school buses and bus stops. And for sure, it continues on social media when the kids arrive home from school and into the night.

Although you might think we have figured this bullying thing out, with the advent of cell phones and social media, bullying and physical confrontations are at an all-time high in many schools. If your kids are being bullied or harassed, please report it. And if your son or daughter is a bully, they are playing a very dangerous game, one that could actually cause them to lose their life. Teach your kids to treat everyone with respect and to never bully other students. Let's all do our part and work together to end bullying and abuse.

The violence that our leaders have allowed to be marketed to our children today is quite shocking. If anything shocks my live audiences at my trainings, it is the entertainment we are selling our children today at places like Walmart, Target, and GameStop. This shocking entertainment includes violent video games, internet pornography, torture films, and sexually degrading and violent music. Kids growing up today are surrounded by guns, death, and violence. A quick Google image search of just a few of the recent movie posters alone is all you need to see to determine why our young people are so fascinated with guns, violence, shootings, and assault rifles.

Grab your phone and do a Google image search of the following movie posters: *Pineapple Express*, *Max Payne*, *Quantum of Solace*, *Transporter 3*, *Legend*, *The Punisher*, *White House Down*, *John Wick*, *Resident Evil*, *The Purge: Anarchy*, *Killing Them Softly*, *The Heat*, *Hansel & Gretel*, *Zombieland*, and *Dawn of the Planet of the Apes*. This will show you that guns, violence, assault rifles, and death are the main themes of many of the movies that young people are watching today. And those are just the posters. Can you imagine what the actual movies are like?

Today's video games take violence and sex to another level, with adult themes being marketed to children. It is one thing to watch violent movies and listen to violent music, but the violent video games are interactive and allow you to participate in the violent acts. Titles like *Call of Duty: Modern Warfare*, *Manhunt*, *Gears of War*, *God of War*, *Mortal Kombat*, *Hatred*, *Dead Space*, *The Evil Within*, *Silent Hill*, *Resident Evil*, *Gears of War 2*, *Soldier of Fortune*, *Dead By Daylight*, *Conan Exiles*, *For Honor*, *Friday the 13th*, *Fortnite*, *Sniper Elite 4*, and the grandaddy, *Grand Theft Auto 5*, promote violence, death, murder, street crime, and guns. *Grand Theft Auto 5*, one of the most successful games ever sold, with over six billion dollars in sales, promotes street crimes, killing cops, prostitution, and the brutal killing of women.

In one pretty realistic scene, you pick up a prostitute and have oral sex and intercourse with her in a vehicle. You then can kill her in a myriad of ways, and it doesn't stop there. You can pull out your phone and photograph her corpse, stomp on her head, and then pull out your gun and shoot her, making her bleed. You can photograph her bleeding corpse, saving these photos to your phone. Lastly, you can pull out a gas can, pour gasoline all over her, and set her on fire. This is something a serial killer might do, so yes, this game is basically teaching our children to be serial killers, and the government has turned their heads and are allowing this to happen.

The game also allows you to take violence to a whole new level. There is a modification you can use, or as they call it, a mod, to modify *Grand Theft Auto V* and turn it into a school shooting video game. It is called the *Columbine Mod*, and you can become Dylan Klebold, shooting police officers and civilians, with the game allowing you to practice carrying out a school shooting-type attack. You can end it by shooting yourself in the head, just like the Columbine killers did.

Video game makers will scream that the game isn't meant to be played by children, knowing full well that most of their players are children, teens, and college students. Unfortunately, the US government doesn't protect children from violent video games. The video game companies rate their own games, and the stores that sell these games make their own rules. It is time we begin regulating video games in the same way we regulate pornography and other adult content. Since they claim the games are really meant for adults, let's make sure the law states that you must be eighteen years old to purchase and play these violent video games. And if a retailer sells these games to those under the age of eighteen, they should open themselves up to fines and prosecution. Will some parents still purchase these games for their children? Of course. But they might pause if they know that the games have such graphic sex and violence that it is actually illegal for children to buy them. If they know the government is basically saying this isn't really meant for children, they might at least give it a second thought. The same could be said for alcohol, tobacco, vaping, and pornography. Some parents still buy those things for their children, but at least they know those items are really meant to be consumed by adults.

With the rise of teen violence, mass murder, and school shootings, our politicians have blamed the weapon instead of the person using the weapon and want to ban assault rifles. The question I want to ask them is, "Why do you think these kids want to use assault rifles in their shootings?" The answer? Because you have allowed the entertainment industry to glamorize these guns to children now for decades, and it is starting to come back to haunt you.

When I first began my company in 1985, launching my forty-year study on teen violence, school shooters were using weapons like their father's revolvers, .22 rifles given to them by their parents, and shotguns used for hunting. There were no rifles used in school shootings back then. Unfortunately, once our leaders allowed these entertainment companies to promote and glamorize these guns to children, we now are seeing the rise in rifles being used in school shootings, mass shootings, and gang shootings.

A lot of killers, especially mass murderers and school shooters, talk about their love for violent video games, and some have stated that they practiced on those games for their crimes. We know the Parkland mass murderer and the Sandy Hook mass murderer played violent video games for upward of fifteen hours per day. The New Zealand mass murderer practiced on *Call of Duty* and recreated the game by mounting a camera on his helmet, live streaming his massacre for all to see, and it looked very similar to his favorite video game. Although I feel there is a connection between these violent games and real life violence, my research states that you need more than one cause to become a juvenile killer. I definitely believe these games play a role in today's violence, mass murder, and school shootings, and although they are only one piece of the puzzle, it is a piece that I see in over 90% of the cases I research.

Another one of my concerns for today's kids, and the innocence of children, is internet pornography. The fact that this graphic and violent sexual content is a click away with no real safeguards is very troubling and frightening. Kids consuming internet pornography can quickly find themselves looking at child pornography as well as torture pornography. It is one thing if an adult wants to view this sexual and violent content, which is totally legal, but children are a different story. A child's brain, which is far from being fully developed, cannot handle this kind of adult content. I have seen the effects on children addicted to porn, resulting in acts of rape and violence, signs of depression, and threats of suicide. Many of the serial killers I interview talk about tracing their violent fantasies back to when they first discovered pornography, usually at a very young age. Serial killers like Ted Bundy, Ed Gein, and Dennis Rader all talked about discovering their father's or grandfather's pornography stash, which started the ball rolling for all of them.

An example of one of these cases is fourteen-year-old Joshua Phillips from Jacksonville, Florida. In 1998, Joshua asked his parents for a computer in his bedroom. They obliged, bought him a computer, and hooked it up to the internet. It is not a surprise that little Joshua discovered pornography pretty quickly, and he soon became addicted to it. The problem with juveniles and pornography is that they don't look at the same content over and over. When it comes to juveniles, pornography is escalatory, meaning teens and children escalate their porn content, needing a bigger dopamine hit to get the same effect. They will continue to search for more shocking content, usually leading them down the road toward torture pornography or child pornography. In the case of Joshua Phillips, he gravitated toward torture pornography, and his favorite website investigators found on his computer was *Cheerleader Torture*. He became addicted to torture pornography at the young age of fourteen, and it had devastating consequences.

Not long after, an eight-year-old girl named Maddie Clifton went missing from her home, disappearing from the same neighborhood Joshua lived in. She had been missing for a week, and the community was searching everywhere for her. Joshua was so concerned that he was on the search crew as well, and he kept her "missing" poster in his bedroom. Unfortunately, Maddie was deceased, and Joshua knew exactly where she was. He slept on top of her every night for a week, as her body lay under his waterbed. Joshua had lured Maddie to his yard, dragged her into his house, and raped, beat, stabbed, and strangled the little girl to death. He then stuffed her dead body under his waterbed. He would go to school every morning, help the search crew look for her after school, and sleep on top of her at night.

Finally, one day his mother was cleaning his room and saw some liquid leaking from under his waterbed. Upon removing a piece of the frame, a set of feet fell out, and Joshua's mother found Maddie. In a state of shock, she called 911, and the police quickly responded. Joshua confessed to the murder. He was convicted and sentenced to life without parole, and he continues to serve his life sentence in a Florida state prison.

It doesn't take too many clicks when viewing porn to stumble across child pornography or torture pornography, which is the scariest part of internet pornography.

Here are the latest porn stats: The average age of first exposure to porn is eleven years old, 33% of porn users are females, and 10% of porn users are under ten years old. There is no telling how much damage the porn industry is doing to our children, and we also know that it has a negative effect on the actors who participate in the filming of these videos. Unfortunately, there is no way to measure the kind of damage this is doing to these young brains, but I do see the consequences in the behavior of teens growing up. I am hoping I can make enough noise to get our politicians and lawmakers to take action and hold the porn companies and producers accountable, and to protect the innocence of our precious children.

The good news is that some states have already begun what I have been asking for—an age verification system—and you do that by making people register online to view porn. I am pretty sure that Florida, Kentucky, and other states have begun this process. If you choose to view internet pornography, the laws should be the same as they are for buying porn at a convenience store. You must be eighteen years old, and to view it, you must register with your ID. And if a porn company doesn't follow these rules and sells pornography to children or allows children to view their content without restriction, they should be charged under our child pornography laws and heavily fined.

Another issue we are dealing with is the movie industry. Today's movies have slowly become more violent, especially with the improvement of special effects. Movies have been known to inspire many killers throughout history, but the new wave of torture films and the graphic violent content has me concerned, especially when they fall into the hands of children. Movies like *Texas Chainsaw Massacre*, *Evil Dead*, *Hostel*, and *Saw* have graced our theaters and streaming services for decades, but due to improvements in technology, and special effects, the recent releases of these franchises have literally become torture pornography. These new films are filled with dismemberment, decapitation, nudity, rape, graphic violence, and pornography.

In the film *Hostel 2*, a woman is strung up naked, while another nude woman lying on the ground slices her to pieces and stabs her, enjoying in ecstasy the blood that is leaking onto her face and body below. She rubs the victim's blood all over her body in enjoyment, then grabs a sickle and slices her throat, killing the hanging woman as blood sprays all over the movie screen. That film was rated R for teens, ages seventeen, eighteen, and nineteen years old, and played on many big screens across the US. The film earned seventeen million dollars and was banned in many countries.

Some killers point to movies as the inspiration for their crimes, while others can be connected to their favorite moves by the crime scene evidence. One of those cases is the murder of two-year-old James Bulger by two ten-year-olds, Robert Thompson and Jon Venables. The case occurred in England, and the boys may have been inspired by the movie *Child's Play*, since both Chucky and the victim were splattered with blue paint and beaten to death. Daniel Gonzalez, also in the UK, was thought to have been inspired by *Nightmare on Elm Street* when he stabbed at least four people to death. In Pittsburgh, Pennsylvania, attorneys claimed that eighteen-year-old Michael Anderson was inspired by the movie *A Clockwork Orange* when he stabbed and strangled a seventeen-year-old female to death. In 2016, two teen girls, inspired by *American Horror Story*, targeted and stabbed one of their grandfathers to death, with robbery as the motive. Michael Hernandez, fourteen, claimed to be inspired by *American Psycho* and *The Silence of the Lambs* when he stabbed a fellow classmate to death inside the school bathroom.

Steven Miles, inspired by the television show *Dexter*, killed and dismembered his seventeen-year-old girlfriend in England, even going so far as to copy Dexter by wrapping her dismembered body in plastic and dumping the body parts in trash containers. Thierry Jaradin was inspired by the *Scream* movies when he used two kitchen knives to stab his female victim thirty times, mutilating her body, wearing a *Scream* costume while he committed the murder. Jake Evans had watched Rob Zombie's *Halloween* movie three times before proceeding to kill two members of his family. He wanted to stab them to death like Michael Myers, but instead chose to shoot them with a revolver to spare them any pain. He killed his sister and mother, but his father survived because he was away on a business trip.

In 1999, inspired by *The Silence of the Lambs*, Anthony Lauritsen attacked and murdered his grandmother, who was at the top of his kill list. He bludgeoned her with a hammer and then, using a lawn edger, he disemboweled her, also nearly decapitating her. It was brought out in court that Anthony had watched that movie several times, and his favorite scene was where Hannibal attacks a police officer and removes his organs. My recent interview with Atlanta serial killer Aeman Presley revealed that he was inspired by the film *300,* and he told me he still remembers the clashing of the swords and the sound they made. He said it drove him to walk around Atlanta and shoot innocent victims. The good news is that movies are rated by governmental authorities, the bad news is that they still easily end up being watched by children of all ages. It would be wise if parents would monitor what movies and entertainment their children are consuming and do their best to protect them from this graphic and violent content.

Another major influence on children and teens today is the music industry that they love so much and are so influenced by. We know these artists influence their fans to wear the same clothing, shoes, or jewelry, so why can't they influence them with their message? The music industry that is geared toward children has become very violent and sexual in nature, even adding nudity to their music videos. Rapper 21 Savage has a music video for his song "All The Smoke," where he decapitates one female and throws her head into the woods. In the same video, he also beats a woman to death by bashing her head in with a hammer, all while wearing an upside down cross on his face.

In the video for her song "Bitch Better Have My Money," Rhianna kidnaps a female victim, stuffs her into a wooden trunk, and takes her away. Once she arrives at a warehouse, she strips her naked, strings her up, and hangs her. The video ends with Rhianna lying naked, covered in money and the victim's blood. How does our society react to this kind of entertainment, mostly aimed at children? They invite her to perform at the halftime show at the 2023 Super Bowl. Oh, and her boyfriend, rapper ASAP Rocky, likes to kill cops in his music videos, whom he represents as pigs, and then butchers them into hot dogs. These are the kind of people our society and companies like the NFL gives a massive platform to.

Cardi B is another top artist with a penchant for violent messages. One of her songs, "Wet Ass Pussy," was the number one song in 2020, winning all kinds of awards. The lyrics and music video are sexually explicit, with the lyrics including words like "pussy," "whores," and suggestions to "gobble" and "swallow me."

In another music video for the song called "Press," Cardi B is shown shooting and killing a bunch of people as she is walking through the video, singing and covered in blood. She is wearing a body suit to make her appear that she is nude. The violent lyrics include suggestions to fuck and kill prostitutes, wear a bulletproof vest, and create a murder scene.

The lyrics to these and many similar songs are easily found online with a simple Google search.

If these kinds of music videos came out in the 1930s, 1940s, and 1950s, they wouldn't only have never been released, but the artist would have probably been arrested for public indecency. And if they told the authorities they wanted to sell this violence and pornography to children, they might have ended up in an insane asylum. If this content was released in the 1960s, 1970s, and even the 1980s, it would probably have come out but wouldn't have been mainstream. It would have been tucked away and only available for those eighteen and older. Remember the old Blockbuster video store? The more graphic content was hidden away in the back room, labeled the "Adult" section. This is where this kind of content would have been found, even in the 1980s, when we still protected the innocence of children.

Fast forward to the 2000s, where this content is available everywhere and to anyone. Children are no longer protected from this graphic content, as they have had their innocence stolen at a very young age. Instead of being locked up in mental institutions or jails, these performers are becoming rich and famous. Rhianna was awarded the Super bowl halftime show, 21 Savage received a Grammy award in 2020, and Cardi B was recently seen on a Zoom interview with President Biden. Fame, fortune, and power are the rewards our society has given these negative role models. And as many of these "role models" release this material for your children, many of them don't allow their own children to consume this content. Many of their children are protected in private schools, and they are protected from negative influences. People like rapper Snoop Dogg talks about bitches and hoes, guns, and the gang lifestyle, all while he lives in a peaceful suburb married to the same woman for nearly thirty years. A double standard, for sure.

Shock rocker Marilyn Manson has been accused of inspiring the Columbine school shooters, but that was incorrect. They enjoyed German bands like Rammstein and probably weren't fans of Manson. But Manson, whose real name is Brian Hugh Warner, has inspired other school shooters I have spoken to, as well as many juvenile killers who loved his music. The ultimate connection was Cleveland, Ohio school shooter Asa Coon, fourteen, who walked into his school, SuccessTech Academy, with two guns, shooting two teachers and two students in 2007. Coon used two handguns, a .22 caliber revolver and a .38 caliber revolver, and was wearing a Marilyn Manson T-shirt. After shooting his victims, Coon walked into a classroom and fatally shot himself in the head. He had been the target of bullies and had suffered from mental issues. I am not blaming Marilyn Manson for this shooting, but there is a connection, for sure.

Many of the killers I interview claim they were inspired by violent entertainment. Joshua Cooke shot both of his parents to death in Virginia after being inspired by the movie *The Matrix*. He was also listening to a song called "Bodies" by Drowning Pool in his headphones as he murdered his parents. The lyrics to that song include letting the bodies hit the floor. Tennessee school shooter Jamie Rouse was inspired by his death metal music, especially Deicide. California school shooter Charles Williams told me he left his father a suicide note before heading to school, including the depressing lyrics to the Lincoln Park song "In The End." Williams took the bus to Santana High School and opened fire, shooting fifteen classmates and killing two. Again, I am not blaming this entertainment for these crimes, but it surely does play a role in these incidents. I believe if these teens weren't obsessed with this violent entertainment, these crimes may not have occurred.

Another cultural landmine parents should be aware of are social media platforms and phone applications. This technology can lead to your children being bullied online, and it can lead to them meeting strangers for sexual activity. Some of these apps allow strangers to track your child's location if they aren't careful with their privacy settings. These apps and platforms change every month, but here is a list of apps that might cause concern for you as a parent or adult:

Down, Omegle, Hoop, Yik Yak, KiK Messenger, Snapchat, Snapsave, Ask FM, 4Chan.com, Yeti, Poof, Whisper, Secret, Yubo, Tinder, Dubsmash, Chat Roulette, Badoo, Slingshot, Wishbone, Bigo Live, Discord, Roblox, Yarn, Twitter, Burn Book, Lipsi, Zepeto, Tellonym, IMVU: 3D Avatar, Tik Tok, Chatous, GroupMe, Tumblr, Periscope, Phhhoto, YouNow, FindMyFriends, Bumble, Instagram, Live.Me, Holla, Hot or Not, and Blendr.

As an example, the popular Snapchat app can fool your children into thinking that the sexually explicit messages and photos they send will disappear, but they can be saved by others. On Instagram, users can now access pornography, and on Discord, users can be exposed to all kinds of dangers, including pornography, hate speech, and interaction with online predators. Omegle is an anonymous video chatting platform that can expose your children to nudity and live sex acts. Hoop allows children to connect with total strangers, swiping through profiles similar to the sex app Tinder. Kik Messenger allows children to meet strangers in chat rooms, many of them adults.

There are also photo vault apps that might look like a calculator, but their sole purpose is to hide photos from others, including parents, school administrators, and police officers. There are also apps that can turn your smartphone into a drug scale, allowing you to weigh drugs in grams or ounces. Along with technology, items that can be purchased on websites like Amazon is mind-blowing. There are drug concealment items like water bottles, Pringles chip containers, Monster energy drink cans, and Axe body spray containers, along with fake tampons. These devices have compartments allowing juveniles to hide their drugs and alcohol from school authorities, parents, and law enforcement officers. On Amazon right now, you can even purchase meth pipes and have them delivered in one day.

Since many predators use these apps to stalk and groom children, you might want to consider using monitoring software to track your child's phone or computer use. Just google "monitoring software for Apple phones," and you should get some results of monitoring products. Some of the names I have seen in the past include Bark.us, Mspy. com, Aura.com, KidsGuard Pro, Norton Family Premier, Net Nanny, PhoneSheriff, My Mobile Watchdog, Qustodio, Boomerang, and Circle Home Plus.

A lot of teens are obsessed with deadly weapons, including firearms, rifles, knives, bombs, swords, and hatchets. Anything our government can do to limit these companies glamorizing firearms to children would be a big help. It is also helpful to understand where teens get their ideas, mainly movies and video games, and keep that in mind as you devise a plan to protect our children.

After the two-year COVID lockdown, which I thought was a horrible idea, the US became very violent. The homicide rate rose from 12,000 homicides to 16,000 homicides, along with an increase in mass shootings, school shootings, and suicides. Understanding that juveniles are fragile today, as well as depressed and suicidal, it would be a big help to eliminate bullying at school, stop confusing kids with adult issues like gender confusion, and just let kids be kids. The suicide rate is higher in teens who are struggling with mental health issues, so we need not add any more stress to the lives of children today. When I was growing up in the 1980s, many of these issues were unheard of, and kids could just be kids. Let's wait until these kids' brains are fully developed so they can process these hard issues when they are mature adults.

The use of drugs, alcohol, and medication can contribute to teen violence, with many of the medications these kids are taking causing possible depression, suicidal thoughts, and homicidal thoughts. Many students today are also vaping with THC. Being a teenager today is tough enough, but adding mind-altering drugs can lead to a disastrous outcome. Another issue facing kids growing up today is the lack of spirituality. Back in the days of *Leave it to Beaver* and *The Andy Griffith Show*, families went to church together on Sunday, and many kids were taught faith in God growing up. When a child has faith in their life, they have a purpose and a reason to live. When you eliminate this from a kid's life and you take away discipline at home and at school, there really isn't any reason for a child to go on. They have no purpose and no reason to live. And this is why so many juveniles are committing the crimes we see them committing, including the school shootings and mass shootings, the family murders, and all of the gang violence.

The last issue destroying this young generation is untreated mental illness. Many kids today are mentally unstable and depressed, with not much to live for. Not only do these kids need therapy and guidance, but some need to be sent away for long-term care. And when these kids become adults, there are few options for them to get free mental health care. Our political leaders have closed many of the facilities that were open to help mentally ill adults, and the ones that are open either have very long waiting lists or their cost prevents the average adult from seeking help. I believe every state should have at least four mental health facilities that resemble a Marriott or Hilton hotel, where those in need can check themselves in for free and stay as long as they feel necessary. Until our government makes this available to our citizens, we will continue to have school shootings, mass shootings, serial murders, and a high rate of suicide.

So where are our leaders, as I asked in the title of this chapter? Why are they not addressing these important issues that I have raised in this chapter? Why are they no longer protecting our children? Why have they put profit before the lives of innocent children? There needs to be laws created quickly to protect our children from violent video games and internet pornography, and to protect our kids from those who wish to do them harm. Please contact your local senators and members of Congress for me, so we can get this accomplished. I would be happy to mail them a free copy of this book if I need to.

Along with our political leaders and lawmakers, where are our women's groups at? Why am I the only person in the US talking about this? How can women sit quietly as these entertainment companies teach young men how to treat women, teach them that woman are to be raped, shot, stabbed, stomped upon, and set on fire. Where are you ladies? Are you okay with children being taught at Walmart to have sex with women, shoot them in the head, steal their money, take pictures of their corpse, and set them on fire as they do in the video game *Grand Theft Auto 5*?

Are you okay with women being stripped naked, dragged into a warehouse, and hanged and murdered like in the Rhianna video "Bitch Better Have My Money?" Every time I speak and show these clips, I ask myself and the audience, "Where are our women's groups at? Where are our civil liberty groups at? Where is the ACLU? Where is the National Organization for Women, or NOW? Where is the National Women's Law Center? Where is RAINN (Rape, Abuse & Incest National Network)? Where is Save The Children? Where is Gloria Allred? Where is Oprah Winfrey? And where is Ellen DeGeneres?" I am tired of fighting this fight alone and, as a man, and I need influential women to stand with me. If you are ready to fight, message me on my website, and let's make some changes together. Women deserve to be respected, honored, and treated with dignity. We can do this together.

To review, what needs to change, and how can we help these kids before they turn to violence and suicide? How can we stop the next school shooter, thrill killer, mass murderer, spree killer, or serial killer?

Solve the fatherless problem with some incentive for parents to stay together.

Enact tougher laws for bullying at schools, and force schools to take bullying incidents seriously.

Punish those who glamorize, promote, and sell violence to our children.

Enact laws to protect children from internet porn, and arrest and fine those who make porn available to children.

Legislate video games and fine those who break these laws.

Punish those who glamorize guns and assault rifles to children.

Add more warnings and limit the mind-altering drugs that are being peddled to our children and teens by doctors as medicine.

Enact laws restricting the news media from reporting the killers' names, so as to not motivate and inspire the next killer.

Allow prayer and religious beliefs back into schools.

Keep political and divisive flags, banners, and signs out of schools so as to not confuse children.

Reopen the hundreds of mental health facilities our leaders have closed, allowing suicidal people to get mental health care at no cost.

Create a watchdog group in Washington, DC to continue to monitor these groups and companies, keeping them in check.

What are some steps you can take as a parent or teacher to help troubled kids before they turn to violence or suicide? The first would be to assemble a list of professionals who could help these troubled teens and children. Professionals should be able to counsel a juvenile who is dealing with sexual issues, suicidal issues, and homicidal issues. You also need to assemble a list of places where parents could send their troubled children for long-term care, meaning six to nine months. My favorite is the Central Florida Behavior Hospital in Orlando, Florida, where kids can go to get long-term care, usually around nine months, and leave the hospital a healthy member of society.

The question I ask my attendees at my live shows is, "Can we save all the kids?" And they usually respond correctly with the answer of "No." But can we save some? And the answer to that one is "Yes!" We might not be able to save all of the troubled kids but we can save some, and that makes our efforts worth it. For those of you who are in the trenches fighting for our children, underpaid, getting verbally abused by dysfunctional parents, we see you. We know you aren't paid enough, but we see you. And I want to thank you from the bottom of my heart for the work you are doing. You are making a difference, so please be encouraged. If you ever need my help, please visit my website and send me an email. I would be honored to help you.

CHAPTER ELEVEN

DON'T BE A VICTIM: A CRIME PREVENTION PLAN

Before I help you devise a safety plan that will help prevent you from becoming a victim of a violent crime, let me first give you an overview of violent crime in the United States without all of the political propaganda. My crime stats come from the FBI's Uniform Crime Report, also called the UCR. Lock in as I walk you through our homicide statistics, mass murder statistics, and agenda-free gun stats. What you read might surprise you as much as it surprised me.

Prior to the COVID lockdown, the US had on average of around 12,000 homicides per year. After the two-year lockdown, homicides rose from 12,000 to around 16,000 per year. If you want to get specific on what types of homicides, how victims were killed, and who the killers and the victims were, just jump on the FBI UCR website; the stats are pretty easy to read and understand.

When we talk about mass murders, a typical year prior to the COVID lockdown was around twenty-four mass murders per year. After the two-year lockdown, mass murders rose to approximately forty per year, almost double the number prior to the COVID lockdown. The FBI's definition of a mass murder is the killing of four people at one time and in one location. Our biased media, whose specialty is to cause fear and panic among Americans, defines mass shootings as shooting four people. Using their definition, nobody has to die to make it a mass shooting, which allows them to use a much higher number than the FBI. In 2023, the FBI reported forty mass murders, while some politicians and mass media outlets reported there were 656 mass shootings that same year.

Where do you think those 656 mass shootings took place? They aren't happening at our schools and colleges, nor are they happening at libraries or movie theaters. So, where are they happening? The mass shootings they are counting are usually gang shootings and drive-bys, occurring in our urban areas and inner cities. If you know anything about street crime, these types of shootings happen nightly in most big cities and are almost impossible to prevent. The truth is, they are counting gang shootings and trying to pass them off as school shootings to cause panic among US citizens and help the biased politicians push their political agendas. So, I would warn you to be very careful about statistics and which ones you trust, and I would never trust a statistic or study done by a political group or the media. I trust the FBI, Homeland Security, and the Secret Service. Now, I do believe that some of the forty mass murders that the FBI counts are deadly gang shootings, so to be clear, if you want to count kids being killed in school shootings or church shootings, that number is much lower, probably about ten or fifteen incidents per year.

Another scare tactic that some of our politicians and media outlets use is a number like "36,000 gun deaths per year in the US." This number was prior to the COVID lockdown, so in all honesty, it is probably higher today. But when we break that number down, it isn't actually what they want you to believe. The 36,000 gun deaths aren't murders, but instead, mostly suicides. Of those 36,000 gun deaths, 22,000 are suicides, which would be "most" gun deaths in the US, 61%. Those are people who usually purchase their guns legally and proceed to kill themselves. They also include approximately 500 accidents per year and 500 justified killings per year, which are people protecting themselves with their gun. So when you defend yourself against an attacker or the police shoot someone trying to kill them, they include those gun deaths as part of the gun problem.

Let's break down that statistic even more. Of the 36,000 gun deaths they speak of, only 13,000 are actually gun homicides, in a country of approximately 340 million people. And if you live in the US, you know that these gun homicides rarely happen in nice suburban towns or safe rural towns. And many people own guns in these areas, so if guns were the problem, there would be plenty of homicides there as well. Instead, 80% of these gun murders happen in our urban areas and inner cities, where gangs, crime, and drug dealers thrive. So when studying the 36,000 gun deaths number, it shines a light on two problems we have in the US: suicide and urban gun violence. And our politicians will do nothing to solve either problem.

If you wanted to solve the US suicide problem, which is nowhere near as high as other counties like China and Japan, you would have to reopen all the mental health facilities our leaders have closed, allowing adults to check in to get free mental health care for as long as they need it. And if you want to stop urban violence, which is a much bigger problem, you would have to spend billions of dollars to improve our inner city schools, offer jobs for inner city kids, and create more opportunities for them to improve their standing in life. These kids have no education, no positive leaders, no family, and no hope.

Another statistic that is important to understand is what types of guns do killers use in the US to commit their crimes? Our political leaders and media talk a lot about assault rifles, which are actually AR-15 rifles. Here is the breakdown of guns used in US homicides:

80% Handguns
10% Shotguns
10% Rifles (2% AR-15s)

As you can see, most murders in the US are handgun murders, and if you remember in the previous paragraph, they occur in the city. So, our gun problem in the US is actually a "handgun in the hood" problem, and not an assault rifle or mass shooting problem. Our politicians want to paint it as an assault rifle problem to further their political agendas, but our problem is criminals and gang members killing each other with illegal handguns, and they will never follow any laws created by our political leaders and lawmakers. It is nearly an impossible problem to solve.

So, when you hear a media outlet or a politician talking about gun violence, and they mention things like "more common-sense gun laws," "banning assault rifles," and "raising the purchase age of guns," you now know two things: either they have no idea what they are talking about, or they are trying to lie to the public to further push their political agendas. Making more laws to stop the 80% of killers who follow no laws? Murder is already illegal, folks. And banning a weapon responsible for 2% of our murders, even though most of those murders also take place in the hood? Even if you banned and confiscated all thirty million assault rifles that are known to exist in the US, you would at best only stop 2% of murders. In reality, those killers would just move to another firearm, like a handgun or a shotgun, and they would continue to kill each other. Do you want a solution? Do you want to fix this problem? How about we stop blaming inanimate objects and get to the heart of this problem, the problem being young people with no hope, and young people with no fathers. That is the only way to change this crime wave that is occurring today in our major cities.

In light of what I just covered, as we devise a safety plan for you and your family, it is quite obvious you don't want to live in an urban area where most of these murders take place. That would be step one, moving your family to a safe neighborhood. And as long as you stay away from buying or selling drugs or sex, and you stay away from gang activity, the chances of you being killed in a safe community are very low. Next, let's take a look at four areas that you can address in your safety plan:

Home Safety
Travel Safety
Vehicle Safety
Condition Yellow, also known as Situational Awareness

Home safety is by far the most important of these areas, since you spend more time at home than anywhere else. This is your castle, your sanctuary, and a place where you should feel safe. After choosing a safe area to live in, there are three things killers have told me in my forty years of interviews that they don't want to see if they choose to victimize you and your family. They are dogs, guns, and cameras, and in that order. I have started telling my live audiences that they must have at least two of these three components, although I would prefer all three. As you can see, a dog is the number one deterrent for crime, and it has always been the killer's number one response. Dennis Rader, "BTK," told me that if I had a dog, my wife Wendi would never become one of his victims. He would skip our house, even if he just saw dog prints in our yard. So, a large dog is a great addition to your crime prevention plan, and by a large dog, I am talking about a German shepherd, Doberman pinscher, Akita, Bullmastiff, Pit Bull terrier, Boxer, Great Dane, Rottweiler, and an American Bulldog. These dogs are deterrent dogs, and much better than a smaller breed dog that just barks.

A gun was number two on this list, although owning a gun isn't for everyone. If you own a gun, it is a great deterrent, and it can save your life or the lives of your loved ones. You will want to make sure to store your gun in a steel gun safe, something similar to a Vapen Gun Safe, and keep it out of reach of children, visitors, and intruders. You also need to train with that firearm and learn how to use it safely. A gun is the ultimate equalizer, and when used properly, it can even the playing field with a dangerous criminal, including a serial killer. Most of the time, when you own a gun, you don't even need to fire the weapon to end a threat, as just displaying it to someone with bad intentions usually neutralizes the threat. There is nothing like having that peace of mind when carrying a concealed weapon, and it helps eliminate the constant fear of being victimized. On the flip side, if you aren't comfortable with a firearm, or you feel that you cannot store it safely, then by all means don't buy a gun.

While we are talking about personal protection devices, let's not give people bad advice, especially women, when it comes to protecting themselves. Suggesting something like a stun gun, pepper spray, or even telling them they should just take a self-defense course like Jiu-Jitsu is very dangerous. Only someone who has no knowledge about violent killers would advise someone to get that close to a bad guy to defend themselves. Law enforcement officers will never get within twenty feet of a dangerous person, shooting them with a taser at a distance, or worse, shooting them with a firearm if they continue to advance toward them. Never give people dangerous advice like this, especially women.

As for me, I own a few different firearms, and they each serve a different purpose. On the daily, especially when I am just walking my dog or checking my mail, I carry a small .380 handgun in my pocket, similar to a Bodyguard by Smith & Wesson. When I think I might actually need a firearm, if I am going into town or out to dinner, I usually holster a Glock-type firearm. And when shit hits the fan, and let's say four thugs are trying to break down my front door, of course I have an AR-15 rifle when I really need protection. I use the same type of rifle that protects politicians and the president, and I use the same type of rifle that law enforcement officers use when the situation is dire. I prefer rifles from Black Rain Ordnance in Missouri.

If you choose not to own a gun, the second best personal protection device would be SOK pepper spray. It is a gel that can be sprayed from twenty to twenty-five feet away, and when someone is hit with this product, they cannot open their eyes. If I couldn't carry a firearm, I would carry SOK. This product can be found at www.sokdef.com, and there you can watch a video of the product in action.

Cameras were number three on the killer's list, and I also want to include security systems as well. Both of these are great deterrents to criminals who may target your home or family. My favorite home security system is SimpliSafe, due to its reasonable price and amazing cameras. It is also easy to install the system yourself. If you choose to just use cameras, my favorites are Ring, as in the doorbell cameras, Nest, which is powered by electricity, and Blink, which is powered by a two-year battery. Many stores like Home Depot, Lowes, and Costco sell kits with these cameras included. I would place cameras on each side of the exterior of your home, and a few cameras inside facing the doors. You will then be able to monitor your home twenty-four hours a day from wherever you are.

Along with cameras, I want you to add two more pieces to your security plan. I want you to add security window film to all of your first floor windows, and I want you to add door armor to all of your exterior doors. This almost makes your home like a fortress, and it gives you peace of mind when you aren't home. StrongGlass by MGT Films provides security to your windows and sliding doors, preventing intruders from entering your home. This product is reasonably priced, and the company will provide you with a free estimate. You can check out their products at mgtfilms.com. Regarding your doors, you need to add security to all of your entry doors, including the garage door, if you have one. This product is reasonably priced, and more information can be found at doorarmor.com.

I would then add some signage to the outside of your home, as well as stickers on your exterior doors. One would be a "Beware of Dog" sign or sticker, and another would be something like "Smile, you're on camera." Signage is a great deterrent, and it should definitely be used at your home to deter those who might target you personally. When it comes to firearms, I would never let people know you have a gun, even if it is a joke. No "Protected by Smith & Wesson" signs, no NRA stickers, and no "Protected by Glock" signs or stickers. The same would apply to your vehicle. Nobody needs to know that you own a firearm. I would also never open carry, as I think the safest way to carry a firearm is to keep it concealed. There are people who will kill you to get their hands on your firearm, so please be careful.

Another place where you spend a lot of time in is your vehicle. If someone locks onto you, they can always follow you to your home. So let's make sure your vehicle isn't a target or an invitation to criminals. Are you giving people too much information about yourself and your family members on your vehicle? Do you have a decal letting people know what school your children attend, or what church your family can be found at on a Sunday morning? Some parents will even add a decal to their vehicle with their children's name on it. Nobody needs to know that your spouse is in the military or that you have a baby on board. And nobody cares about your political affiliation. A military sticker lets people know that your spouse may often be out of town, and a "baby on board" sticker lets criminals know that you will be distracted when you stop at a store or a mall. I would skip all stickers and decals for your vehicle and protect your privacy. The same can be said for your luggage when traveling. When you travel, never fill out a luggage tag with your personal information, and never attach a luggage tag or a business card to your luggage. Nobody needs to know who you are or where you live. Remember, the airline will tag your bags and track your bags for you, so there is no need for you to add an additional tag.

Last, but most important, is living in a state of what I call "Condition Yellow," or what others might call "situational awareness." In my training, there are four stages of situational awareness: Condition White, Condition Yellow, Condition Red, and Condition Black. Condition White is being oblivious to what is happening around you, and many people live in this condition on a daily basis, thinking crime won't happen in their community. Condition Yellow is being aware of your surroundings at all times, keeping your head on a swivel, and being prepared should evil pay you a visit. Condition Red is taking action and fighting evil, defending your life and the lives of your loved ones. And Condition Black is being in shock mode, freezing, and probably becoming a victim of a rape, a robbery, or possibly a murder.

When you live in Condition White and bad shit happens, you usually move to Condition Black, and you usually die.

If you live in Condition Yellow and something bad happens, you are prepared and can move to Condition Red, which is fight mode. The chances of an intruder breaking into your home is low, and the chances of you being in a mass shooting is rare. But if it ever happens to you, I want you to be prepared, and I want you to survive.

What does living in Condition Yellow mean? When I go to a restaurant with my wife, I always place my back to the wall, facing the door of a restaurant. Condition Yellow means I never stay on the first floor of a hotel or apartment. Condition Yellow means I sit in the back row of the movie theater, near the stairway, should I need to take a shot down the stairs, never allowing anyone to sit behind me. Condition Yellow means when I exit a grocery store, I survey the parking lot as I walk toward my vehicle, instead of looking at my phone. Always be aware, and always have a plan. Like the saying goes, "Be polite. Be humble. And have a plan to kill everyone in the room." Always be prepared, and never be taken by surprise.

One last bit of advice: Now that you live in the suburbs or a rural community, there are a few more things you can do to not invite crime and criminals into your world. Here is my list of don'ts:

Don't join a gang
Don't buy or sell drugs
Don't buy or sell sex
Don't date strangers online, with apps like Tinder
Don't sell stuff to strangers online, with apps like Facebook Marketplace
Don't run or jog outside, never at night, and never alone
Don't marry or date a crazy person, and if you don't believe me, just watch *Dateline*, *48 Hours Mystery*, or *20/20*. I would rather be alone than with someone who is dangerous and unstable.

This plan doesn't guarantee your safety, but if you implement the steps I have discussed in this chapter, you and your family will be much safer and live with a greater sense of peace than before.

SELECTED PHOTOS

SPEAKING TRUTH TO EVIL

Phil & Wendi with Michigan serial killer Matthew
Macon, known as "The Mid Michigan Monster."

Phil & Wendi with Indiana serial killer William "Clyde" Gibson, who is also a necrophile and a cannibal.

Phil & Wendi with long haul trucker serial killer Dellmus Colvin, who killed upwards of 50 victims.

Phil interviewing Indiana serial killer William "Clyde" Gibson, who had a woman buried in his backyard, and was arrested with a woman's severed breast on his vehicle's center console.

Phil with New York Serial Killer Robert Spahalski, whose twin brother was also a killer.

Phil with juvenile serial killer and satanist Sean Sellers, Phil's first face-to-face interview with a killer.

Phil and Wendi with Florida Vampire thrill killer Rod Ferrell.

Phil with serial killer David Berkowitz, known as "The Son of Sam." Berkowitz was one of Phil's early face-to-face serial killer interviews.

Phil with two Tennessee school shooters,
Jamie Rouse and Jacob Davis.

APPENDIX A

THE LONGEST LIST OF BLACK SERIAL KILLERS EVER PUBLISHED

Most people can barely name one Black serial killer, and the most common answer would be Wayne Williams, "The Atlanta Child Killer," and Lee Boyd Malvo and John Allen Muhammad, "The DC Snipers." In reality, there are more than 1000 Black serial killers, making them 38% of all serial killers in US history. In this list are 1036 Black serial killers, and even if you don't agree that all of them are serial killers because some might be classified as spree killers or gang killers, there are easily 1000 names on this list that most would define as serial killers.

Also, America's deadliest male serial killer is a Black male, Samuel Little, "The Choke and Stroke Killer," and America's deadliest female serial killer is a Black female, Roberta Elder, known as "Atlanta's Mrs. Bluebeard." Also, America's youngest modern-day serial killer is a Black male named Craig Chandler Price, known as "The Warwick Slasher." With the recent change of the FBI's definition of a serial killer, from three to two victims, they are also beginning to include those who kill in the process of robberies, and those who kill for financial gain. Some of the most notable Black serial killers are listed below, in the event you want to look up some of their cases.

Disclaimer: Some of the serial killers listed in this section could be innocent, or they may have killed more or less victims than listed. My information comes from three sources: Media reports, police files, and court records. As you know, I wasn't present at the actual murders, so there is no way I can tell if someone might be innocent.

Joshua Julius Anderson, 5 victims

Jake Bird, The Tacoma Axe Killer, 46 victims

Henry Brisbon, The I-57 Murderer, 3+ victims

Wesley Brownlee, The Stockton Serial Killer, 6 victims

Rufus Cantrell, King of Ghouls Grave Robber, Black HH Holmes

Jarvis Roosevelt Catoe, DC Strangler, 8-11 victims

Billy Chemirmir, 22-30 victims

Nathaniel Robert Code Jr., The Cedar Grove Killer, The Shreveport Serial Killer, 8-12 victims

Alton Coleman and Debra Brown, 8 victims

Dellmus Colvin, The Interstate Strangler, 40-50 victims

Paul Durousseau, The Jacksonville Strangler, 9 victims

Roberta Elder, Atlanta's Mrs. Bluebeard, 13 victims

Lorenzo Fayne, 6 victims

Kendall Francois, The Poughkeepsie Killer, 8-10+ victims

Lonnie Franklin Jr., The Grim Sleeper, 10-68 victims

Carlton Gary, The Stocking Strangler, 4-9 victims

Alfred Gaynor, Big Al, 9-10 victims

Lorenzo Gilyard, The Kansas City Strangler, 6-13+ victims

Fred Glover, 15 victims

Mark Godeau, The Baseline Killer, The Baseline Rapist, 9 victims

Harrison Graham, The Corpse Collector, 7 victims

Vaughn Greenwood, The Skid Row Slasher, 11 victims

Geoffrey Griffin, The Roseland Killer, 7-8 victims

Robert Hayes, The Daytona Beach Serial Killer, 4+ victims

Ivan Hill, The 60 Freeway Killer, The Southside Slayer, 9+ victims

Calvin Jackson, Manhattan's West Side Killer, 9 victims

Charles Jackson Jr., The East Bay Slayer, 8+ victims

Elton Manning Jackson, The Hampton Roads Killer, 12 victims

Pearl Jackson, Odelle Jackson, Peyton Johnson, The Axeman of Birmingham, 14-15 victims

Ray Shawn Jackson, The Gillham Park Strangler, 6 victims

Wilbur Lee Jennings, The Ditchbank Murderer, 6+ victims

Milton Johnson, The Weekend Murderer, 5-17 victims

Vincent Johnson, The Brooklyn Strangler, 5-6 victims

Andre Jones & Freddie Tiller, 8 victims

Anthony Joyner, The Elderly House of Horrors, 6-18 victims

Posteal Laskey Jr., The Cincinnati Strangler, 7 victims

Derrick Todd Lee, The Baton Rouge Serial Killer, 7+ victims

Samuel Little, The Choke and Stroke Killer, 93 victims

Franklin Lynch, The Day Stalker, 3-13 victims

Jerry Marcus, The Tuskegee Strangler, 7 victims

Hulon Mitchell Jr., Yahweh ben Yahweh, 15 victims

Eddie Lee Mosley, The Rape Man, 8-16+ victims

Gerald Parker, The Bedroom Basher, 6 victims

Craig Chandler Price, The Warwick Slasher, 4 victims

Cleophus Prince, The Clairemont Killer, 6 victims

Anthony Robinson, The Shopping Cart Killer, 4+ victims

Marc Sappington, The Kansas City Vampire, 4 victims

Morris Solomon, The Sacramento Slayer, 7 victims

Erno Soto, Charlie Chop-Off, 4-5 victims

Anthony Sowell, The Cleveland Strangler, 11 victims

Lonnie V. Spells, The Trucker Murderer, 12 victims

Timothy Wilson Spencer, The Southside Strangler, 5 victims

Edward Surratt, The Shotgun Killer, 11-18+ victims

Brandon Tholmer, The West Side Rapist, 12-34 victims

John Floyd Thomas, The Westside Rapist, The Southland Strangler, 7-15+ victims

Maury Troy Travis, The Bi-State Strangler, 12-17+ victims

Chester Turner, The Southside Slayer, 16+ victims

Henry Louis Wallace, The Taco Bell Strangler, 11 victims

Carl Eugene Watts, The Sunday Morning Slasher, 15-100+ victims

Nathaniel White, 6 victims

Nicholas Lee Wiley, The Syracuse Serial killer, 3-7 victims

Wayne Williams, The Atlanta Child Killer, 24-30 victims

The Zebra Murderers, 73 victims

The two main reasons I am so passionate about this and am writing about this are: one, our law enforcement community is unaware of this problem, and two, our racist American news media outlets choose to ignore this crime wave so they don't appear racist. Both of these reasons are dangerous and result in innocent people being killed, especially Black women and Black children. It is time to stop playing politics and the race card, begin doing the work to sound the alarm to the public, and begin saving lives. I don't have a racist bone in my body, but I am one of the only people who will talk about these cases and talk about the victims who were killed by these serial killers, many of whom are Black. The media doesn't seem to be interested in them, or in these cases. So please understand why I am doing this, and what my motivations are. Here is the longest list of Black serial killers ever published, in alphabetical order.

MOHAMED S. ABDULKADIR: Killed two male victims, shooting one to death in 2009 in Nebraska, and then stabbing an inmate to death in 2011 in prison.

TONY ALVIN ABLES: Killed at least four victims in Florida from 1970 to 1990, raping, bludgeoning, shooting, strangling, and smothering them with a pillow. His victims included one male and three females, and he was released from prison to kill again.

KEITH ADAMS: Killed three male victims in Florida between the years of 2001 and 2005, shooting and bludgeoning his victims to death.

SALEEVAN ISSE ADAN: Killed three Black males in Georgia, strangling them to death from 2001 to 2009. His last victim was a fellow inmate.

CURTIS LAMONT ADKINS: Killed three male victims in Florida, shooting them to death in 2004.

DERRICK ANTWAN AGEE: Killed three Black victims in Georgia between the years of 1997 and 2000, shooting his victims to death.

THOMAS AIKENS: Killed eleven victims in New York, shooting to death ten males and one female in 1980.

RANDY ALANA: Killed one male and two females in California between 1983 and 2013, bludgeoning, stabbing, and strangling his victims to death. One victim was a fellow inmate, and he was released from prison to kill again; his last victim was a female federal defense investigator.

ANDRE STEPHEN ALEXANDER: Killed four victims in California between 1978 and 1980, shooting and stabbing two males and two females to death. One of his victims was a female Secret Service agent.

BILLY ALEXANDER: Killed three victims in Florida in 1991, shooting three Haitian immigrants to death. He told me a lot has changed since his crimes, and he has had a long road to recovery and redemption.

CARUTHERS ALEXANDER: Killed two victims in Texas between 1973 and 1981, raping and strangling them to death. One victim, nineteen, was abducted from her vehicle in a staged car accident. He was released from prison to kill again, and he was executed by lethal injection in 2001.

HENRY C. ALFORD: Killed two victims in North Carolina in 1963. It is from this case that we get the term "Alford plea," allowing a suspect to plead guilty in court but still maintain their innocence.

FRANKLIN DEWAYNE ALIX: Killed four male victims in Texas during the years of 1997 and 1998. His victims were raped and shot to death, and while he was in custody, he confessed to three more murders, multiple rapes, and multiple kidnappings. He was executed in 2010.

BILL ALLEN: Killed three male victims in Illinois in 1982, shooting them to death.

HOWARD ARTHUR ALLEN: Killed three elderly women in Indiana between the years of 1974 to 1987, robbing, bludgeoning, and stabbing them to death. He was sentenced to death in 1988, but this was later commuted to a life sentence.

JAMES F. ALLEN: Killed three male victims in Illinois between the years of 1969 and 1984, shooting his victims to death. He was released from prison to kill again. He sent me a letter saying that if I spoke to a friend of his first victim, he would cooperate with me. He was recently exonerated of one murder.

QUINCY JOVAN ALLEN: He killed four White victims in North Carolina, South Carolina, and Ohio in 2002. His victims were robbed, set on fire, and shot to death, and he recorded his murders into a tape recorder, calling himself "Weird Man." He killed three males and one female from

1968 to 1988. He recently had his death sentence commuted to life in prison without parole in South Carolina.

ROBERT SYLVESTER ALSTON: This former dishwasher from North Carolina killed four women between 1991 and 1993, raping them, strangling them, mutilating them, decapitating them, dismembering them, and dumping their body parts in multiple locations.

KING PHILLIP AMMAN REU-EL, FORMERLY KNOWN AS PHILLIP CHEATHAM: Murdered three victims in Kansas, shooting one male and two females to death between 1994 to 2003.

DARRYL MARTIN ANDERSON: Killed three and possibly five victims in Maryland during the years of 2012 and 2013, both male and females. His victims were all shot to death, and some were raped. He was already serving a life sentence for another murder when he was sentenced to 240 years in prison for shooting two women to death in 2013. He flipped off the court when he received his sentence.

DICKIE EDGAR ANDERSON JR.: Killed two White females in Connecticut during 1997 and 1998. He raped, strangled, and shot his victims to death, and he is suspected of more murders.

EMMANUEL ANDERSON: Killed one White female with an ice pick and shot two Black women to death in Tennessee and Illinois during 1934 and 1935. The victims were also raped and bludgeoned to death.

JOSHUA JULIUS ANDERSON: Killed five to seven victims in Oklahoma in 2006 and 2007. He killed both men and women of multiple races, and his most gruesome crime was a son and his elderly mother. He forced them to have sex, shot and killed them both, and ate part of the elderly women's brain.

RASHAWN T. ANDERSON: Killed two male victims in Kansas, one in 2005 and one in 2006, shooting his victims to death.

ROBERT ANDERSON: Killed one male and two females in Florida in 1912, shooting his victims to death.

TYRONE ANDERSON: Killed one male and three females in Missouri between 1975 and 1994, shooting, stabbing, and strangling his victims to death.

JESSE JAMES ANDREWS JR.: Killed three males and one female in Alabama and California between the years of 1966 and 1979, shooting and strangling them to death. In 1979, he killed three victims by shooting and stabbing, and he sodomized the female victim before killing her.

JOSHUA WAYNE ANDREWS: Killed four males and one female in Virginia and other states between the years of 2000 and 2002, shooting his victims to death.

PATRICK FRANKLIN ANDREWS: Killed three males in West Virginia and Washington, DC between 1997 and 2007, shooting and stabbing his victims to death. His 2007 case was the stabbing murder of a fellow inmate.

ANTWAN ANDRE ANTHONY: Killed at least four males and one female in North Carolina in 2012, shooting his victims to death. He is suspected of more murders, and his last crime was a triple murder at a store called Hustle Mart. He sent me a letter stating that he still had appeals, and he wouldn't talk about anything until his appeals were over.

MICHAEL LEE ANTHONY: This serial rapist turned serial killer in Michigan is responsible for at least two murders of Black females in 2001 while living in his elderly mother's basement. When he was arrested, he had two corpses in his apartment who had been raped and strangled or smothered to death. One was located under a pile of clothes, and one was in a freezer.

DEREK DANIEL ARCHIE: Killed one White male and one White female in Florida in 1975, raping, suffocating, and strangling his victims to death.

JAMES ARMSTRONG: Killed three males in Pennsylvania in 2009 and 2010, shooting his victims to death.

NOAH ARNOLD: Killed two males in Washington and Idaho, one in 1917 and one in 1923, shooting his victims to death.

TYRONE L. ARNOLD: Killed two females in Missouri, one in 1988 and one in 2011, raping and strangling his victims to death. He was released to kill again.

QUENTIN ARNWINE: Killed two White males in Colorado, one in 2006 and one in 2007, shooting his victims to death.

ROSCOE ARTIS: Killed three young Black females and possibly more in North Carolina in 1983, bludgeoning, raping, and dumping their bodies in a field. He was convicted because of DNA evidence, and he sent me a letter saying that he was willing to help me with my project.

LAZALE DELANE ASHBY: Killed one male and one female in Connecticut, one in 2002 and one in in 2003, raping, strangling, and shooting his victims to death.

ROBERT ELLWOOD ASKINS: Killed nine Black females in Washington, DC between 1938 and 1972. His victims were raped, strangled, poisoned, and shot to death. He was the serial killer responsible for "The Freeway Phantom" murders in the early 1970s, in which six women were abducted and killed.

BENJAMIN THOMAS ATKINS: "The Woodward Corridor Killer" and "The Highland Park Strangler" was a homeless crack addict turned serial killer who raped, tortured, and strangled with a cord at least eleven Black female crack addicts in Michigan in 1991 and 1992. He also enjoyed having sex with their corpses.

JAMES D. ATTERBURY: Killed two male victims in Florida between 1982 and 1984.

EDWARD AUGUSTINE: Killed three Black males in Louisiana between 2007 and 2010.

JOHN MILTON AUSBY: Killed three White females in Washington, DC in 1971, raping and shooting his victims to death.

ALFONSO AUSTIN JR.: Killed two female victims in Florida in 1976.

RUFUS LEE AVERHART: Killed two White male victims in Indiana, one in 1972 and one in 1981, shooting his victims to death.

RICKY ALLEN AZMOE: Killed three victims in Florida between the years of 1987 to 1990, shooting his victims to death.

HAROLD CLEVELAND BAIN: Killed two victims in Florida, one in 1958 and one in 1981, shooting his victims to death.

CHRISTOPHER NEAL BAKER: Killed two Black males in Alabama in 2012, shooting his victims to death.

EDWARD BAKER: Killed six victims in New York, Texas, and New Mexico between 1888 and 1891, bludgeoning and shooting his victims to death.

ANTHONY BALAAM: "The Trenton Strangler" sodomized and strangled to death four Black female prostitutes in New Jersey from 1994 to 1996, dumping their bodies in vacant lots.

ANTHONY ROZELLE BANKS: Killed a male and a female in Oklahoma, one in 1978 and one in 1979, shooting his victims to death.

DAVID EARL BANKS: Killed one Black female and two Black males in Illinois in 1990, raping, stabbing, and strangling his victims to death.

CLINTON BANKSTON JR.: Killed one White male and four White females in Georgia between April and August of 1987 at the age of sixteen. He stabbed a couple to death and also hacked three others to death with a hatchet.

JAMES ANTONIO BARNES: Killed between three and twenty Black victims in Illinois, Indiana, Louisiana, Mississippi, and Tennessee between 1988 to 1992, shooting his victims to death. He explained that he had a feeling that made him feel cold and numb, and it could only be relieved when he killed. He described his victims as "the vermin of the earth."

JEROME SIDNEY BARRETT: Killed four White women in Tennessee in 1975. The victims were raped and strangled to death, and he bragged that he killed "four blue-eyed bitches," one of his victims being a nine-year-old Girl Scout delivering cookies in her neighborhood. He is suspected of more murders.

LAMAR BASKIN JR.: Killed two females in Texas, a seventy-one-year-old female in 1990, and another woman in an office park. His victims were stabbed to death, and he was arrested through DNA.

ANTHONY DEVIAN BATES: Killed two Black males and one Black female in Georgia in 1996. His victims were shot to death, and he said in court, "If I had a chance to do it again, I can't say that I wouldn't."

ANTHONY GEORGE BETTLE: Killed his wife in 1987 at a Marine base and was sent to a federal prison in Georgia. While incarcerated, he murdered a male corrections officer with a hammer in 1994, which landed him on death row.

PATRICK BAXTER: Killed three females in New York between 1987 and 1990, raping, shooting, and stabbing his victims to death. His victims were fourteen, nineteen, and twenty-five years old. He told me, "I'm no psycho, socio, or any other personality disorder, at least none that the shrinks could diagnose."

CARL LAMONT BAYLESS: Killed three victims in Ohio between 1970 and 1974, shooting his victims to death. He killed his first victim at the age of fourteen.

HOWARD MILTON BELCHER: Killed four gay Black men while working as a prostitute in 2002 in Georgia. He robbed, raped, and strangled his victims to death, although he claims he is innocent. He has sent us dozens of letters and drawings, with a mix of threats, sexually charged poetry, rants about his innocence, and numerous prayers and Bible verses.

MICHAEL BERNARD BELL: Killed five Black victims in Florida between 1989 and 1993, shooting his victims to death. One of his victims was a two-year-old boy.

WILLIE FRED BELL: Killed two White males in Georgia in 2001, stabbing his victims to death.

SHIQUAN BELLAMY: Killed four Black males and one Black female in New Jersey in 2010, shooting his victims to death. Two of the victims were a recently engaged couple.

MALCOM BERNARD BENSON: Killed two victims in Michigan, one in 1995 and another in 2015, after being released from prison to kill again. He also sexually assaulted a female after he was released from prison.

SHEDDRICK DEON BENTLEY: Killed two White males in Florida, on in 2004, and one in 2016, strangling and stabbing his victims to death. The first victim was stabbed 150 times and his body was found in a dumpster.

NORMAN BERNARD: Killed three male victims in California in 1983, shooting his victims to death. He claimed he was helping the homeless by putting them out of their misery. He attempted to kill another victim in North Carolina, severing his penis and shooting him. The letters he sent me are hard to understand and really make no sense.

ALTON ALONSO BEST: Killed six Black victims in Washington, DC during the years of 1986 and 1987. The victims were raped, stabbed, and strangled to death, and he is a suspect in the Suitland Murders in Maryland, although he was only officially charged with one murder.

BRIAN RICARDO BETHELL: Killed three men in Florida in 2006 with robbery as the motive. A Bahama native, his victims were older men.

MARKO BEY: Killed one White and one Black female in New Jersey, one in 1983 and one in 1984, while he was a teenager. The victims were raped, beaten, and strangled to death.

YUSUF ALI BEY IV: He ordered others to kill one White male and two Black males in California in 2007, one victim being a journalist. The victims were all shot to death, and racism was one of the motivations.

TONY EDWARD BIGOMS: Killed two Black females in Tennessee, one in 2002 and one in 2012, raping, strangling, stabbing, and dismembering his victims.

DARRELL BERNARD BILLINGSLEA: Killed two Black males in Texas in 1989, and after his release from prison, he killed his ex-girlfriend in 2008, who was one of his prison penpals. His victims were shot and stabbed to death. He has sent me several letters telling me he is into Islam, and that he is innocent. He rants about the Texas court system and sends poems with titles like "Tears I've Cried in the Hood."

JAKE BIRD: "The Tacoma Axe Killer" killed between twenty-seven and forty-four White victims in sixteen states, including Washington, Utah, Nebraska, and Kansas. He killed his victims between 1935 and 1949, raping, shooting, stabbing, strangling, and bludgeoning them to death. His preferred weapons were an axe and a hatchet, and he killed both men and women evenly.

DARRYL WAYNE BIRDOW: Killed one Hispanic male and one White male in Texas in 1993. He would invade his victims' homes and strangle them to death with a coat hanger, and then steal their valuables.

RODNEY TROY BIXLER: He raped and killed three White females in Kentucky in 2000 and was also a serial rapist. His victims were raped and strangled to death, He was cooperative in his letter to me, telling me he hopes to tell his story and help others on the outside.

THERON BLACK: Killed a Black male and a Black female in Florida, one in 1959 and one in 1976, shooting his victims to death.

TERRY A. BLAIR: Killed nine Black females in Missouri from 1982 to 2004. His victims were raped, bludgeoned, and strangled to death. He has been cordial and workable with me, corresponding and answering my questions, and doing an interview with me. He hinted that there were more victims, but because of his children, he didn't want to discuss them.

ELMORE BOGAN: Killed two Black females in Ohio in 1988, raping and strangling them to death. One of his victims was only fifteen years old.

CLIFFORD STANLEY BOLDEN: Killed three male victims in California between 1979 and 1986, stabbing them to death. One of his victims was found in a bathtub.

MARTSAY BOLDER: Killed two Black males in Missouri, one in 1973 and one in 1979, shooting and stabbing his victims to death. His second victim was the stabbing death of a fellow inmate.

ARTHUR JEROME BOMAR: Killed and raped three victims in Pennsylvania and Nevada between the years of 1978 and 1997, bludgeoning one male and raping and bludgeoning two female victims to death. One of his victims was a Nevada police officer, and he was released from prison to kill again. One of his victims was beaten to death with a tire iron, and it is thought he had sex with one of his victims after death.

WILLIE BONNER: Killed three victims in Florida between 1992 to1998, raping and shooting his victims to death. He killed again after being released from prison, and he is suspected in more murders.

GEORGE AARON BOOKER: Killed one male and two females in New Jersey between 1971 and 1985, raping, bludgeoning, strangling, and stabbing his victims to death.

DONALD EUGENE BORDERS: Raped and smothered to death three elderly White females in North Carolina in 2003. He was arrested due to a DNA match.

RUFUS BOSWELL: Killed two victims in Florida, one in the 1980s and one in the 1990s, shooting his victims to death.

JOSEPH BOWEN: Killed three White males in Pennsylvania between 1971 and 1973, shooting and stabbing his victims to death. His first murder was that of a police officer. While in prison, he stabbed the warden and deputy warden of the prison, killing the warden.

CHARLES ANTHONY BOYD: "The Bathroom Slayer" killed one White and two Black females in 1986 and 1987 in Texas. The victims were raped, drowned, strangled, suffocated, and stabbed to death.

LUCIOUS BOYD: "The Lady Killer" killed between three and thirteen victims in Florida and Louisiana from 1993 to 1999, raping and stabbing his victims to death. One victim was murdered when she ran out of gas on her way home from church.

MICHAEL JOE BOYD: Killed one White male and one Black male in Tennessee, one in 1983 and one in 1986, shooting his victims to death. He killed again after being released from prison.

WILFORD BRADFORD: Killed two victims in Florida, one in 1976 and one in 1990, stabbing his victims to death.

JAMES OPELTON BRADLEY: Killed three females in North Carolina between 1988 and 2014, bludgeoning and strangling his victims to death. He first killed his eight-year-old stepdaughter and was released from prison to kill again. He is a former US Army sergeant.

WILLIAM J. BRADLEY: Killed one White male and one Black male in Ohio, one in 1963 and one in 1984. His victims were bludgeoned and shot to death.

BUD BRADSHAW: Killed three Black victims in Kansas between 1904 and 1935, shooting and stabbing his male and female victims to death.

JOSEPH BRANT: Killed four females in Louisiana between 2007 and 2008, raping, shooting, stabbing, and strangling his victims to death, and setting one of them on fire.

MICHAEL JEROME BRAXTON: Killed two Black males in 1993 in North Carolina, shooting his victims to death. In 1996, he continued his killing spree when he stabbed a fellow inmate to death.

MCARTHUR BREEDLOVE: Killed a White male and a White female in Florida, one in 1974 and one in 1978, stabbing his victims to death. He was also convicted of two rapes in California as well.

JAMES DENNIS BREWER: Killed one White male and one White female in Indiana, one in 1977 and one in 1978, bludgeoning and shooting his victims to death.

ANTHONY RAY BRILEY, JAMES DYRAL BRILEY, LINWOOD EARL BRILEY: "The Briley Brothers" killed between ten and twelve victims in Virginia in 1979. The victims were shot, bludgeoned, and stabbed to death, and included both men and women. Linwood committed the first murder at the age of sixteen when he shot a female neighbor dead as she was hanging clothes on a clothesline. One of their victims was found dead with a pair of scissors and a fork sticking out of his back.

SIDNEY RUFUS BRINKLEY: "The City Line Stalker" killed four White and Black females in Pennsylvania in 1979, raping, strangling, bludgeoning, and stabbing his victims to death. He also had sex with their corpses, and he had a plan to kill five people at his trial, including the judge.

HENRY OMAR BRISBON JR.: "The I-57 Killer" killed four victims in Illinois from 1973 to 1978, his first murder taking place when he was seventeen years old. His victims were robbed, raped, shot, and stabbed to death, and his last murder victim was a cellmate. He is also known for stabbing serial killer John Wayne Gacy in prison. As he walked out of the courthouse after being sentenced to death, he yelled, "You'll never get me. I'll kill again. Then you'll have another long trial. And then I'll do it again."

EUGENE VICTOR BRITT: Killed between ten and eleven females in Indiana in 1995, raping, beating, stabbing, and strangling his victims to death. He was released from prison to kill again, and one of his victims was only eight years old. His MO was to sodomize his victims' dead bodies. I have talked with Britt many times, but he is a little difficult to communicate with.

DONALD BROADNAX: Killed a friend by shooting him to death in 1977 in Alabama and was sent to prison for several years. A few years after his release in 1994, he moved in with a woman who had been visiting him in prison. When she came to visit him at work one day with her four-year-old grandson, he killed them both, bludgeoning them to death.

RICKY HENRY BROGSDALE: "The Peeping Tom Killer" killed two Black males and two Black females in 1987 in Washington, DC, raping, shooting, and strangling his victims to death. Some of his victims were shot through the windows of their homes with a .22 caliber handgun.

ANTOINE & DON BROOKS: Killed at least three Black males and females in Louisiana in 2011 and 2012, shooting his victims to death during drug transactions.

GRADY BROOKS: Killed between eleven and nineteen victims in Georgia between the years of 1931 and 1933, at the age of seventeen and eighteen. He raped, strangled, and slashed his victims to death with a knife and an axe. He confessed to eleven murders but may have killed many more.

JOHN BROOKS: Killed nine victims in Louisiana in 1986, shooting his victims to death. He also attempted to kill two more victims, and most of his victims were Black. He was arrested at the age of fifteen for molesting an eight-year-old female, and he began his killing spree at the age of twenty.

JOSEPH JAMES BROOKS: Killed a Black female and a Black male in Maryland, one in 1983 and one in 1993. His victims were shot and stabbed to death.

SHELLY ANDRE BROOKS: Killed between seven and twenty mostly Black female prostitutes in Michigan between 2001 and 2006. His victims were raped, strangled, and bludgeoned to death with rocks, concrete, bricks, and sticks. He is suspected of killing more victims, and he was arrested because his last victim survived and went to police. He has been cordial and open about his crimes and wants to share information that might help others.

DEVAUGHNDRE MONIQUE BROUSSARD: Killed two Black males in California in 2007, shooting his victims to death.

ALI MUHAMMAD BROWN: Killed one White male and three Black males in Washington and New Jersey in 2014, shooting them to death. He claimed it was his war against infidels.

BROADUS BROWN: Killed a victim in Florida in 1974 and was sent to prison. He was paroled, and in 1987, he shot his girlfriend to death in front of her eight-year-old son.

CHARLES BROWN: Killed one male and one female in Florida, one in 1961 and one in 1964, shooting and stabbing his victims to death.

CURTIS DON BROWN: "The Bandit" killed between three and eighteen women in Texas in 1985 and 1986. His victims were raped, shot, bludgeoned, and strangled to death. He wrote me and respectfully declined an interview.

RAYMOND BROWN: Killed five victims in Alabama between 1960 and 1987, raping and stabbing his victims to death. Three victims were killed when he was just fourteen years old, in a triple homicide, where he stabbed the victims to death and slit their throats. He was sent to prison and later released to kill again. This time, he killed his live-in girlfriend and her ten-year-old daughter. His girlfriend was stabbed numerous times, including in the vagina and anus, and was cut wide open. The ten-year-old was raped and stabbed to death.

JACOB PATRICK BROWN: Killed two Black males in Washington, one in 1990 and one in 1996, shooting them to death.

JAMES CORNELIUS BROWN: "The Escort Killer" killed four Black females in 2011 in Michigan. The victims were raped and strangled, and he liked to kill prostitutes in pairs. He claims he is innocent and his interview was coerced. He asked me, "How can I be a killer if the people you say I killed had no cause of death?"

JOHN HENRY BROWN: Killed one victim in 1963 and one victim in 1986 in Georgia, shooting them both to death.

LATECE MEGALE BROWN: Convicted of one murder in 2003, but he admits to killing many more in California. His known victim is a sixteen-year-old female who was raped and murdered, and he is responsible for more rapes as well. His response to me regarding an interview was "I wouldn't care if you worked for the devil and came to steal my soul, my only concern is that you make this risk worthwhile because speaking to you can be hazardous to my health."

MATTHEW BROWN: Killed three Black females in Louisiana in 1984 and 1985, raping and stabbing his victims to death.

VERNON BROWN: Killed three and possibly six females between 1980 and 1986 in the states of Indiana, Missouri, and Texas. The victims were raped, stabbed, and strangled to death. He was also a child molester, and some of his victims were children.

WILLIAM VINCENT BROWN: Killed two and possibly five Black females in 2003 in Maryland, raping, bludgeoning, and strangling his victims to death.

WILLIE ARTHUR BROWN: Killed three to five Black males in Michigan between 1979 and 1999. The victims were gay men who were strangled to death as Brown worked as a prostitute. He explained that since he has been incarcerated, he has "devoted a greater majority of my time speaking to young adults about the disadvantages of committing crime."

WILLIE BROWN JR.: Killed two victims in Michigan, one in 1968 and one in 1971, stabbing his victims to death.

WESLEY BROWNLEE: "The Stockton Serial Killer" killed seven victims as he drove the streets of Stockton,

California, shooting people at night. Most of his victims were homeless men.

EUGENE ALVIN BROXTON: Killed between five and seven victims in Texas in 1991, shooting, stabbing, and strangling his victims to death.

DAVID LANCE BRUCE: Killed between three and as many as thirty Black females in Ohio in 2005, raping, strangling, and stabbing them to death.

PHILIP MICHAEL BRYANT: Killed three Black males in Virginia and New York in 2009 and 2010, shooting his victims to death. The victims were dismembered with an axe and placed inside dumpsters. One of them was an off-duty corrections officer.

TOMMY LEWIS BUCHANAN: Killed two Black females in Wisconsin, one in 1977 and one in 1987, strangling his victims to death.

DAVID BULLOCK: Known as "The .38 Caliber Killer," Bullock killed six victims in New York in 1981 and 1982. Five of his victims were male, and one was a female. He worked as a prostitute and shot his victims to death, offering him a high. When asked why he did it, he explained, "It's fun!" When explaining why he did what he did, he explained, "I was in the Christmas spirit. It made me happy. I enjoy what I do." He wrote me a few letters and one time chided me for not asking how he was doing, saying, "You were remiss and failed to ask about my health, well-being, and if I needed anything. This lack of concern is no way to earn respect... this is check, not checkmate!" He is a talented artist and has sent me drawings of Wendi and me.

LESLIE LEON BURCHART: "The Golden Years Killer" murdered between seven and fourteen elderly women in

1996 in Virginia. His victims were raped, bludgeoned, and strangled to death.

JERMAINE DERRICK BURGESS: Killed four elderly victims in Pennsylvania between the years of 2001 and 2008, raping, bludgeoning, and strangling them to death. He is suspected of more murders. He responded that he was in the hole, or the segregated housing unit, and he would have his people check me out. He also asked what many ask me, "There's plenty of people incarcerated for multiple murders, so why did you contact me?"

NATHAN BURKETT: Killed four victims in Nevada and one victim in Mississippi between 1978 and 2002, raping, strangling, and burning them to death. He also killed his mother in 1982 and buried her body in her yard.

ADRIAN WAYNE BURKS: Killed one victim in California in 2005 and later killed four victims in a quadruple homicide in Kansas in 2009. His victims were shot and strangled to death. They included one male and four females, and one victim was only three years old.

EUGENE MCARTHUR BURNEY: Killed three Black females in Florida between 1966 and 1984, strangling his victims to death. In 1966, he strangled his wife to death and was sent to prison for only eight years. In 1984, he strangled two more females to death.

KEITH LAMONT BURNS: Killed between three and seven females in Michigan between 1989 and 1995, raping and strangling his victims to death. He was convicted because of DNA and is suspected of more murders.

THURMAN LEVONE BURNS: Killed one Black male and one Black female in North Carolina, one in 1988 and one in 2006, shooting his victims to death.

FRED BURTON: Killed three White males in Pennsylvania between 1971 and 1973, shooting and stabbing his victims to death. His first murder was the shooting of a police officer. While in a Pennsylvania prison, Bowen continued his killing spree, stabbing to death the warden and deputy warden of the prison.

WYATT ELLIS BUSBY: Stabbed one victim to death in 2016 in Texas. While incarcerated in 2023, he stabbed and beat his cellmate, serial killer Billy Chemirmir, to death. Chemirmir was making rude comments about Busby's children.

PHILLIP REESE BUSH: Killed five White males and females in West Virginia between 1974 and 1982, shooting his victims to death.

JAMES ELROY BUTLER: Killed two Black males and one Black female in North Carolina between 1978 and 1998, shooting and stabbing his victims to death.

RAYMOND OSCAR BUTLER: Killed three males in California in 1994 and 1995, shooting and stabbing his victims to death. The 1994 murders were a double homicide, when Butler was only eighteen years old.

ROBERT JOE BUTLER: Killed three victims in Texas and Kansas from 1955 to 1992, stabbing them to death. His last victim was his wife, and he was able to kill again after being released.

ARTHUR CAIN: Killed three victims in Illinois between 1980 and 2015, strangling his victims to death. He was sentenced to seventy years in prison for the 1980 murder, and after being paroled in 2015, he killed a twenty-one-year-old female, whose body was found in an alley.

VINCENT BYRON CALHOUN: Killed two victims in Michigan, one in 2004 and one in 2006, shooting his victims to death.

PERCY LAMONTE CAMEL: Killed two Hispanic males in California, one in 2009 and one in 2010, shooting his victims to death.

JOSEPH CAMPBELL: Killed one male and one female in Illinois, one in 1913 and one in 1915, bludgeoning his victims to death.

RUFUS CANTRELL: Killed nine victims from 1900 to 1903 in Indiana, bludgeoning, poisoning, and shooting eight males and one female to death. He also robbed graves to supply skeletons to a medical supply company. When they complained about needing fresher specimens, he began killing living people.

PATRICK OHARA CAPLE: Killed between three and four Black males in Georgia in 1994, shooting his victims to death.

JONATHAN DANIEL CARR & REGINALD CARR: "The Wichita Massacre" and "The Wichita Horror" was a crime wave carried out by two brothers who raped, robbed, and killed three White males and two White females in Kansas in 2000. They could be classified as spree killers as well since their crimes took place in one month, but their crimes included rape and torture, making them more like serial killers. One of the Carr brothers resides next door to Dennis "BTK" Rader in the El Dorado Correctional Facility.

CONNELL L. CARROLL: Killed two White females in Florida, one in 2009 and one in 2011, shooting his victims to death.

TAURUS JERMAINE CARROLL: Killed two victims in Alabama, shooting a female to death in 1995, then stabbing a fellow inmate in 2009.

CHARLES LENDELLE CARTER: This chef turned serial killer killed four and possibly six victims in Georgia from 1992 to 2005. The victims were raped, shot, stabbed, and strangled to death. He claims to have hunted victims for fifteen years and is suspected of more murders.

CLARENCE CARNELL CARTER: Killed a Black male in Ohio in 1988, shooting the victim to death. While in custody, he beat and stomped a fellow inmate to death, landing him on death row.

SAMUEL CARSON: Killed nine victims in Washington, DC from 1989 to 1996.

ROBERT ANTHONY CARTER: Killed two victims in Texas in 1981, robbing and shooting his victims to death, all while he was seventeen years old. One of his victims was also only seventeen.

STEPHEN NATHANIEL CARTER: Shot to death two males, one in Hawaii and one in Massachusetts, in 1917.

JARVIS THEODORE ROOSEVELT CATOE: Known as "The DC Strangler," he killed between eight and thirteen female victims in Washington, DC and New York between the years of 1935 and 1941, raping, mutilating, and strangling his White and Black victims to death. He would pose as a handyman, and once the victims let him inside the house, he strangled them to death. He explained that he was motivated by detective magazines.

CHRISTOPHER BERNARD CAVINESS: Killed one Black male and two Black females in North Carolina in

1988 and 1989, bludgeoning and strangling his victims to death. His male victim was his own father.

BEN CHANEY: Killed two White males and two White females in Florida and South Carolina in 1970, shooting his victims to death. He was the brother of slain civil rights leader James Chaney.

DAMON LOPEZ CHAPPLE: Killed two White victims, one in 1984 and one in 1988 in Washington. The victims were bludgeoned and stabbed to death. White in prison, he was charged with raping a fellow inmate.

ROBERT CHARLES: Shot to death nine male victims in Louisiana and Mississippi in 1900.

XAVIER DEMARK CHASE: Killed one male and one female in Michigan, one in 1990 and one in 2007, shooting his male and female victims to death. He was released from prison to kill again.

STANLEY BRENT CHATMAN: Killed four Black victims in Alabama between the years of 2005 and 2013, shooting his victims to death. After being released for the 2005 murder, he killed again. And while on bond awaiting trial, he killed two seventeen-year-old twin brothers. He also shot and paralyzed their mother. He explained to me that his mother was killed when he was two years old, and his father left a week after that.

JUAN CHAVEZ: Killed four White males and one Hispanic male in California between 1986 and 1989, strangling his victims to death.

PHILLIP DELBERT CHEATHAM JR.: Killed three to four victims in Kansas between the years of 1994 and 2003, killing again after being released from prison.

BILLY CHEMIRMIR: Killed between twenty-two and thirty mostly White elderly men and women in Texas. He would pose as a maintenance worker or medical person to gain entrance to the victims' homes, then smother them with a pillow. Chemirmir was born in Kenya and had a violent criminal past. While incarcerated in Texas, he made sexual comments about his cellmate's children, and that cellmate, Wyatt Busby, killed him in 2023.

ERVIN E. CHERRY: Killed three Black females in Florida in 1993 and 1994, strangling his victims to death. He said they reminded him of his mother, and he would have kept killing if he hadn't been caught. He wrote several letters to me and when I began to ask questions, he responded, "Your questions bring back memories of my tainted sin-filled past life employed with the advocates of Satan... I'm no Ted Bundy or Ed Gein or Jack the Ripper... I have a conscience."

ELROY CHESTER: Killed three males and two females in Texas in 1997 and 1998, shooting, beating, and strangling his victims to death. His last murder victim caught him trying to rape two young girls. A documentary was made about him called *Killing Time*.

SAM CHINN III: Killed three Black females in New York and Texas between 1989 and 1995, raping, stabbing, and strangling his victims to death. He may have more victims in California and Illinois.

WILLIAM JENNINGS CHOYCE: Killed three females in California between 1988 and 1997. He raped, strangled, and shot his victims in the head, and then posed their dead bodies.

LEONARD CHRISTOPHER: "The Frankford Slasher" killed between seven and nine White females in

Pennsylvania between the years of 1985 and 1990, raping, bludgeoning, and stabbing his victims to death.

RUDOLPH CHURCHILL: Killed two Black females in Pennsylvania in 1989, raping and strangling his victims to death.

EARL CLANTON JR.: Strangled to death two Black females, one in Virginia and one in New Jersey in 1972 and 1981.

JOHN CLARK: Killed between seven and eight victims in Tennessee, Virginia, Alabama, Illinois, and Ohio between 1908 and 1924. He killed both men and women, and his weapon of choice was an axe.

MICHAEL CLARK, NATHANIEL BURSE & GARLAND JACKSON: Known as "The De Mau Mau Murders," this Black gang murdered between ten and twelve White victims in Illinois in 1972 with racial motivations. Clark wrote me several letters, and he has explained how he would label himself as "a disgruntled, confused Vietnam veteran, that was ignorant with misplaced values that committed very heinous crimes." Some of their murders were multiple victims, like the Corbett family of four.

ROYAL CLARK JR.: Killed one White female and one Black female in California, one in 1980 and one in 1989, raping and strangling his victims to death. His 1989 victim was a fifteen-year-old who was strangled with an electrical cord. He was serving a death sentence for killing a fourteen-year-old in 1980 when he confessed to the second homicide.

TOM CLARK: Killed three victims in Mississippi.

VERNON LEE CLARK: Killed between four and seven White females in Maryland between 1979 and 1989, raping, stabbing, bludgeoning, shooting, and strangling his victims to death. He met some of his victims while doing yard work for them.

KEITH BERNARD CLAY: Killed three male and one female in Texas in 1993 and 1994, robbing and shooting his victims to death. His 1993 victims were a triple homicide of a father and his two children aged ten and thirteen. The victims were bound and violently killed by stabbing, beating, and shooting.

GREGORY CLEPPER: Killed between eight and fifteen female prostitutes in Illinois between 1991 and 1996. His victims were raped and strangled to death, and his last victim was found stuffed inside his bedroom closet. He bragged to police that he killed as many as forty women.

WILLIE CLISBY: Killed one male and one female in 1979 in Alabama, stabbing his victims and bludgeoning them to death with an axe.

EDWIN WILLARD COACHMAN: Shot and stabbed to death two Black females in Florida, one in 1958 and one in 1969.

NATHANIEL ROBERT CODE JR.: Known as "The Shreveport Serial Killer," he killed twelve Black victims in Louisiana between the years of 1984 and 1987, stabbing, strangling, and cutting the throats of his victims. He also posed their bodies by turning them over face down in their own blood, which was his signature. His last three victims were his grandfather and his two young nephews. Four of his victims were the Cheney-Culbert family, which earned him the nickname "The Cedar Grove Killer."

WILLIE ANDREW COLE: Killed two males and one female in Tennessee and New York between 1960 and 2005, bludgeoning and stabbing his victims to death.

ALTON COLEMAN & DEBRA BROWN: This serial killer and spree killer couple raped, bludgeoned, shot, and strangled two males and six females in Ohio, Michigan, Indiana, Wisconsin, and Illinois in 1984. They also committed rapes and other violent crimes, and their victims included a seven-year-old, a nine-year-old, and a fifteen-year-old.

ROBERT GLEN COLEMAN: Killed three victims in Louisiana in 2003, robbing, shooting, and stabbing his victims to death. One of his victims was a retired seventy-year-old minister, and another was his wife.

FREDRICK COLLINS: Killed one White male and one White female in Pennsylvania, one in 1924 and one in 1932. His victims were raped, bludgeoned, stabbed, and strangled to death. While serving time for murder, he was visiting the prison doctor's home as part of his work release, when he raped and killed the doctor's daughter. While he was being executed, he smiled and said he was glad he did it.

DELLMUS CHARLES COLVIN: Known as "Heavy," he killed between six and fifty-two mostly truck stop prostitutes while working as a long-haul truck driver from 1982 to 2005. The victims consisted of mostly White females, one Black female, and two White males, and were all strangled to death. When he describes his crimes, he explains, "I've been hunting such a long time, I've been trucking since 1980, and I averaged one to three murders per year. Hell, I lost count years ago."

TERRELL EARL COMBS: Killed two Black males in Virginia, one in 2006 and one in 2008, shooting his victims to death.

ADAM COMEAUX: Killed three White females in Arkansas and Louisiana in 1985, raping and bludgeoning his victims to death.

ANTHONY H. COOK & NATHANIEL COOK: These two brothers worked as long haul truck drivers and killed nine White victims in multiple states, including Oregon and Ohio, from 1973 to 1981. Their victims were raped, shot, stabbed, and bludgeoned with a baseball bat and a concrete block, and their crimes were racially motivated. Their victims included four males and five females, and they preferred to kill couples.

MICHAEL COOK: Killed two elderly White females in California, one in 1996 and one in 1998, robbing, raping, and burning his victims to death.

ROBERT LEE COOK: Killed four male victims in Pennsylvania and New Jersey in 1985 and 1986, robbing, shooting, and stabbing his victims to death.

JESSE LEE COOKS: Killed one White male and one White female in California, one in 1973 and one in 1974, shooting and stabbing his victims to death. His crimes were racially motivated, as Cooks was one of the "Zebra Killers," a racially motivated killing group.

CLEOPHUS COOKSEY JR.: Killed nine victims in Arizona in 2017, his last victims being his own mother and stepfather. His victims were all shot to death, and one was sexually assaulted. He had rapped about killing people in YouTube videos, and police suspect there may be more victims. Cooksey is the grandson of civil rights leader Roy Cooksey.

DAVID COOPER: Killed two children in New Jersey in 1993 and 1995, raping and strangling them to death.

SAMUEL JAMES COOPER JR.: Killed five males in North Carolina, in 2006 and 2007, some of his victims being killed in armed robberies. He has sent me many letters and called me several times.

HERBERT COPELAND: Killed between six and twelve White victims, including four police officers in Washington, DC, Illinois, Texas, and North Carolina from 1909 to 1918. His male and female victims were all shot to death and included both White and Black victims. He confessed before he was hanged in 1925 that he was responsible for twelve unsolved murders.

SAMUEL DEWAYNE COPELAND: Killed a Black male in Tennessee in 1991 and was released from prison to kill again, when he stabbed his girlfriend to death in 2015.

MICHAEL CORBETT: Killed five victims with Freddie Glenn in Colorado in 1975, shooting and stabbing his victims to death. Their last victim was Karen Grammer, the younger sister of actor Kelsey Grammer. Grammer was raped by the two, then stabbed in the throat and left to die in a mobile home. She crawled to a neighbor's porch but died when nobody answered the door.

KEITH SHAWN COSBY: Killed two White males in California, robbing and stabbing his victims to death.

WALTER COTTON: Killed three White males in Virginia in 1899 and 1900, bludgeoning and shooting his victims to death. He confessed to more murders and was sentenced to death. He was hanged in 1900, and his body was also riddled with bullets.

LUZENSKI ALLEN COTTRELL: Killed three male victims in South Carolina in 2002, shooting his victims to death. One of his victims was a police officer.

BERNARD COUSAR: Killed one Black and one Hispanic male in Pennsylvania in 1999, robbing and shooting his victims to death.

CLIFTON COUSINS: Killed between five and fifteen victims in Ohio and Kentucky between 1987 and 1989. His victims were shot, stabbed, and strangled to death. He has been very cordial with me and willing to help me with my project.

JUAN COVINGTON: Killed five male and female victims in Pennsylvania between the years of 1998 and 2005. He worked at a hospital during the murders, even killing some of his co-workers. His victims were shot to death, and his crimes were motivated by delusions from his paranoid schizophrenia.

DEXTER COX: Killed three White victims in Tennessee in 2007 and 2008, shooting his victims to death. His 2008 victim was a police officer who Cox killed at the officer's home.

FREDERICK PETE COX: Killed one White and two Black females in Florida in 1997, raping and shooting his victims do death. He had been active in the military and also worked as a corrections officer.

DONALD LAVELL CRAIG: Killed two young females in Ohio, one in 1995 and one in 1996, abducting, raping, and strangling the twelve- and thirteen-year-old girls to death.

LOUIS CRAINE: Killed five Black female prostitutes in California between the years of 1985 and 1987. His victims were raped and strangled to death.

ANDRE CRAWFORD: Known as "Dre," "The Englewood Rapist," and "The Invisible Man," he killed eleven Black female prostitutes in Illinois between 1997 and 1999, raping, beating, stabbing, and strangling his victims to death. He also enjoyed having sex with their corpses and was connected to his victims through DNA. He told me he grew up in an abusive and broken home and was a drug user most of his life. He explained that he killed for sex, lust, anger, and revenge.

DAVON CRAWFORD: Shot to death six Black male and female victims in Ohio between the years of 1995 and 2009. After killing his first victim, he was sent to prison but was released to kill again. His last five victims were all killed in a mass shooting inside a Cleveland home, and included his wife, her sister, and her three children, ages two, two, and five. He shot himself in the head while being pursued by police, killing himself.

JAMEL SHALEKE CRAWFORD: Killed four males in Virginia in 2001 and 2002, robbing and shooting his victims to death.

LUCIUS CRAWFORD: Killed two to three victims in New York between 1993 and 2012, stabbing them to death. He is also responsible for a stabbing spree in South Carolina and has proclaimed that "there is a devil inside of me."

DEWITT CRAWLEY: Killed a seventeen-year-old Black male in 1970 in Pennsylvania at the age of eighteen, stabbing him to death. He spent five years in prison and was released to kill again. In 1983, he killed his two teen nieces and their father in his nieces' home. The crime scene was horrendous and included the hanging, drowning, and bludgeoning of the three victims. The two young girls were also sexually assaulted.

JAHMELL CROCKAM: Killed one White male and one Black male in New Jersey, one in 2010 and one in 2011, shooting them to death. His 2011 victim was a police officer trying to pick him up for a warrant.

JAMES M. CROMWELL: Killed two White females in Kansas, one in 1987 and one in 1991, raping and strangling his victims to death.

JAMES CROWSON: Killed between three and four male victims between the years of 1957 and 1974 in Pennsylvania, robbing and shooting his victims to death.

TIMOTHY LAVAUN CRUMITIE: Known as the serial killer pastor, he killed two males and two females in North Carolina, one in 2005, and three in 2016. He was released to kill again, and all of his victims were shot to death.

MICHAEL TYRONE CRUMP: Killed two Black female prostitutes in Florida, one in 1985 and one in 1986. The victims were robbed, raped, and strangled to death.

JASON ANDRE CRUZ: Killed two Black males in Kansas, one in 2007 and one in 2008, shooting his victims to death.

EDWARD LEE CUMMINGS: Killed two White females in North Carolina, one in 1983 and one in 1985, shooting his victims to death.

STEVEN CUNNINGHAM: Killed two female victims in New York, one in 1989 and one in 1993, raping and strangling them to death. His 1989 victim was fifteen years old, and his 1993 victim was a teacher, his girlfriend's sister.

JOSEPH DANCLAIR: Killed two females in New York in 2015, raping and strangling them to death.

CHARLES EDWARD DANIELS: Killed two Black females in Louisiana, one in 1965 and one in 2000, bludgeoning and stabbing his victims to death.

EARL LLEWELLYN DAUGHTREY JR.: Killed three to four White victims in Georgia and Alabama, raping and ligature strangling his victims to death. He is suspected of more murders in Florida and Georgia, and he met some of his victims while doing odd jobs.

JAMES EDWARD DANIELS: Killed four male victims in New York and New Jersey between the years of 1963 and 1984, shooting his victims to death. He was released from prison to kill again, and one of his victims was a state trooper.

RICHARD C. DANIELS: Killed four White females in Pennsylvania between the years of 1940 and 1942, bludgeoning his victims to death.

BRIAN RANARD DAVIS: Killed between two and six Black females in Texas in 2007, stabbing and burning his victims to death. Some of his victims were dumped under bridges.

CECIL EMILE DAVIS: Killed three White females in Washington between 1993 and 1997, raping, drowning, smothering, and strangling his victims to death. He was cordial with me and wants to help me with my project.

CURTIS A. DAVIS JR.: Killed four Black males in Illinois between 1989 and 2012, shooting his victims to death.

DARON DUANE DAVIS: Killed an eleven-month-old female in South Carolina in 1994, beating his infant daughter to death. He was sent to prison and released to kill again, and this time he beat his five-month-old daughter to death.

GIRVIES L. DAVIS: Killed six White males and three White females in Illinois in 1978 and 1979, robbing, shooting, and stabbing his victims to death. For four of his murders he had a co-defendant, Richard Holman, and the crimes earned them the nickname "The .22 Caliber Killers." Davis said it was easier to kill witnesses than wear a mask.

GREGORY DAVIS: Killed four Black females in Mississippi and Georgia in 1986 and 1987, robbing, raping, beating, and strangling his victims to death. He was cordial in his correspondence with me and is willing to help me with my project.

KENNETH RAY DAVIS: Killed two females in Tennessee, one in 1999 and one in 2000, raping and strangling his victims to death.

LARRY DAVIS: Killed two Black victims in New York, one in 2010 and one in 2011, bludgeoning and strangling his victims to death. His first victim was his girlfriend, and his second victim was his grandmother, whom he kept in his bedroom closet for days.

ROBERT DAVIS: Killed two male victims in West Virginia, one in 1935 and one in 1949, shooting and stabbing his victims to death.

ROBERT EARL DAVIS: Shot two victims to death, one in Illinois and one in Indiana, in the years 1985 and 2011.

VON CLARK DAVIS: Killed two Black females in Ohio, one in 1970 and one in 1983, shooting and stabbing his victims to death. His first victim was his wife, who was stabbed to death in front of his children. He was released to kill again; this time he shot his girlfriend to death.

WILLIAM HOWARD DAVIS: Killed five to six Black males from 1998 to 2008 in Georgia, shooting his victims to death.

MICHAEL DEAN: Killed three Black males and one Black female in Tennessee in 2011 and 2012, robbing and shooting his victims to death.

EUGENE T. DECASTRO: Killed three White victims in North Carolina from 1982 to 1992, stabbing his victims to death. His first murder occurred when he was just seventeen years old, and he was released from prison to kill again. His last two murders were an elderly couple who were stabbed and beaten to death.

ALVIN CORNELIUS DEDRICK: Killed two Black males in Washington, one in 1994 and one in 2000.

TONY DEGRAFREED: Killed two Black females in Indiana, one in 1994 and one in 2014, stabbing and shooting his victims to death. Both of his victims were his wives, and he was released to kill again after shooting his first wife.

JAMES DEMOUCHETTE: Killed three males in Texas between 1976 and 1983, shooting and stabbing his White and Black victims to death. His 1976 crime was a double murder of two Pizza Hut clerks, and he was sent to death row. He was known as the "Meanest Man on Death Row," where he stabbed a fellow inmate to death.

BENNIE EDDIE DEMPS: Killed two victims in 1971 in Florida, shooting his victims to death. He was sent to death row and stabbed a fellow inmate to death.

MICHAEL GLENN DENNARD: Killed a White male and a Black male in Texas in 1985, shooting his victims to death.

JEROME DENNIS: Killed five Black females in New Jersey in 1991 and 1992. His victims were raped, bludgeoned, stabbed, and strangled to death, and one of his victims was only sixteen years old.

WALTER DIAZ: Killed one White male and one White female in New York in 1993, robbing and shooting his victims to death.

DENNIS TYREE DIGGS: Killed three male victims in Maryland in 2015 and 2016, shooting his White and Black victims to death.

ANDREW DILLON: Killed five White females in Pennsylvania between 1990 and 1995, raping, bludgeoning, stabbing, and strangling his victims to death. His victims were elderly and ranged in age from sixty-seven to eighty-six.

SAMUEL JEFFERSON DIXON: Killed two males and two females in California in 2000 and 2001, raping, bludgeoning, smothering, and stabbing his victims to death. There was some talk that he said he had read a book about Jeffrey Dahmer and was inspired by him.

ALGERNON DELIN DOBY: Killed two victims in Arkansas, one in 1990 and one in 1999, robbing and shooting his victims to death.

CORNELIUS DODSON: Killed three Black males and one Black female in Missouri in 1974 and 1975, shooting and strangling his victims to death.

HOWELL DONALDSON: Killed three Black males and one White female in Florida in 2017, shooting his victims as they exited the city bus.

MIKE DONNELLY: Killed three White males in Washington and Idaho between 1911 and 1923, shooting his victims to death.

CHRISTOPHER JORDAN DORNER: Killed three males and one female in California in 2013, shooting his victims to death. This ex-cop also killed two police officers, and his crimes could be considered a spree killing.

DAMIEN LAMONT DORRIS: Killed two men and three women in Michigan between 1993 and 2004, shooting his victims to death.

JESSIE DOTSON: Killed five males and two females in Tennessee between 1994 to 2008. His victims were shot and stabbed to death. His 2008 crime was the mass murder of a family called the "Lester Street Massacre," which was the worst mass murder in Memphis history, including children aged two and four. He was released to kill again, when he killed the family.

JOSHUA DOTSON: Killed five victims in Memphis, Tennessee between 2019 and 2024, shooting his victims to death. His victims include his former girlfriend and her unborn child. He called himself a serial killer, and he called himself "Michael Myers."

JOHNNY DOUGLAS: Killed three female victims in Illinois between 1994 and 1997, raping and strangling his victims to death.

RONNIE DONTELL DRANE: Killed four Black victims in Indiana and Kentucky in 2002 and 2003. His two male victims were shot, and his two female victims were raped and strangled to death.

DARRELL DEWAYNE DRAUGHN: Killed one Black male and one Black female in Louisiana in 2000, robbing, shooting, and stabbing his victims to death. He stabbed a sixty-four-year-old woman to death and shot an eight-year-old boy in the back of the head with a shotgun.

CHARLES LEE DUFFY: Killed ten victims in Georgia between 1994 and 1997, robbing, bludgeoning, raping, and shooting his victims to death. He has corresponded with me and is cordial and wants to help me with my project. He explains that he is "tired of hurting people" and wishes that he would have received a death sentence "so I don't have to deal with a lot of situations." He also admits, "Yes, I killed more than two people and I have really grown to hate that."

GLEN LEON DUKES: Killed between two and four victims in Texas in 2012. His victims were raped, shot, and strangled to death. He is suspected of four more murders, and one of his victims was tied to a chair, suffocated, and set on fire.

JOSHUA DUKES: Killed four male victims in Mississippi in 2015 and 2016, robbing and shooting his victims to death.

ZOLLIE EDWARD DUMAS: Killed two Black females in Nevada, one in 1988 and one in 2014, stabbing his victims to death. He was released to kill again after the first murder, this time stabbing his fifty-nine-year-old girlfriend to death.

JERRY LEE DUNBAR: Killed two Black females in Virginia in 1989, strangling his victims to death. He then placed their bodies under hotel beds.

DAVE DUNNHAM: Killed Black males and one Black female in South Carolina and Maryland in 1930 and 1931, shooting, stabbing, and bludgeoning his victims with an axe. Two of his victims were a mother and son.

AHMOND SUKARNO DUNNIGAN SR: Killed two to three Black females in Georgia in 1993, raping, torturing, burning, and drowning his victims. He has been cordial and willing to help me with my project.

PAUL DUROUSSEAU: "The Jacksonville Serial Killer," "The Killer Cabbie," and "The I-95 Killer" killed between seven and nine Black females in Georgia and Florida from 1997 to 2003, including two who were pregnant. He may have murdered others when he was stationed in Germany in the early 1990s, and his victims were tied up, raped, and strangled to death with a cord. He met many of his victims when he worked as a cab driver. He sent a letter claiming he is innocent of these crimes, and he was shocked that we believed the media reports and police investigation.

ELBERT C. DYE: Killed two White males in Wisconsin, one in 1937 and one in 1952, bludgeoning his victims to death.

TORIN DYSON: Killed two males and one female in Missouri in 2001, robbing and shooting his victims to death. Two of his victims were a couple shot execution style.

JEFFREY EADY: Killed three Black females in South Carolina in 2013, robbing and shooting his victims to death.

JAMES EALY: Killed one male and four females in Illinois between 1982 and 2006, strangling his victims to death. His first crime was a quadruple homicide, the victims being a pregnant woman and her three children. The last victim was a Burger King worker who was stabbed with a screwdriver and strangled with her uniform bow tie.

JOSEPH R. EBRON: Killed three Black males in Washington, DC and Texas between the years of 1994 and 2005, shooting and stabbing his victims to death. His first murder occurred when he was fifteen years old, his second murder when he was seventeen years old, and his last murder was a fellow inmate.

JAMES EDWARDS: Killed one male and two females in Illinois, New York, and Ohio in 1974. His victims were robbed, bludgeoned, and shot to death.

KWAUME LARAY EDWARDS: Killed three Black males in Virginia between 2006 and 2014, shooting his victims to death. He killed his first victim at the age of seventeen.

ROBERTA ELDER: Dubbed "Atlanta's Mrs. Bluebeard," she killed thirteen victims in Georgia by poisoning, beginning in 1938 with her first husband. Twelve more victims followed, including another husband, who was a minister, and several children, grandchildren, other family members, and some friends. She is America's deadliest female serial killer.

NATHAN ELGIN: Killed one male and seven females in Texas in 1884 and 1885, stabbing and bludgeoning his victims with an axe.

WALTER EARL ELLIS: "The Milwaukee North Side Strangler" killed one White female and nine Black females in Wisconsin from 1986 to 2007. He targeted female prostitutes and runaways, one being only sixteen years old. His victims were raped, beaten, shot, strangled, and stabbed to death.

WILL ELLIS: Killed seven male victims in Kentucky, Mississippi, Alabama, and Georgia in 1905.

DUANE WILLIAM ELTON: Killed two Black female prostitutes while stationed at Fort Lewis in Washington in 2014. One of his victims was only fourteen years old, and the victims were driven to a remote area and shot several times. He explained that he wanted oral sex, and his wife wouldn't give it to him.

ANDREW RAYMOND ENGRAM: Killed two victims in Arkansas, a male in 1975 and a female in 1997. The victims were raped, stabbed, and strangled to death, and he killed again after being released from prison.

KEVIN SEDELL EPPS: Killed two White females in Washington, one in 1990 and one in 1994, raping and stabbing his victims to death.

MARK JAMES ROBERT ESSEX: Known as "The New Orleans Sniper," he killed nine mostly male victims in Louisiana in 1972 and 1973. His victims were all shot to death, and he also wounded thirteen others. His crimes were racially motivated.

SANUEL PIETRO EVANS: Killed two White males in Washington, one in 1968 and one in 1972, shooting and stabbing his victims to death.

FREDERICK ANTONIO EVINS: Killed two White females in South Carolina, one in 2002 and one in 2003. His victims were raped, stabbed, and strangled to death, and he is also responsible for more rapes. He has been cordial to me and was excited to help with my project.

JOHN WESLEY EWELL: "The Grim Creeper" killed two males and two females in California in 2010, strangling his victims to death. He received his nickname because he was a copycat of "The Grim Sleeper." His last two victims were a married couple, and his MO was to enter their homes and bind their hands behind their backs. He usually bludgeoned or strangled them to death.

STANLEY FAISON: Stabbed to death two Black males in Michigan, one in 1965 and one in 1987.

LORENZO FAYNE: Killed six Black victims in Illinois and Wisconsin between 1989 and 1993. The victims were raped, bludgeoned, stabbed, sodomized, and strangled to death. Five of his victims were children and teens, some as young as six and nine years old. He explained to me that he preferred sex after death so they didn't scream or fight back.

JT FELDER: Killed two males in Texas and Georgia, one in 1988 and one in 1998, stabbing his victims to death.

MATTHEW FELIX: Killed one male and one female in New York, one in 1985 and one in 1999, stabbing his victims to death.

JOHN ERROL FERGUSON: Killed eight to twelve victims in Florida between 1974 and 1978, known as "The Carol City Murders." The victims were robbed, raped, shot, and stabbed to death. He had two co-defendants, Marvin Francois and Beauford White. They were all sentenced to death and executed.

JACK DEMPSEY FERRELL: Killed two Black females in Florida, one in 1981 and one in 1992, shooting his victims to death. Both of his victims were his girlfriends, and he was released from prison to kill again.

CHARLES FIELDS: Killed one Black male and one Hispanic male in Texas in 2015, robbing and shooting his victims to death. He committed his crimes as a teenager.

STEVIE LAMAR FIELDS: Killed one Black male and one Black female in California, one in 1974 and one in 1978. His victims were bludgeoned and shot to death.

RONALD LEO FISHER: Killed between two and three Black males in Georgia between the years of 2005 and 2009, shooting his victims to death. One of his victims was only seventeen years old.

LANCE EDWARD FLEMING: Responsible for "The Bathtub Killings," he killed three females in California and Michigan between 1977 and 1981, shooting and stabbing his victims to death. His victims were female roommates, and all of them were found dead in the shower, resembling the Hitchcock movie *Psycho*. In 1982, he walked out of prison posing as a visitor and escaped but was returned.

JOHN BILL FLETCHER JR.: Killed two females in Washington in 1987. His victims were raped and stabbed to death. He also raped at least six other women, who survived.

LAWRENCE DONNELL FLOOD SR.: Killed two Black males in North Carolina and New Jersey, one in 1994 and one in 2007, shooting his victims to death. His first victim was only sixteen years old.

HENRY ANTAWON FLORENCE: Killed two White males in Florida, one in 1998 and one in 1999, bludgeoning and shooting his victims to death.

NORMAN KEITH FLOWERS: Killed three females in Nevada in 2005, raping, strangling, and shooting his victims to death.

RICHARD JEROME FLOWERS: Killed one Black male and one Black female in Alabama, one in 1979 and one in 1996, bludgeoning and shooting his victims to death. When he was fourteen years old, he killed a neighbor for sexually abusing his sister. At seventeen, he killed again and was sent to prison. Released from prison to kill again, he murdered a female co-worker in 1996.

WENDELL FLOWERS: Killed one White and one Black male in North Carolina, one in 1981 and one in 1989, shooting and stabbing his victims to death. His second victim was a fellow inmate, whom he stabbed thirty-one times.

JEREMIAH FOGLE: Killed one Black male and two Black females in Florida between 1986 and 2011, shooting his victims to death. His victims included two wives and the pastor of a church.

ROBERT FORD: Killed five victims in Idaho and Washington between the years of 1915 and 1923, raping and shooting his victims to death.

RONALD N FORTE: Killed two Black males in Nebraska, one in 1977 and one in 1991, robbing and shooting his victims to death.

LINWOOD EARL FORTE: "The Nightstalker" killed one elderly male and two elderly females in North Carolina in

1990. His victims were raped, stabbed, strangled, suffocated, and set on fire.

MELVIN EARL FORTE: Killed one White male and one White female in California, one in 1981 and one in 1982, shooting his victims to death.

JAMES LEE FORTUNE: Killed two male victims in Maryland, one in 1995 and one in 2008, shooting his victims to death.

JAMES FOSTER: Killed four Black females in New York in 1963, raping and strangling his victims to death. One of his victims was fifteen years old.

JAMES FOUNTAIN: Killed two Black females in New York, one in 1977 and one in 1994, raping, dismembering, and stabbing his victims to death.

KENDALL FRANCOIS: "The Poughkeepsie Killer" killed eight mostly White female prostitutes in New York between 1996 and 1998. His victims were strangled to death, and he stored their bodies in his home to have sex with their corpses.

JOHN WAYNE FRANKLIN: Killed three White victims in Kansas in 1968, robbing and shooting his male and female victims to death.

LONNIE DAVID FRANKLIN JR.: "The Grim Sleeper" killed at least seventeen but more likely upward of sixty-eight Black females in Los Angeles, California between 1985 and 2007. He took a fourteen-year break from killing, hence the Sleeper nickname. His victims were raped, shot, and strangled to death.

MICHAEL V. FRANKLIN: Killed two Black males in Florida, one in 1998 and one in 2000, robbing and shooting his victims to death.

QUAWN MOSES FRANKLIN: Killed two White males in Florida in 2001. His victims were robbed and shot to death, and he also attempted to kill at least two others. He has been cordial in his writings and wishes he had met someone like me who might have helped him when he was a troubled teenager.

WILLIAM LONNIE FRANKLIN: Killed three Black males in Illinois between 1976 and 1981, robbing and shooting his victims to death.

RAY MCARTHUR FREENEY: Killed two Black females in Texas in 2002, raping, strangling, and stabbing his victims to death.

LAVELL FRIERSON: Killed two male victims in California, one in 1972 and one in 1978, shooting his Black and Hispanic victims to death. He had gang affiliations yet was released to kill again. His second victim was an airline employee who was shot execution style.

JOHN LEONARD FULLER: Killed two Black males in Washington, one in 1987 and one in 2000, shooting and stabbing his victims to death.

FREDDIE L. GALLOWAY: Shot to death two Black males in Florida, one in 1966 and one in 1975.

KENNETH EARLE GALLOWAY: Killed two victims in Washington, one in 1988 and one in 1995, bludgeoning his victims to death. His victims were infants, and he has also assaulted other children.

DEADRICK EUGENE GARRETT: Killed two Black males in Tennessee, one in 2007 and one in 2009, shooting and stabbing his victims to death.

CARLTON MICHAEL GARY: "The Stocking Strangler" killed nine elderly White females in New York and Georgia between 1970 and 1978, raping and strangling his victims to death.

LOUIS BERNARD GASKIN: "The Ninja Killer" killed between three and nine White victims in Georgia and New York between 1986 and 1989. He dressed as a Ninja and shot through the victims' house windows at night with a .22 caliber rifle, robbing and killing his male and female victims.

JOHNNY LEE GATES: Killed two White females in Georgia in 1976, raping and shooting his victims to death.

LOVENE STERLING GATES: Killed one White and one Black victim in Oregon in 2007, robbing and shooting his victims to death. These victims were killed on the same day, which would make him a spree killer, but the crime has a serial killer feel to it.

ANDRE CLEVELAND GAY: Killed between four and five Black victims in Georgia between 1990 and 2014, shooting his male and female victims to death. He was released from prison to kill again, and two of his victims were a couple shot dead and left on the side of the road. He wrote me and was friendly, saying he is interested in helping me with my project. He had a co-defendant named Richard Augusta Wilson.

ALFRED J. GAYNOR: "Big Al" killed ten females in Massachusetts between the years of 1995 and 1998, raping, sodomizing, and strangling them to death. He enjoyed sex with his victims after death. The son of one of his victims attacked him with a chair in court, causing significant damage.

HUBERT GERALDS JR.: Known as "The Englewood Strangler," he killed between five and seven Black prostitutes in Illinois in 1994 and 1995. His victims were raped and strangled to death, and he preferred to have sex with victims when they were unconscious.

ROBERT A. GIBBS: Killed two Black males in Ohio, one in 1971 and one in 1983, bludgeoning and shooting his victims to death.

GREGORY DEVON GIBSON: Killed one White and one Black victim in North Carolina, one in 1992 and one in 1998, robbing, shooting, and bludgeoning his victims to death with a hammer. His first murder took place when he was sixteen years old, when he killed a ninety-year-old female. He eventually hung himself in his jail cell.

MOSE GIBSON: Killed seven White victims in California, Arizona, Louisiana, and Florida between 1908 and 1920, bludgeoning his male and female victims to death.

NATHAN GILES: Killed four females in New York between 1963 and 1978, robbing, shooting, and stabbing his victims to death.

LORENZO J. GILYARD: Known as "The Kansas City Strangler," he was a trash worker by day and a serial killer by night, strangling thirteen White and Black female prostitutes to death in Missouri between 1977 and 1993. His victims were raped and strangled to death. Many of his victims were found with a cloth stuffed into their mouths. He wrote me and told me he was innocent, blaming the justice system for his incarceration.

FREDDIE LEE GLENN: Killed five victims with Michael Corbett in Colorado in 1975, shooting and stabbing their victims to death. Their last victim was Karen Grammer, the younger sister of actor Kelsey Grammer. Grammer was repeatedly raped by the two, then stabbed in the throat and left to die in a mobile home. She crawled to a neighbor's porch but died when nobody answered the door.

FRED GLOVER: Killed fifteen males and females in Alabama between 1919 and 1923, robbing and bludgeoning his victims with an axe. His victims included fourteen White victims and one Black victim.

CHARLES GOODLETT: Killed two males in Tennessee, one in 1946 and one in 1978, robbing, shooting, and stabbing his victims to death.

ROHAN JEROME GOODLETT: Killed two Asian males in Maryland in 2011, robbing and shooting them to death.

ANTWONE GOOLSBY: Killed three Black males and females in Washington between 2002 and 2009, shooting his victims to death.

JOHN GORDON: Killed three victims in Mississippi between 1895 and 1897.

JOHN GORDON: Killed two males in Pennsylvania, one in 1992 and one in 2011, shooting his victims to death.

ROMALIS GORDON JR.: Killed three females in Louisiana and Florida between 1993 and 2006, shooting his victims to death. While in prison, he confessed to the Florida murder, where he shot a female spring breaker to death and left her on the side of the road.

MICHAEL L. GORMAN: Killed two Black females in Missouri, one in 1988 and one in 1989, raping, shooting, and strangling his victims to death.

MARK GOUDEAU: "The Baseline Killer" killed one male and eight females near Baseline Road in Arizona in 2005 and 2006. His victims were robbed, raped, and shot to death. He was also known as "The Baseline Rapist" and was convicted of several rapes and kidnappings as well.

KWAUHURU GOVAN: Killed one Black male and one Black female in New York, one in 2004 and one in 2005, smothering his victims to death. One of his victims was seventeen years old, and it is thought he kidnapped her to test out his sex toy inventions. Her ligature marks were possibly made by a sex chair, and he had the drawings of the chair on his person. One of his victims was a nineteen-year-old male relative, who was dismembered.

JAMES WILLIE GRACE: Killed one White and one Black male in North Carolina in 1976, shooting his victims as a sniper.

ANDRE LORENZO GRAHAM: Killed one White male and two White females in Virginia in 1993, robbing and shooting his victims to death. His co-defendant was Mark Arlo Sheppard.

HARRISON FRANK "MARTY" GRAHAM: "The Corpse Collector" killed between seven and nine Black females in Pennsylvania between 1983 and 1987, raping, bludgeoning, and strangling his victims to death. He kept the corpses in his apartment so he could have sex with them. He told me that growing up, he was involved in all three triad behaviors (bedwetting, animal cruelty, and fire starting). He also told me he was always under the influence of drugs, and he claimed he killed because of his anger. About his victims, he told me that there was no begging for mercy, and those he targeted wouldn't be able to survive.

FREDDIE GRANT: Killed three Black females in South Carolina in 2011 and 2012, raping, shooting, and smothering his victims to death. His youngest victim was only fifteen years old, and he has been cordial and willing to help me with my project.

WALDO GRANT: Killed four males in New York between 1973 and 1976, and his victims were stabbed and beaten to death with a hammer. All of the victims were gay men, and some of them were dismembered. He explained that he had "an uncontrollable urge to kill."

KENNETH GRANVIEL: Killed one Black male and six Black females in Texas in 1974 and 1975, raping and stabbing his victims to death. Five of his victims were a family, which included three women and two children. When Granviel was sixteen, he raped and attempted to strangle his own mother, and when he was released, he sexually assaulted his own brother. He is suspected in two unsolved murders.

JAMIEL DOUGLAS GRAVES: Strangled to death two Black females in Virginia in 2012. One of the victims was found in his closet.

COLEMAN WAYNE GRAY: Killed one male and two females in Virginia in 1984 and 1985, shooting his victims to death. Two of the victims were a mother and daughter.

MARCOS GRAY: Killed one male and one female in Illinois in 1993, robbing and shooting his victims to death.

RONALD ADRIAN GRAY: Killed four White females in North Carolina in 1986 and 1987, raping, shooting, and stabbing his victims to death. He is also responsible for numerous rapes.

CLEO JOEL GREEN III: "The Red Demon" killed three Black females in Kentucky in 1983, raping, strangling, and bludgeoning his victims to death. One of his victims was a seventy-six-year-old female who was decapitated. He attacked other females who survived, like the stabbing of a seventy-three-year-old with a pair of scissors, and the attempted rape of a sixty-nine-year-old who had no legs. When he tried to rape her, she grabbed his testicles and squeezed them until he passed out.

DESHAWN LEON GREEN: Killed three Black males in Florida in 2009, shooting his victims to death.

GREGORY VICENTE GREEN: Killed one Black male and four Black females in Michigan between 1991 and 2016, shooting and stabbing his victims to death. After killing his wife, he was released to kill again. Green married the daughter of the pastor who advocated for his release, and years later, he murdered all four of her children in a fit of rage.

LARRY CRAIG GREEN: Known as "The Zebra Murders," he killed twelve White victims in California in 1973 and 1974, shooting and stabbing his nine male and three female victims to death. His murders were racially motivated, and he was part of a group of four killers who called themselves the "Death Angels." They are suspected in possibly seventy-three or more murders, and his co-defendants were Manuel Moore, Jessie Lee Cooks, and JCX Simon.

TRAVIS DWIGHT GREEN: Killed two White females in Texas, one in 1998 and one in 1999, raping and strangling his victims to death.

VAUGHN ORRIN GREENWOOD: "The Skid Row Slasher" killed eleven male victims in the skid row area of Los Angeles, California between 1964 and 1975. His victims were bludgeoned and stabbed to death, and they had their throats cut. He also staged the bodies and drank their blood, leaving cups of blood around the body, and leaving rings of salt as well.

DARNELL GRIFFIN: Killed two females in Hawaii, one in 1980 and one in 1999, raping and strangling his victims to death. He was released from prison to kill again.

GEOFFREY GRIFFIN: "The Roseland Killer" killed eight Black females in Illinois in 2000, raping, bludgeoning, stabbing, and strangling his victims to death.

JEFFERY LEE GRIFFIN: Killed one male and two females in Texas in 1978 and 1979, abducting and stabbing his victims to death. One of his victims was stabbed forty-nine times and dumped in a trash bin, and another victim was a seven-year-old male.

RICHARD GRISSOM JR.: Killed four to five White females in Kansas and Missouri between 1977 and 1989. His victims were kidnapped, raped, strangled, and stabbed to death, and he began killing at the age of sixteen. He was released from prison to kill again, and the later victims were all college students.

EDRIC DASHELL GROSS: Killed two White females in California, one in 2001 and one in 2002, raping and strangling his victims to death. He was arrested thanks to a DNA hit.

VINCENT DARRELL GROVES: Killed between sixteen and twenty-four victims in Colorado between 1978 and 1988, raping and strangling his victims to death.

FREDERICK LEE GUDE: Killed one female and two males in Georgia between 1969 and 2004, shooting and stabbing his victims to death. He was released from prison to kill again, this time stabbing his girlfriend to death with an ice pick.

STANLEY LEE GUIDROZ: Killed one male and one female in Washington and Louisiana, one in 1983 and one in 2011, stabbing his victims to death. His victims included his son and his wife.

JEFFERY LEE GUILLORY: Killed between three and eight Black females in Louisiana between 1999 and 2002, bludgeoning and strangling his victims, and then staging their bodies. He wrote me and told me nothing is off limits, except for his middle name, "Lee." "Don't call me Lee!" He is suspicious but willing to help me.

WILLIAM MARVIN GULLEY: Killed three victims in Georgia in 1994, robbing, kidnapping, bludgeoning, torturing, and stabbing his victims to death.

JAMES GUZMAN: Killed two White males in Florida, one in 1982 and one in 1991, robbing and stabbing his victims to death. He used a sword to kill one of his victims.

MATTHEW GUZMAN: Killed between two and four male victims in Florida in 2010, shooting his victims to death.

HUBERT A. HACKNEY: Killed three Black males in Washington, DC in 1973, shooting his victims to death.

KEVIN BERNARD HALEY & REGINALD JEROME HALEY: These two brothers killed eight females in California between 1982 and 1984, raping, bludgeoning, shooting, and strangling their victims to death. They are also suspected of sixty rapes, and most of their homicide victims were in their seventies and eighties.

CHARLES JEROME HALL: Killed two White males in Georgia, one in 1983 and one in 2014, bludgeoning and shooting his victims to death.

DEWAIN HALL: Killed two Black females in California in 1989, shooting two prostitutes to death

ABDULLAH TANZIL HAMEEN: Killed two male victims in Pennsylvania and Delaware, one in 1980 and one in 1991, shooting his victims to death. He was arrested and eventually executed by lethal injection.

ARTHUR L. HAMILTON: Killed two victims in Florida, one in 1965 and one in 1974.

LLOYD WAYNE HAMMOND: Killed three Black males in Kentucky in 2006, shooting his victims to death.

TEVIN HAMMOND: Killed between three and six Black males in Pennsylvania in 2013, robbing and shooting them to death. Although robbery was his motive, he enjoyed the act of killing.

KEVIN L. HAMPTON: Killed one Black and two White females in Indiana between 2000 and 2004. He raped and strangled his victims to death and was arrested because of a DNA match. He explained, "I had to kill some people to stop them from calling the cops on me," and "Is there still bodies that I have never been to court on? Yes!"

THOMAS J. HAMPTON: Killed five victims in Florida, Georgia, and South Carolina between 1887 and 1901.

WILLIAM HENRY HANCE: "The Chairman of the Forces of Evil" killed one White and two Black elderly females in Georgia in 1977 and 1978, raping and bludgeoning them to death.

LARRY SHANNON HANKERSON: Killed between two and three Black males in Georgia in 1994, shooting his victims to death.

JOHN COLEMAN HARDAWAY: Killed one male and one female in Oregon, one in 1996 and one in 2011, bludgeoning and shooting his victims to death. He was released from prison to kill again, and when released, he beat his girlfriend to death.

PAUL HARRINGTON: Killed five Black victims in Michigan between 1975 and 1999, shooting his victims to death. He killed his first wife and two daughters in 1975 and was never charged. In 1999, he killed his second wife and his three-year-old son.

AMBROSE HARRIS: Killed two White victims in New Jersey, his second victim being a fellow inmate.

CARL HARRIS: Killed three Black victims in Georgia in 1993, raping and strangling his victims to death. One of his victims was an infant.

DEWAYNE LEE HARRIS: "Chilly Willy" killed three female prostitutes in Washington in 1997 and 1998, raping, stabbing, and strangling his victims to death. The victims had their wrists and ankles bound with shoelaces and were gagged with their own panties. He has been very difficult to deal with, making constant threats, and finally sending me a card and letter telling me, "Thank you for your bullshit and your waste of time," and "You are using high profile cases to make money off of us, find yourself another factory lab rat for your book." He has claimed that he committed thirty-two more murders, and he may be telling the truth.

EARL CARL HARRIS: Killed five or six Black females in Missouri, Indiana, and Michigan between 1928 and 1938, shooting and stabbing his victims to death.

JAMES HARRIS: Killed one Black male and one Black female in Pennsylvania, one in 1982 and one in 2015, raping, shooting, and strangling his victims to death.

MICHAEL DARNELL HARRIS: Killed five elderly White females in Michigan in 1981 and 1982. His victims were raped, stabbed, and strangled to death. He sent me several copies of trial records and attorney notes as he claims he is innocent of his crimes. "Your info is wrong, in March of 2016 a new DNA test result vindicated me of serial murders."

RALPH HARRIS: "The Pill Hill Rapist" killed six males in Illinois between 1992 and 1995, robbing, raping, and shooting his victims to death. He is responsible for more rapes.

ROBERT WAYNE HARRIS: Killed four males and two females in Texas in 1999 and 2000, and his victims were kidnapped, raped, and shot to death. His later murders came in a mass shooting at his former workplace, killing five people. When he was eight years old, he watched his father kill his mother, then commit suicide. When he was fifteen, he attacked his aunt with a hammer.

LESTER HARRISON: Killed one male and six females in Illinois between 1951 and 1973, raping, bludgeoning, strangling, and stabbing his victims to death. Some of his victims were beaten with bricks, and he ate a part of his last victim's body, saying it turned him on to see women suffer. He also enjoyed keeping trophies from his victims.

KENNETH HARTLEY: Killed a Black male and a Black female in Florida, one in 1986 and one in 1991, shooting his victims to death.

WAYNE LAMARR HARVEY: Killed three White males and one White female in Michigan between 1975 and 1984, shooting his victims to death.

JOSEPH HARWELL: Killed between three and six Black females in Ohio between 1989 and 1997, raping and strangling his victims to death. He lived in the same neighborhood as fellow serial killer Anthony Sowell and was arrested because of a DNA match.

MELVIN HAUSER: Killed three Black males in Pennsylvania between 1966 and 1987, shooting and stabbing his victims to death.

SAMUEL CHRISTOPHER HAWKINS: "The Traveling Rapist" killed two females in Texas, one in 1976 and one in 1977, raping and stabbing his victims to death. One of his victims was twelve years old, and he also confessed to over forty rapes.

THOMAS WILLIAM HAWKINS JR.: Killed three Black females in Pennsylvania between the years of 1980 and 1989, raping, strangling, and stabbing his victims to death. He killed his first victim when he was only fourteen years old, strangling a fifteen-year-old female to death. He was released to kill again, and this time it was his fourteen-year-old niece, who was raped and strangled with a phone cord, and then stabbed with a fork.

TIMOTHY ANDREW HAWKINS: Killed three Black females in Maryland between 1988 and 2003, strangling and stabbing his victims to death.

ROBERT TYRONE HAYES: Known as "The Daytona Beach Killer," he killed three and possibly seven females between 2005 and 2016, most of his victims being sex workers. All of them were shot in the head. The initial profile of the killer was a White male, which is very common in law enforcement.

SAMUEL JOHNSON HAYES: Killed two victims in Georgia, robbing and shooting his victims to death.

THOMAS A. HENDERSON: Killed between two and five Black victims in Ohio between 1996 and 1998, shooting his male and female victims to death.

JOHN RUTHELL HENRY: Killed one Black male and two Black females in Florida between 1975 and 1985, stabbing his victims to death. His first victim was his wife, who was stabbed thirty times, and he was sent to prison. He was released from prison to kill again, and he did so, killing his second wife and his four-year-old stepson, stabbing them to death.

WILLIAM MORGANHERRING: Killed two White victims in North Carolina in 1994, raping and strangling his victims to death. One of his victims was sodomized after death.

EARL HICKS: Killed three White females in Illinois and California in 1937 and 1938, raping and bludgeoning his victims to death.

MONROE HICKSON: Known as "Blue Boy" and "Bluecorns," he killed two males and two females in South Carolina in 1946, robbing, bludgeoning, and shooting his victims to death. Some of them were killed with an axe. In 1966, he escaped prison and was never apprehended.

CLARENCE HILL: "The Duck Island Killer" and Sunday school teacher killed six victims, three couples in New Jersey between 1938 and 1940, shooting his victims to death. The victims were parked in an area called Duck Island and were killed with a 12-gauge shotgun. One of his victims was only sixteen years old.

IVAN JEROME HILL: Known as "The 60 Freeway Slayer" and "The 60 Freeway Killer," he killed one male and eight females in California near the I-60 Pomona freeway between 1979 and 1994, shooting and strangling his victims to death.

MARK ANTHONY HILL: Killed three White females in Washington between 1989 and 1997, shooting, stabbing, and strangling his victims to death.

THEODIS HILL: Killed five females in Missouri and Arkansas between 2006 and 2009, raping and strangling his victims to death. He is suspected of additional murders, and he told me, "I have five murders they know of but I must be honest today, there are many more in other states. I was a very sick person...I think I have demons in me."

WALTER HILL: Killed five Black victims in Alabama and Georgia between 1952 and 1977, shooting and stabbing his male and female victims to death. His first murder was when he was seventeen years old, and he was released to kill again. Three of his victims were killed in the same house, all shot in the back of the head.

WARREN LEE HILL: Killed a Black male and a Black female in Georgia, shooting and beating his victims to death. His first victim was his girlfriend, and his second victim was a fellow inmate.

DOUGLAS HINES JR.: Killed two females in Texas and California, one in 1973 and one in 1991, raping, robbing, and stabbing his victims to death. He was released from prison to kill again.

EARL HINES: Killed two male victims in Colorado in 1990.

RONALD HINTON: Killed three White females in Illinois between 1996 and 1999, robbing, raping, and strangling his victims to death. His eight-year-old daughter saw a composite sketch on television and told her teacher it was her daddy, which led to his arrest. He explained he was a troubled teen and wished that someone like me would have reached him before he began his life of crime, hanging with shady characters.

ANTHONY JEROME HIPP: Killed one male and one female in North Carolina, one in 1978 and one in 1995, bludgeoning and stabbing his victims to death. He killed again after being released from prison, stabbing one of his victims thirty-four times.

TONY RENZELL HOBSON: Killed a male and a female in Georgia and Kentucky, one in 1983 and one in 1992, robbing and stabbing his victims to death.

WILLIE JAMES HODGES: Killed three elderly White females in Florida, Ohio, and Alabama between 2001 and 2003, raping, stabbing, shooting, and bludgeoning his victims to death with a hammer. He claimed I was just like the prison system, suspecting he was guilty of multiple murders. He emphatically defends himself, stating that he isn't a mass murderer or a serial killer, and claims innocence.

PHILLIP DYLAN HOLLAND: Killed one male and one female in Florida, one in 1981 and one in 1988, stabbing his victims to death.

HAROLD HOLMAN: Killed one White male and two White females in California between 1972 and 1980, robbing, raping, and bludgeoning his victims to death. His nickname is "Spiderman," as he would crawl up the outside of buildings to enter people's homes, sneaking in their upper story windows.

RICHARD L. HOLMAN: Killed six White males and three White females in Illinois in 1978 and 1979, robbing, shooting, and stabbing his victims to death. For four of his murders, he had a co-defendant, Girvies Davis, and the crimes earned them the nickname "The.22 Caliber Killers."

ALVIN C. HOLMES: Killed two victims in Florida, one in 1956 and one in 1972, shooting his victims to death.

DARRYL LAMONT HOLMES: Killed two White males in South Carolina in 1996, robbing and shooting his victims to death.

EDWARD J. HOLMES: Killed three victims in Maryland and Washington, DC in 1973, raping, bludgeoning, and stabbing his victims to death. At nineteen years old, he killed three children, ages nine, eleven, and twelve. Holmes was the janitor of a local school.

WILLIE JAMES HOLMES: Killed four Black victims in Pennsylvania in 1978 and 1979, robbing, shooting, strangling, and stabbing his male and female victims to death. He was a contractor who knew his victims, and some even attended church with him.

LEON CORNEAL HOLSTON: Killed four young males in Florida between 1962 and 1966, raping and stabbing his victims to death.

JAMIE HOOD: Killed one White male and one Black male in Georgia in 2010 and 2011, shooting his victims to death. One of his victims was a police officer.

JOHN MICHAEL HOOKER: Killed one Black male and two Black females in Oklahoma between 1971 and 1988, shooting and stabbing his victims to death. He killed his first victim at the age of seventeen, was sent to prison, and later was released to kill again. He then killed his girlfriend and her mother.

RAYMONT HOPEWELL: "Money" killed one Black male and four Black females in Maryland between 1999 and 2005, raping and strangling his victims to death. He experienced all three of the homicidal triad warning signs (animal torture, fire starting, and bedwetting). He has been cordial and is willing to talk about the murders that the police don't know about.

JAMES F. HORTON II: Killed two males in Illinois and California, one in 1971 and one in 1982, shooting and bludgeoning his one White and one Black victim to death with a hammer.

ANGELO HOWARD: Shot five Black males to death in Ohio in 2002 and 2003.

EARL HOWARD: Killed one male and one female in Ohio, one in 1972 and one in 1991, shooting his White and Black victims to death. He was sent to prison for the first murder and later released to kill again.

GARY HOWARD: Killed two victims in Florida, one in 1978 and one in 1986.

GENE HOWZE: Killed one Black male and one Black female in Florida, one in 1970 and one in 1972, shooting his victims to death.

ARENZA DOUGLAS HUBBARD: Killed one Black male and one Black female in Michigan, one in 1997 and one in 2006, shooting and running over his victims.

FRANK M. HUBBARD: Killed two victims in New Jersey, one in 1969 and one in 1981, robbing and shooting his victims to death. He was sent to prison and released to kill again.

ROBERT JEAN HUDSON: Killed two victims in Texas, one in 1987 and one in 1999, shooting and stabbing his victims to death. He was sent to prison and released to kill again, which he did. His last murder was the stabbing of his ex-girlfriend and her eight-year-old son. Thankfully, the son survived.

VINCENT HUDSON: Killed three Black females in Illinois in 2004, raping, strangling, and bludgeoning his victims to death. He described a recent incident in prison that left him permanently blind: "My eyes got ripped out of my skull and has changed my life." He has been cordial and is open to helping me with my project.

WILLIAM LOUIS HUFF: Killed two White female children in Arizona in 1967, raping, bludgeoning, stabbing, strangling, and dismembering his victims. His victims were six and seven years old.

MICHAEL HUBERT HUGHES: "The Southside Slayer" killed between eight and twelve and possibly as many as forty-four Black females in California between 1986 and 1993, raping and strangling his victims to death. He is one of the deadliest killers in California history. He enjoyed posing his victims after he killed them, and one of his victims was only fifteen years old. He had his attorney send me a letter stating that he didn't want to speak to me, stating that "he wished me to inform you in no uncertain terms that he wants no further communications from you whatsoever." He can kill little girls, but he doesn't have the balls to write me back.

TOMMIE COLLINS HUGHES: Killed one male and two females in Texas in 1996 and 1997, robbing and shooting his victims to death.

WILLIE HUGHES: Killed between two and three males in Michigan and Pennsylvania between 1933 and 1960, bludgeoning and strangling his victims to death.

LENDELL HUNTER: Killed between two and three females in Georgia between 1970 and 1974, raping and beating his victims to death. He is suspected of more murders.

RICHARD LOUIS HUNTER: Killed four elderly Black females in Georgia in 1986, raping and strangling his victims to death. He is suspected of more murders.

SAMUEL LEE IVERY: "The Ninja of God" killed four Black females in Missouri, Illinois, and Alabama in 1992, robbing, hacking, and stabbing his victims to death. Some of his victims were bound, and some decapitated.

THOMAS TRESHAWN IVEY: Killed two to three White females in South Carolina and Alabama in 1992 and 1993, shooting his victims to death. In 1993, he and another inmate escaped from jail while awaiting murder charges and went on a crime spree, killing a thirty-year-old male and a police officer in South Carolina. He was sentenced to death, and on execution day, he slit his own throat. He survived, and the execution was carried out.

ANTHONY J. JACKSON: Killed between five and eight White females in Massachusetts in 1972, raping and strangling his victims to death.

ANTHONY L. JACKSON: Killed between two and three White and Black victims in Florida during the years of 1984 and 1985, shooting his victims to death. He is suspected in more murders, and he explained his broken home to me, growing up with no father, and how everyone in his family has been to prison or jail. He told me his schooling ended in the seventh grade. He reminisced that "there are so many things that I do wish that I could have changed about my life, but once we cross a certain line we can't go back."

CALVIN JACKSON: Killed nine White females in New York in 1973 and 1974, raping, strangling, stabbing, and smothering his victims to death. He enjoyed having sex with their corpses, and some of his victims were elderly. His MO would be to sneak into his victim's home, smother

her with a pillow, and have sex with her corpse. One of his victims was sculptor Eleanor Platt.

CHARLES JUNIOR JACKSON: Known at "The East Bay Slayer," this handyman killed one male and seven females in California between 1975 and 1982. His victims were raped, stabbed, and strangled to death, and one of his victims was eleven years old. He is suspected in more murders.

EARL LLOYD JACKSON: Killed two to three elderly Black females in California in 1977, robbing, raping, and bludgeoning his victims to death. One of his victims was raped with a wine bottle, and two of his victims were eighty-three and ninety years old. He sent me a Christmas card and told me to drink some spiked eggnog.

ELTON MANNING JACKSON: The "Hampton Roads Killer," also known as "The Norfolk Gay Killings," killed twelve gay males in Virginia between 1987 and 1996, strangling his seven White and five Black victims to death. He preferred ligature strangulation.

HOMER LEE JACKSON: Killed four Black females in Oregon between 1983 and 1993, raping and strangling his victims to death. One of his victims was fourteen years old.

LARRY KENNETH JACKSON: Killed two Black females in Oklahoma between 1985 and 1994, shooting and stabbing his victims to death. While serving a prison sentence for his first murder, he escaped while working on a prison work crew and was picked up by his current girlfriend. They went to a hotel to have sex and do drugs, and he ended up stabbing her and slashing her with a box cutter, cutting her jugular vein.

LENOIS JACKSON: Killed one Black male and one Black female in Pennsylvania and Tennessee in 1989, shooting his victims to death.

LEROY JACKSON JR.: Killed one male and one female in Illinois, one in 1953 and one in 1954, robbing and stabbing his victims to death. He also committed over 100 rapes.

O'DELLE JACKSON & PEYTON JACKSON: Killed ten males and four females in Alabama between 1919 and 1923, robbing and bludgeoning their victims with an axe.

RAY SHAWN JACKSON: "The Gillham Park Strangler" killed six Black females in Missouri in 1989 and 1990, raping and strangling his victims to death. He would lure women to a secluded area with drugs and choke them unconscious. He would wake them up, rape them, and strangle them to death. He would then pose their bodies in provocative poses to shock first responders.

RICHARD HILLIARD JACKSON: Killed one Black male and one Black female in Maryland, one in 1972 and one in 1976, bludgeoning and strangling his victims to death. His first victim was his infant stepson, and he was sent to prison but was released to kill again. The second victim was an elderly female.

ROBERT BERNARD JACKSON: Killed two victims in North Carolina, one in 2016 and one in 2017, robbing and shooting his victims to death. He had co-defendants, and one of his victims was a store clerk.

WILLIAM ROGER JACKSON: Killed eleven males and one female in New York in 1980, robbing and shooting his victims to death.

ERNEST JAMES: Killed two White males in Florida, one in 1983 and one in 1986, bludgeoning and stabbing his victims to death. His crimes were racially motivated.

EUGENE H. JAMES: Killed two White females in Maryland and Washington D.C. in 1948, stabbing his victims and then cutting their throats.

RICHARD JAMES WHITE: "Babyface" killed between six and fifteen males in Georgia, Massachusetts, New York, and Pennsylvania between 1991 and 1994, shooting his Black and Hispanic victims to death. He claimed they were revenge killings for his brother's death, and he thought a witch doctor made him invisible to police.

SHAWN JAMES JARRETT: Killed two females in Pennsylvania and Michigan, one in 1982 and one in 2014, raping and strangling his White and Hispanic victims to death. He was sent to prison for his first murder, then released to kill again. His second victim was a co-worker, who was killed and dumped alongside a road.

DOJUAN CARLOS JEFFERSON: Killed two Black males in Kentucky, one in 1997 and one in 2014, shooting his victims to death.

STEVEN JEFFERSON: Killed two Black females in Tennessee, one in 1991 and one in 2009. His victims were raped and bludgeoned to death, and he was released from prison to kill again.

CECIL C. JENKINS: Killed between four and five females in Indiana in 1998, raping, strangling, and stabbing his three White and one Black victim to death.

JOHN CORNELIUS JENKINS: Killed between five and thirteen Black victims in Michigan between 1979 and 1989, shooting his mostly male victims to death. He was released from prison to kill again. He has been cordial with me, and he told me he would like to tell his story, which, as he explains, is three-fold. "Back then, now, and the future. Because I have a life story to give, the bad, good, and my transformation as well."

JONATHAN LYNN JENKINS: Killed one White male and one Black male in North Carolina in 1998 and 1999, strangling his victims to death.

NIKKO A. JENKINS: Killed three males and one female in Nebraska in 2013, robbing and shooting his victims to death. He killed all of his victims after leaving prison, claiming demons commanded him to kill.

TYREE AMONDRICK JENKINS: Killed three males in Florida between 2006 and 2008, robbing and shooting his victims to death. His first two victims were teenagers.

WILBUR LEE JENNINGS: Known as "The Ditchbank Killer" and "The Ditchbank Murderer," he killed between five and nine mostly Black females in California between 1981 and 1984. His victims were raped, strangled, and bludgeoned to death. The bodies of his victims were found in canals and irrigation pipes, which led to his nickname.

DANTE JETER: Killed two males in Maryland, one in 2006 and one in 2008, robbing, bludgeoning, and stabbing his Black and Hispanic victims to death. One of his victims was the murder for hire of a dentist, for which he was paid $1000 by his cousin.

ANDREW JETT: Killed two Black females in Rhode Island, bludgeoning and stabbing his victims to death. His first murder was his girlfriend, for which he was sent to prison, then he was released to kill again. His second murder was his new girlfriend, who was stabbed to death.

KEVIN GREGORY JOHNS: Killed three Black males in Maryland between 2002 and 2005, bludgeoning, stabbing, and strangling his victims to death. His first murder victim was his uncle, who was stabbed and strangled to death. He was sent to prison, where he killed two fellow inmates, one on a prison bus.

RONNIE JOHNS: Known as "The 44-Caliber Killer," he killed three males and one female in Michigan in 1991, robbing and shooting his mostly Black victims to death. He also attempted to kill four others.

ALVIN JOHNSON: Killed three victims in California, Oregon, and Utah between 1972 and 1983, raping, bludgeoning, and stabbing his victims to death. He teamed up with serial killer Wilbur Lee Jennings for his California murder. He was hit in the head with an axe as a child, which causes him problems in life. He killed his first male victim in 1972 and was sent to prison, only to be released to kill again. His next victims included an elderly female and a couple who were raped, tortured, beaten with a shovel, resulting in the death of the male.

AMON JOHNSON: Killed one White male and two White females in Oklahoma in 1944, robbing and stabbing his victims to death.

CEDIL J. JOHNSON: Killed four males in Tennessee between 1980 and 1985, bludgeoning and shooting his victims to death. His first murder was a triple homicide at a convenience store, and one of the victims was a twelve-year-old male. He then killed a fellow inmate in prison.

DAVID EUGENE JOHNSON: Killed one White female and one Black female in Florida, one in 1998 and one in 2001, robbing, bludgeoning, and stabbing his victims to death. His first murder took place when he was just fifteen years old when he killed a prostitute, but he was never charged with that crime. When he was seventeen, he stabbed a local author to death. He bragged that he tried to cut the head off the author.

DAVID JOHNSON IV: Killed three Black males in Indiana in 2015, shooting his victims to death.

DAVID LEE JOHNSON: Killed two victims in Michigan, one in 1978 and one in 1994, shooting his victims to death.

EDDIE JAMES JOHNSON: Killed four victims in Illinois and Texas between 1975 and 1987, raping and shooting his White and Hispanic victims to death. He was sent to prison for murder and was later released to kill again. His second murder was a triple murder in Texas, and the victims included a couple and their ten-year-old daughter, whose bodies dumped in a ditch.

ELDRED L. JOHNSON JR.: Killed one male and one female in New York, one in 1995 and one in 1996, stabbing his victims to death.

EMANUEL JOHNSON: Killed two White females in Florida in 1988, raping, robbing, and stabbing his victims to death. One of his victims was a seventy-three-year-old female.

JAMES EARL JOHNSON: Killed two White females in Massachusetts, one in 1992 and one in 1993, raping and strangling his victims to death. He is suspected in more murders.

JOHNNY RAY JOHNSON: He killed between four and five females in Texas in 1994 and 1995, raping, bludgeoning, and strangling his victims to death. He would smoke crack with his victims, have sex with them, kill them, and then have sex with their corpses.

JUSTIN ALBERT JOHNSON: Killed two Black female children in Mississippi, one in 1990 and one in 1992, raping, strangling, and sodomizing his victims. The two three-year-olds were abducted from their homes, and their bodies were thrown into a body of water. He explained that a voice in his head made him do it. He was arrested on a DNA hit.

MATTHEW STEVEN JOHNSON: Killed three female prostitutes in Connecticut in 2000 and 2001, raping, bludgeoning, and strangling his Black and Hispanic victims to death. He is suspected in at least two more murders. He was sent to prison for attempted murder and was released to kill again. That's when he began his prostitute murder spree, raping them, strangling them, and stomping them to death.

MELVIN JOHNSON: Killed one Black male and three Black females in Illinois between 1984 and 1988, raping, stabbing, smothering, and strangling his victims to death. Two of his victims were young females killed on Halloween night in 1984, ages ten and twelve. He never did time for that murder but was sent to prison for molestation. After he died, he was tied to his murders through DNA.

MICHAEL A. JOHNSON: Killed four Black females in Illinois between 2008 and 2010, raping and strangling his victims to death.

MILTON JOHNSON: Known as "The Weekend Murderer" and "A Summer of Terror," he killed seventeen White victims in Illinois in 1983, raping, shooting, and stabbing his victims to death. His victims included two police officers, seven males, and ten females.

MONTELL JOHNSON: Killed between two and four Black victims in California and Illinois from 1990 to 1994, bludgeoning and shooting his victims to death. He claimed to have killed thirty people at his trial.

RAYMOND EUGENE JOHNSON: Killed one Black male and two Black females in Oklahoma between 1995 and 2007, bludgeoning his victims with a hammer, shooting them, and setting them on fire. He was sent to prison for his first murder and released to kill again. His second and third murders were the beating death of his girlfriend and her infant daughter, whom he killed with a hammer. He then set their bodies on fire. He responded to me and offered to help me, talking about his conversion to Christianity and his involvement with an outside church. He explained, "I ask that you get to know me and not my past mistakes or failures because I am not my mistakes nor am I my failures."

SHAWN "STEVE" ANTHONY JOHNSON: Killed three elderly White females in Florida in 1963, raping and strangling his victims to death. He attempted to kill at least two more victims.

STRESSLA JOHNSON: Killed two Black females in Oregon in 1987, raping and strangling his victims to death. One victim was found nude on her bed in her apartment, strangled with a phone cord. She had been sexually assaulted and sodomized.

THOMAS JOHNSON: "Hucklebuck" killed two victims in Florida, one in 1987 and one in 1992, shooting his victims to death.

VINCENT JOHNSON: "The Brooklyn Strangler," also known as "The Williamsburg Slayer," killed five to six female prostitutes in New York in 1999 and 2000, raping and strangling his Black and Hispanic victims to death. He also enjoyed having sex with their corpses.

VINCENT ALLEN JOHNSON: Killed three male and female victims in Oklahoma between 1979 and 1991, shooting his White and Black victims to death.

JOHN JOHNSTON: Killed five males in West Virginia, Georgia, and Pennsylvania between 1895 and 1903, robbing and shooting his victims to death.

AKEEM R. JONES: Killed four Black males and one Black female in Nebraska between 2009 and 2015, shooting his victims to death. One of his crimes was the double homicide of a couple in 2015.

ANDRE JONES: Killed eight victims in Illinois, beginning with a triple murder that took place in 1971 when he was fourteen years old. The three victims were shot and stabbed to death. Seven years later, he murdered an elderly couple in their home, decapitating the male and stabbing the female to death. Then in 1979, he went on a spree killing with Freddie Tiller, his co-defendant.

BRYAN MAURICE JONES: "The Dumpster Killer" killed four Black female prostitutes in California in 1985 and 1986, raping, sodomizing, stabbing, and strangling his victims to death. He also set his victims on fire, and some of his victims were found in dumpsters.

DANIEL O. JONES: Killed between four and five Black females in Missouri between 1998 and 2001, raping and stabbing his victims to death. He committed these murders while he was out on parole for raping a high school teacher.

DONTE JAMAL JONES: Killed two Black males in Pennsylvania, one in 2010 and one in 2011, shooting and stabbing his victims to death.

GEORGE ALARICK JONES: Killed one Black male and one Black female in Texas, robbing and shooting his victims to death. His male victim was an adult who was abducted from a shopping mall, robbed, shot twice in the head, and dumped.

GEORGE LAMAR JONES: Killed three Black females in Wisconsin and Mississippi between the years of 1972 and 1997, stabbing and strangling his victims to death.

HENRY LEE JONES: "Burn" killed at least four White victims in Florida and Tennessee in 2003, robbing, raping, and stabbing his mostly male victims to death. The victims also had their throats cut. He corresponded with me and explained that he is waiting for his attorney to give him permission to talk to me, and he asked me for a television, since his is broken.

JA'MARI ALEXANDER JONES: "The Tuba Man" killed two males in Washington, one in 2008 and one in 2012, bludgeoning and shooting his victims to death. One of his murder cases was a nightclub shooting.

JEFFERY GERALD JONES: Killed between three and four males in California in 1985, bludgeoning his mostly White victims to death. He surprised his victims in the public restroom and beat them to death with a claw hammer.

JESSE JONES: Killed two White males and two White females in South Carolina in 1942, robbing and bludgeoning his victims to death. The victims were killed with an axe, and two of his victims were elderly.

JOE WILLIE JONES: Killed two males in Louisiana, one in 1947 and one in 1980, stabbing and shooting his Black and Hispanic victims to death.

KELVIN JONES: Killed two males in Pennsylvania, one in 1998 and one in 1999, shooting his Black and Hispanic victims to death.

MARTIN JONES: Killed two White males in New York, one in 1985 and one in 1987, robbing and bludgeoning his victims to death.

MILTON JONES: Stabbed to death one male and one female in New York between 1970 and 1981.

PETER GERARD JONES: Killed one White male and one White female in Michigan, one in 1997 and one in 2014, robbing, stabbing, and strangling his victims to death. He killed his first victim in 1997, a male, and was sent to prison. He was released to kill again, and he strangled and stabbed an eighty-four-year-old female to death.

STEVEN ANTHONY JONES: Killed one male and one female in California in 2004, robbing, bludgeoning, and shooting his victims to death. He also raped and attempted to kill numerous other victims, and his female victim was beaten to death with a hammer. In prison, he has continued his string of violence, raping and attacking other inmates and corrections officers.

SYDNEY JONES: Killed thirteen people in Alabama and other states in 1914, shooting and strangling his victims to death.

KEYDRICK DEON JORDAN: Killed one White female and one Black female in Florida, one in 1991 and one in 1992, robbing, shooting, and strangling his victims to death. In his last murder, he dressed the dead victim and placed her body sitting in a chair before setting the house on fire. He has been cordial with me and concerned that if he talks to me, it could affect his chance at a possible parole. He explained, "My past has not defined me, for I am no longer that same nineteen- or twenty-year-old."

ANTHONY JOYNER: Known as "The Elderly Home of Horrors," he killed six to seven elderly White females in Pennsylvania in 1983, raping, strangling, drowning, and smothering his victims to death. He targeted those who lived in nursing homes and is suspected of at least eighteen murders.

ARTHUR JAMES JULIUS: Killed one Black male and one Black female in Alabama, one in 1972 and one in 1978, raping, bludgeoning, and strangling his victims to death. One of his victims was his cousin, whom he raped and strangled to death.

KWAN KEARNEY: Killed two Black males in Washington, DC in 2010, shooting his victims to death. One of his victims was a seventeen-year-old student.

AROHN MALIK KEE: Known as "The East Harlem Rapist," he killed three females in New York between 1991 and 1998, raping, strangling, burning, torturing, and suffocating his teen victims to death. He also raped four other young girls, and he sells "rape cards" in prison.

MELVIN MOORIS KEELING: Killed three White females in Ohio and Indiana in 2005, raping and shooting his victims to death. One of his victims was only thirteen years old. Featured on *America's Most Wanted*, he shot himself to death before being taken into custody.

LEROY KEITH: Killed three White males in Ohio and New York between 1934 and 1956, robbing and shooting his victims to death.

HORACE EDWARD KELLY JR.: Killed three White victims in California in 1984, raping and shooting his male and female victims to death. One of his victims was an eleven-year-old boy who was shot between the eyes. He wrote me, and it is hard to decipher a letter with sentences like, "Even while end California yes and trouble case open to know I been out of mind for the last 36 years."

LEROY A. KELLY: Killed two Black males in Washington, one in 1985 and one in 1988, shooting his victims to death.

EDWARD DEAN KENNEDY: Killed three males in Florida between the years of 1978 and 1981, shooting his White victims to death. He escaped from prison while serving time for one murder, and he killed his final two victims on the run, one being a state trooper.

LEONARD KIDD: Killed fourteen Black victims in Illinois between 1980 and 1984, stabbing and setting his six male and eight female victims on fire. Already on death row for a quadruple murder, where he stabbed four people to death and set them on fire, he was connected to the mass murder of ten children who died in a fire seven years earlier.

DEAN KILGORE: Killed two male victims in Florida between the years of 1978 and 1989, robbing, raping, shooting, and stabbing his White and Black victims to death. While in prison, in 1989, he killed his lover in prison, a fellow inmate, stabbing him with a shank.

PETRIE KIMBROUGH: Killed four females in Kentucky, Indiana, and Illinois between 1912 and 1919, raping, bludgeoning, and strangling his White and Black victims to death.

COREY LYNN KING: Killed five Black females in California in 2008, bludgeoning, stabbing, and strangling his victims to death. Three of his victims were ages nine, eleven, and thirteen.

JAMES DONALD KING: Killed two Black females in North Carolina, his first wife in 1967, and his second wife in 1988, shooting them both to death. His second wife was found shot to death in the school yard where she worked.

ROBERT LEE KING: Killed three Black females in Mississippi and Tennessee between 2005 and 2009, stabbing his victims to death. His 2005 victim was his girlfriend.

ARTHUR KINLAW: Killed four females in New York and New Jersey between 1982 and 1984, bludgeoning and shooting his White and Hispanic victims to death. His 1982 victim was a teenager whose body was dumped in a cemetery.

ANTHONY KIRKLAND: Killed five females in Ohio from 1987 to 2009, raping and strangling his White and Black victims to death. Two of his victims were thirteen and fourteen years old, and some of the victims' bodies were burned. His first murder was the 1987 murder of his girlfriend, and he was sent to prison but was released to kill again.

JIMMY TODD KIRKSEY: Killed two males and one female in Nevada and California in 1988, bludgeoning, shooting, and stabbing his victims to death.

DONALD KLINE: Killed three White victims in Michigan between 1985 and 1996, raping, stabbing, and strangling his male and female victims to death. He killed his girlfriend forty-eight hours after being released from a mental hospital, and one of his victims was a sixteen-year-old boy, who was strangled to death. He wrote me a strange letter in the third person, with bad grammar, claiming his innocence. He claims, "I been lock up most all of my life I did not have the time to carry out multiple murders."

THOMAS OTIS KNIGHT: Killed four White victims in Florida between 1974 and 1980, shooting and stabbing his male and female victims to death. In 1974, he murdered a Miami couple after forcing them to withdraw $50,000 from a bank. He was able to escape prison and while on the run, he murdered a store clerk. He was sentenced to death and while on death row, he stabbed a corrections officer to death.

DERRICK KORNEGAY: Killed one male and one female in New York, one in 1986 and one in 1987, shooting his victims to death.

CURTIS LEE KYLES: Killed two White females in Louisiana, one in 1984 and one in 2010, shooting his victims to death. He shot a sixty-year-old female to death in 1984, was sent to prison, and was released to kill again, kidnapping and shooting another female to death.

ROBERT CHARLES LADD: Killed one male and three females in Texas between 1978 and 1996, raping, bludgeoning, and stabbing his White and Black victims to death. He committed a triple murder in 1978, was sent to prison, and was released to kill again.

EDWARD LEWIS LAGRONE: Killed six Black victims in Texas between 1977 and 1991, shooting his male and female victims to death. Arrested for a 1977 murder and sent to prison, he was released to kill again. And he did, killing a family of three, including a ten-year-old female, whom he impregnated. He was subsequently arrested and eventually executed.

KEITH LAMAR: Killed six males in Ohio between 1989 and 1993, bludgeoning and strangling his White and Black victims to death. While serving a prison sentence for a 1989 murder, he was involved in a prison riot, which resulted in him killing fellow inmates with several other inmates called the "Death Squad."

AVERY MARTEZ LAMPKINS: Killed two Black males in Virginia, one in 2002 and one in 2015, shooting his victims to death. He killed his first victim when he was only seventeen years old.

DENNIS LANE: Killed two Black females in Georgia in 2021 as a registered sex offender. He would have sex with his victims' corpses and film the acts on his cell phone, then dump their bodies behind a shopping center.

DONALD LANG: Killed two Black females in Illinois, one in 1965 and one in 1972, raping, stabbing, and strangling his victims to death. He is suspected in more murders but couldn't be convicted because he was deaf, mute, unable to read or write, and didn't know sign language or lip reading. After his first murder, he was sent to a mental hospital but was released to kill again. A book and movie was made about his case, titled *Dummy*. He died in 2008.

POSTEAL LASKEY: "The Cincinnati Strangler" and former cab driver killed seven elderly White females in Ohio in 1965 and 1966, raping, stabbing, and strangling his victims to death. He is also responsible for many rapes.

KYLAN M. LAURENT: Killed two Black females in Louisiana and Texas in 2011, strangling his victims to death. He is thought to have killed as many as twenty-two victims, but when police were pursuing him, he jumped into the Mississippi River and drowned.

MICHAEL D. LAWRENCE: Killed two females in Michigan, one in 2012 and one in 2013, shooting and strangling his Black and Hispanic victims to death. He killed a six-year-old in a drive-by shooting in 2012, and he killed his child's mother in 2013.

DERRICK TODD LEE: "The Baton Rouge Serial Killer" killed between eleven and fourteen females in Louisiana between 1992 and 2003, raping, stabbing, strangling, and bludgeoning his mostly White victims with a hammer. One victim was stabbed more than eighty times, and he enjoyed having sex with their corpses.

DONALD EDWARD LEE: Killed two victims in Florida, one in 1986 and one in 1988.

TARRANCE LEE: Killed three Black victims in Indiana between 1986 and 2012, shooting, stabbing, and strangling his two male and one female victims to death. His 2012 case was the murder of his estranged wife, who was strangled to death.

TOBIAS CHANO LEE: Killed two males in Georgia and South Carolina in 2004, shooting his White and Black victims to death.

DEVERNON LEGRAND & STEVEN STRONG LEGRAND: "The Bishop" and his son killed twelve Black victims in New York and New Jersey between 1963 and 1975, bludgeoning, shooting, and strangling their victims to death. Two of their victims were teen sisters.

REGINALD SINCLAIR LEWIS: Killed three males in New Jersey and Pennsylvania between 1977 and 1983, shooting and stabbing his victims to death.

TRAVIS LEWIS: Killed three victims in Arkansas between 1994 and 2020, committing his first murder when he was only sixteen years old. He was sent to prison for a double homicide, and while in prison, the female victim's daughter befriended him. Upon his release from prison, she hired him to work at her bed and breakfast. In the end, he would also kill her, and when running from the police, he jumped into a lake a drowned.

TYRONE ANTWAN LEWIS: Killed three Black males in Maryland between 2005 and 2011, robbing and shooting his victims to death.

WILLIAM CHARLES LEWIS: Killed two victims in Georgia in 2001, shooting his one female and one male victim to death. He shot numerous people, some surviving the attack, and he left a note at each scene that read "Jack."

WALTER LIGHTBURN: Killed three males in Florida between 1981 and 1986, shooting his White and Black victims to death. He was part of a religious sect and had a few co-defendants.

CARLIS LINDSEY: Killed three Black victims in Florida in 1991, shooting his male and female victims to death.

TYVARUS LEE LINDSEY: Killed three males and two females in Minnesota between 2005 and 2007, robbing, bludgeoning, and shooting his White and Black victims to death. One of his crimes was a home invasion triple murder, and one of the victims was only fifteen years old.

HARRY LITTLE SR.: Killed three Black victims in Missouri between 1977 and 2014, bludgeoning and shooting his one male and two female victims to death. In 1977, he committed a double homicide, with one of the victims being his estranged wife. He was sent to prison but was released to kill again, which he did, stabbing and shooting his longtime girlfriend.

KEITH D. LITTLE: Killed two Black males in Maryland and Washington, DC between 2003 and 2011, shooting and stabbing his victims to death. He killed his boss in DC, shooting him six times. He was found not guilty of that crime, and eight years later, in 2011, he killed his current boss, stabbing him forty times and leaving a knife protruding from his neck.

SAMUEL LITTLE: Known as "The Choke and Stroke Killer," Little is considered America's deadliest serial killer, suspected of killing ninety-three victims all across the US. Due to his amazing memory, he was able to work with law enforcement to close fifty cases with his drawings of his victims. Little and I had been talking so long that when I first started communicating with him, he told me he was innocent. He explained, "You are on the wrong road, I am not a murderer. I have been everything else, God knows... I have a long record of violence with women and men for that matter, but I have never killed anyone."

JEROME LIVAS: Killed three females in Georgia in 1977, raping, bludgeoning, and strangling his two White and one Black victim to death.

WILL LOCKETT: Going by the name Petrie Kimbrough, he killed four victims in multiple states including Kentucky, between 1912 and 1920. His victims were stabbed, strangled, and bludgeoned, and one of his victims, a ten-year-old, had her head crushed with a rock.

PERRY DEWAYNE LOCKRIDGE: Killed two Black males, one in Indiana in 1972, and one in Ohio in 1994, shooting his victims to death. When he was fifteen, he killed his brother with a shotgun, and he may have been released to kill again.

FRANKLIN DARIEL LOFTON: Killed two males in Illinois, one in 2006 and one in 2007, robbing and shooting his White and Black victims to death.

ROBERT LONBERGER: Killed two Black females in Ohio, one in 1975 and one in 1996, stabbing his victims to death.

RONALD CLINTON LOTT: Killed two elderly White females in Oklahoma, one in 1986 and one in 1987, raping and strangling his victims to death. His victims were eighty-three and ninety-three years old.

RONDELL LOVE: Killed one male and one female in Louisiana in 1997, shooting and stabbing his victims to death, slashing the throat of one of his victims.

LAURENCE ALVIN LOVETTE: Killed four to five White victims in North Carolina in 2008, robbing and shooting his male and female victims to death. He was only seventeen years old at the time of his crimes. He has been cordial and explained, "I've been in and out of trouble since I was eleven or twelve years old, and I got locked up on these charges when I was seventeen. I'm twenty-six years old now."

FRANKLIN LYNCH: "The Daytime Stalker" killed thirteen elderly White females in several cities in California between the years of 1981 and 1987, raping, robbing, bludgeoning, and strangling his victims to death. He wrote to me defending himself and claiming he is innocent of his crimes. He is also the prime suspect of ten unsolved murders.

WILLY SUAREZ MACEO: Killed two males in Florida in 2022, stabbing and shooting his victims to death. He attempted to kill a third victim, and when he wasn't murdering people, he was selling real estate.

DARYL LINNIE MACK: Killed two White females in Nevada, one in 1988 and one in 1994, raping and strangling his victims to death.

ULYSSES GILLIS MACK: Killed one male and two females in Indiana in 1929, bludgeoning his White and Black victims to death with an axe.

ANTOINE ARELUS MACKEY: Killed two males in California in 2007, shooting his White and Black victims to death. One of his victims was a journalist, and his co-defendant was Yusuf Bey.

JUSTIN KEITH MACKIE: Killed three Black males in Pennsylvania in 2013, shooting his victims to death. One of his victims was a cab driver.

MATTHEW EMMANUEL MACON: Known as "The Mid Michigan Monster," he killed seven females in Michigan between 2004 and 2007, raping, bludgeoning, strangling, and stabbing his six White and one Hispanic victim to death. He was a career criminal and a sex offender. He has been cordial in speaking with me and was friendly when we visited him in prison. Most of his victims were middle-aged women who lived alone, and he enjoyed stripping them and hanging them, all while he ate a sandwich.

RONALD MACON: Killed three Black females in Illinois in 1999, raping and strangling his victims to death. He is suspected in more murders. He has been cordial and wants to help me, stating, "If me sharing my story helps anyone, I'm more than happy to help."

MICHAEL MADISON: Killed three Black females in Ohio in 2013, raping, bludgeoning, and strangling his victims to death. He placed their bodies in plastic bags and hid them in his garage, his back yard, and his basement. He may have killed more victims and enjoyed the act of killing. I have visited him on Ohio's death row, and he explained that he killed for enjoyment's sake and not for sex, because as a drug dealer, he had all the sex he wanted. He was also mentally abused by his mother, which may be the reason he is an anger-driven serial killer.

MUZIWOKUTHULA MADONDA: Killed three males and one female in Ohio and New Mexico in 2011, robbing and shooting his victims to death. He was in the US studying theology at a seminary.

JOHNNIE S. MALARKEY: Killed seven males and three females in California in 1993, robbing and shooting his White and Hispanic victims to death. One of his crimes was a mass murder at a bar, where he fatally shot eight victims.

JOE MALONE: Killed five White females in Texas between 1890 and 1898, raping and shooting his victims to death.

VICTOR KING MALONE: Killed three Black female prostitutes in Michigan in 1984 and 1985, raping, shooting, and strangling his victims to death. He is suspected of killing as many as eleven people.

JOHN PETER MALVEAUX: Killed four females in Louisiana in 1997, strangling his victims to death. He attacked more women who survived his strangulation attempts.

LEE BOYD MALVO, JOHN ALLEN MUHAMMAD: Known as "The DC Snipers" and "The Beltway Snipers," they shot and killed ten males and six females in a sniper shooting spree in Georgia, Louisiana, and Maryland in 2002. The killing spree lasted ten months, and they killed six White, six Black, two Hispanic, and two Asian victims.

ANDY MANN: Killed two males and one female in Minnesota in 1929 and 1930, shooting, strangling, and burning his White and Black victims to death.

ARTHUR MANN: Shot to death two victims in Georgia and Florida, one in 1991 and one in 2007.

CLYDE JAMES MANNING: Killed eleven Black males in Georgia in 1921, bludgeoning, shooting, and drowning his victims.

EUGENE MANNING: Killed four males in Arkansas and Mississippi between 1908 and 1912, robbing, bludgeoning, and drowning his White and Black victims to death.

WILLIE JEROME MANNING: Killed one male and three females in Mississippi in 1992 and 1993, robbing, shooting, and stabbing his White and Black victims to death. Some of the victims were run over with a vehicle.

KEITH DEVON MANUEL: Killed two Black females in North Carolina, one in 2006 and one in 2009, stabbing his victims to death. His last victim was his girlfriend.

JERRY MARCUS: "The Tuskegee Strangler" killed seven to fifteen Black females in Mississippi from 1971 to 1987, raping and strangling his victims to death. He is suspected of killing more victims in Alabama, Georgia, Mississippi, and Tennessee.

LAMONT WALDRON MARSHALL: Known as "The Heritage Hill Murders," he killed five White females in Michigan between 1970 and 1980. His victims were raped, stabbed, and strangled to death, and he is suspected in more homicides.

ARTHUR JAMES MARTIN: Killed two Black males in Florida, one in 1997 and one in 2009, shooting his victims to death. He was sent to prison for the first murder and later released to kill again.

DERRICK L. MARTIN: Killed two White victims in Indiana, one in 1992 and one in 2007, raping and beating his victims to death. He is suspected in more murders.

JAMES DAVID MARTIN: Killed one Black male and two Black females in Maryland, New York, and Pennsylvania between 1989 and 2005, strangling his victims to death. In 1989, he strangled and sodomized a male, killing him. Sent to prison, he was released to kill again, and he did, strangling and raping a fourteen-year-old female. He also strangled and stabbed a relative, who survived. While in prison, he began communicating with a woman, whom he married. When he was released again, he strangled her to death. He is suspected of more murders.

JESSE MARTIN: Killed four Black males in Washington, DC in 1973, shooting his victims to death.

PATRICK A. MARTIN: Killed one male and one female in Michigan, one in 2002 and one in 2009, bludgeoning and smothering his White and Black victims to death. His last murder was the shooting death of his pregnant girlfriend.

SAMUEL MARTIN: Killed three males in Indiana between 1900 and 1903, bludgeoning his White and Black victims to death.

WILLIE "WASH" MARTIN: Killed seven White females in Arkansas between 1920 and 1925, raping and bludgeoning his victims to death. The victims were beaten with rocks, tree branches, and pipes.

GLENFORD J. MARTINEZ: Killed two Black females in Illinois, one in 1992 and one in 2008, shooting his victims to death. He was sent to prison for the first murder and released to kill again. He killed his ex-girlfriend as she left church, then committed suicide.

MORRIS ODELL MASON: Known as "The Killer for the Eastern Shore," he killed two White elderly females in Virginia in 1978, raping, stabbing, bludgeoning with an axe, and setting his victims on fire. He also raped two teen girls, killed an eighty-six-year-old, and nailed one of his murder victims to a chair by her wrists and tied her with rope.

CALVERT LEE MASSEY: Killed two Black females in Michigan, one in 1999 and one in 2004, raping and strangling his victims to death. His 2004 victim was hung by a rope in her closet. She was nude from the waist down, her hands were handcuffed behind her back, and she had burn marks on her body.

BEN T. MATHIS: Killed one male and two females in Alabama in 1963 and 1964, strangling and stabbing his White and Black victims to death.

ERIC MATTHEWS: Killed one Black male and three Black females in Louisiana and Indiana between 1994 and 1998, strangling and smothering his victims to death. His victims included his two ex-girlfriends, his wife, and his one-year-old stepson, whom he threw in a trash bin. He has been cordial and is willing to help me, and I also heard from his fiancée. He explained, "The murders that I regrettably committed were domestic. Over the past several years, I've grown a passion and strong desire to convey the warning signs that could potentially save the lives of women across the world that are in abusive relationships."

JESSE LEROY MATTHEW JR.: Known as "The Back to School Killer," he killed two White females in Virginia, one in 2009 and one in 2014, raping and strangling his victims to death. His victims were both college students.

YNOBE KATRON MATTHEWS: Killed two White females in Texas, one in 1999 and one in 2000, raping and strangling his victims to death.

KEVIN EDWARD MATTISON: Killed two males in Pennsylvania and Maryland, one in 1994, and one in 2008, robbing and shooting his victims to death.

LARKIN MCCLOUD: Killed one White male and three White females in Nebraska in 1917, raping, bludgeoning, strangling, and stabbing his victims to death.

RICKEY BERNARD MCCOY: Killed one White male and five Black males in Georgia in 1994 and 1995, robbing and shooting his victims to death.

JEREMIAH MCCRAY: Killed one White male and four White females in Virginia, Ohio, Georgia, and Alabama between 1956 and 1958, raping, robbing, and bludgeoning his victims to death.

ERIC L. MCDADE: Killed two females in Florida, one in 1995 and one in 2010, shooting and stabbing his victims to death. After his first murder, he was sent to prison and released to kill again. This time, he stabbed a female classmate to death.

DAMIEN MCDANIEL: Killed fourteen victims in Alabama in 2023 and 2024, shooting his victims to death. His victims included a firefighter, a UPS worker, and he also opened fire at a night club.

JAMES MCDANIEL: Killed one White female and three White males in Texas and Illinois between 1978 and 2007, shooting and drugging his victims to death.

ROBERT HENRY MCDOWELL: Killed two White females in North Carolina, one in 1969 and one in 1979, stabbing his victims to death. His victims were also cut with a machete. He is now a practicing Muslim and has been cordial in our exchange of letters.

REGINALD MCFADDEN: Killed three to four White victims in New York and Pennsylvania between 1969 and 1994. His victims were stabbed, bludgeoned, smothered, and strangled to death, and his crimes had racial overtones. He has been pretty cordial in our communications, but he won't work with us unless we pay for thousands of dollars of college credits. He explained that he saw his first murder when he was seven years old, and that affected him for the rest of his life.

RICHARD M. MCFALL: Killed two White males in Oklahoma, one in 1990, and one in 2010, shooting his victims to death.

RAYMON MCGILL: Killed two victims in New York, one in 2000 and one in 2004, robbing, shooting, and stabbing his one male and one female victim to death. He is also responsible for some rapes.

EDWARD GEORGE MCGREGOR: Killed one White female and three Black females in Texas between 1990 and 2006, raping, stabbing, and strangling his victims to death. Some of his victims were found dead in their bathtubs, and he was only seventeen years old when he killed his first victim. He is suspected of more murders and was arrested on a DNA hit.

CRAIG MCINTOSH: Killed two males in Ohio, one in 2012 and one in 2013, shooting his victims to death.

CALVIN MCKELTON: Killed one Black male and one Black female in Ohio, one in 2008 and one in 2009, shooting and strangling his victims to death. He first killed his girlfriend, and then killed his friend who had helped him dispose of her body.

ANTHONY MCKNIGHT: "The East Bay Serial Killer" killed between five and eight Black female prostitutes in California in 1985, raping, bludgeoning, sodomizing, and stabbing his victims to death. He also dismembered some of his victims, and his victims included a thirteen-year-old and a seventeen-year-old.

GREGORY B. MCKNIGHT: Killed two males and one female in Ohio between 1992 and 2000, shooting his one White and two Black victims to death. He killed again after being released from prison, and one of his victims was a college student who was found wrapped in a rug in his bedroom inside his trailer.

LAMON J. MCKOY: Killed one White female and one Black female in New York, one in 2003 and one in 2004, raping and strangling his victims to death. As a teen, he killed his cousin, and he is suspected in more murders. He has been cordial in our correspondence but asked for $10,000 to work with us, which obviously we don't do.

ELTON OZELL MCLAUGHLIN: Killed two Black males and two Black females in North Carolina between 1974 and 1984, bludgeoning and shooting his victims to death.

RALPH MCLEAN: Killed two White males in Maryland in 1995, shooting his victims to death. His two victims were police officers, and he was killed in a shootout while being taken into custody.

LEROY MCNEIL: Killed four to six Black females in North Carolina between 1976 and 1983, robbing, shooting, and drowning his victims.

LAMARQUES DEVON MCWILLIAMS: Known as "Four Acres Homes," he killed between six and ten Black female prostitutes in Texas in 2006 and 2007, raping, stabbing, and strangling his victims to death. He is also suspected of numerous rapes and was apprehended because of a DNA hit.

JAMES MEALEY: Killed four males and one female in North Carolina and Virginia between 1900 and 1903.

LEON MEANS: Killed four females in Michigan between 1989 and 2014, shooting and stabbing his victims to death. In 1989, Means was a prison escapee, and he killed two females while on the run.

JOSHUA TERRELL MEBANE: Killed a male and a female in Maryland and Washington, DC in 2012, shooting his victims to death. He randomly shot a couple walking their dog, killing the female. He also killed a cab driver.

MICHAEL MELVIN: Killed four males and one female in New Jersey in 2004 and 2005, shooting his Black and Hispanic victims to death. His 2004 case was a quadruple homicide, and his 2005 case was the killing of a witness of the 2004 crime.

KEVIN JERMAINE MERCER: Killed two Black males in South Carolina, one in 2000 and one in 2002, robbing and shooting his victims to death.

HENRY MEREDITH: Killed two Black males in Louisiana in 1996, shooting his victims to death.

ALVIN ALLEN MERRIT: This registered sex offender is accused of killing at least three White females in Florida between 1994 and 2002, raping and strangling his victims to death. He was only convicted of sex crimes and has been released from prison.

AARON C. MICHAEL: Killed one Black female and two Black males in Pennsylvania between 2005 and 2009, shooting his victims to death.

DAVID STEPHEN MIDDLETON: Known as "The Cable Guy" and "Big Dave," he killed between three and four White females in Nevada and Colorado between 1993 and 1995, raping and suffocating his victims to death. He was a former Miami police officer, and he had made tapes of himself with prostitutes.

FRANK MIDDLETON, JR.: Killed one White female and one Black female in South Carolina in 1984, raping and strangling his victims to death. He was able to kill those two females when he escaped from a prison work crew.

GREGORY DEWAYNE MILLER: Killed two Black females in Georgia, one in 2002 and one in 2008, bludgeoning his victims to death.

HAYWOOD EUGENE MILLER: Killed one White male and two White females in Colorado in 2016, shooting his victims to death.

JEREMY WAYNE MILLER: Killed two males in Texas, one in 2014 and one in 2015, shooting his victims to death. One of his victims was a security guard, and one was his friend.

JOSEPH LEWIS MILLER: Killed two White males in Pennsylvania, one in 1959 and one in 1981, shooting his victims to death.

GRANT MINOR: Killed one White female and one Black female in New York, one in 1970 and one in 1980, strangling his victims to death.

HULON MITCHELL: Killed fifteen males in Florida and New Jersey between 1981 and 1986, bludgeoning, shooting, and stabbing his victims to death. His crimes were racially motivated, and his victims included eleven White, three Black, and one Hispanic male.

ROY MITCHELL: Killed six White males and two White females in Texas in 1922 and 1923, raping, bludgeoning, and shooting his victims to death.

TONY GARRETT MITCHELL: Killed two Black females in Tennessee in 2002, raping and shooting his victims to death. He has been cordial and willing to help me with my project.

WILLIAM GERALD MITCHELL: Killed one White female and one Black female in Mississippi, one in 1974 and one in 1995, raping, strangling, sodomizing, and running over his victims with a vehicle. He killed again after being released from prison.

JESSIE RAY MOFFETT: Killed one male and one female in California, one in 1979 and one in 1987, bludgeoning and shooting his victims to death.

KASEY JACK MONROE: Killed two White females in North Carolina in 1985, raping and shooting his victims to death.

ASHANTI MONTGOMERY: Killed two males in Pennsylvania in 2013, shooting his victims to death. The cooling off period was short, so he may be considered a spree killer, but I believe he would have kept on killing if he hadn't been arrested.

MANUEL MOORE: Known as "The Zebra Killings" and "The Death Angels," these racially motivated killers, who were Black Muslims, took place in San Francisco in 1973 and 1974, killing thirteen and as many as seventy-three White victims. Their victims were shot and stabbed to death, and they killed males and females. They were convicted of fifteen murders and ten attempted murders and were named the Zebra Killings because police used the Z channel on their police radios when discussing the case.

THOMAS JAMES MOORE: Killed two Black victims in Florida, one in 1990 and one in 1993, shooting his male and female victims to death.

MARK S MOORE-EL: Killed two victims in Missouri, one in 1975 and one in 1993, shooting his victims to death.

JAMES LEWIS MORGAN: Killed one Black male and one Black female in North Carolina, one in 1976 and one in 1997, shooting and stabbing his victims to death. He was released from prison to kill again. He sent me a strange, rambling letter laced with the names of dozens of celebrities and listing the many accomplishments he said he is responsible for, including music, basketball, and more.

MARSHALL MORGAN SR.: Killed four Black victims in Illinois between 1977 and 2001, shooting his male and female victims to death.

WILLIAM MORGANHERRING: Killed two Black females in North Carolina in 1994, stabbing and strangling his victims to death. His first victim was a disabled roommate, who was bound and had her throat slit. His second victim was strangled and sodomized.

CORY DEONN MORRIS: "The Crackhead Killer" killed between five and eleven Black females in Arizona and Oklahoma in 2002 and 2003, strangling his victims to death, and having sex with their corpses. He is suspected of more murders.

ROBERT I MORRIS: Killed two Black males and two Black females in Pennsylvania between 1995 and 2003, smothering his victims to death.

WINSTON MOSELEY: Killed three White females in New York in 1963 and 1964, raping, shooting, and stabbing his victims to death. He also enjoyed having sex with their corpses.

PETER LUCAS MOSES: Killed one Black male and one Black female in North Carolina in 2010, shooting his victims to death. He killed a four-year-old male because he thought he was gay, and then he killed an adult female because he was afraid she would call the police.

TERRY MOSES: Killed three White victims in California between 1976 and 1978, raping and shooting his male and female victims to death.

BARRY WENDELL MOSLEY: Killed three Black females in California in 1999 and 2000, raping and strangling his victims to death. One of his victims was a female teenager, and another was an elderly neighbor. He began his killing spree at the age of seventeen, and he is responsible for numerous rapes. He has been cordial and willing to help me with my project.

EDDIE LEE MOSLEY: Known as "The Rape Man," he killed between thirteen and thirty-three Black females in Ft. Lauderdale, Florida between the years of 1973 and 1987, raping and strangling his victims to death.

WINSTON MOSELEY: Killed three victims in New York in 1963 and 1964, stabbing and shooting his victims to death. One of them was Kitty Genovese, and another of his victims was only fifteen years old.

JOSEPH ELI MOSS: Killed two victims in Pennsylvania, one in 2001 and one in 2007, shooting and stabbing his victims to death. He was released from prison to kill again.

KORI ALI MUHAMMAD: Killed four White males in California in 2017, shooting his victims to death. His crimes were racially motivated.

MICHAEL MULLINS: Killed three to five Black females in Tennessee between 1999 and 2012. His victims were raped, stabbed, bludgeoned, and strangled to death. He is suspected of numerous rapes and more murders.

DAWUD MAJID MU'MIN: Killed a cab driver in Virginia in 1973 and was sentenced to forty-eight years in prison. He escaped prison and killed a female carpet store owner, raping her and stabbing her sixteen times. He tried to sneak back into the prison but was caught.

DONALD MURPHY: Killed five to twelve Black females in Michigan in 1980, raping, bludgeoning, stabbing, and strangling his victims to death. He confessed to six murders but was only charged with two.

FLOYD MURRAY: Killed one Black male and one Black female in Texas, one in 1987 and one in 2013, shooting his victims to death.

HENRY CARLTON MYERS: Killed three Black males in Florida and Georgia between 1993 and 2005, shooting and stabbing his victims to death. He has been cordial and wants to help me with my project, explaining, "I have been praying for a chance to do some good in my life, not wanting it to end like this."

EDDIE RICKY NEALY: Killed two White females in California, one in 1985 and one in 1988, raping, bludgeoning, and strangling his victims to death. One of his victims was a fourteen-year-old female. and he is suspected of numerous rapes and murders.

STANLEY NELSON: Killed three Black females in California in 1970, bludgeoning and strangling his victims to death.

VINCENT L. NEUMAN: Killed two White males in South Carolina in 1993, shooting his victims to death.

ANDRE NEVERSON: Killed two Black females in New York in 2002, shooting his victims to death.

HUEY NEWTON: Killed one male and one female in California, one in 1967 and one in 1974, shooting his Black and White victims to death.

ROBERT NIXON: Killed six females in Illinois and California between 1936 and 1938, raping and bludgeoning his one Hispanic and five White victims to death.

SHERMAN LOUIS NOBLE: Killed four Black males in Kentucky between 1985 and 1987, robbing, bludgeoning, and shooting his victims to death. Some of his victims were elderly, and some were beaten to death with a hammer.

DEMPSEY B. NOLAN JR.: Killed five males in Indiana and California in 1996 and 1997, robbing and shooting his White and Black victims to death.

THOMAS NOLDEN: Killed one male and one female in Wisconsin in 1945, robbing and bludgeoning his victims to death.

MICHAEL WAYNE NORRIS: Killed two males and one female in Texas between 1979 and 1986, shooting his White and Black victims to death. Two of his victims were his ex-girlfriend and her two-year-old son, and he was released from prison to kill again.

EUGENE HOLLIS NUNNERY: Killed three Hispanic males in Nevada in 2006, robbing and shooting his victims to death. He targeted Hispanics, and he told the judge, "I'd do it again."

JAMES OLBERT: Killed two Hispanic males in New Jersey, one in 2011 and one in 2012, shooting his victims to death.

LOUIS OLIVER: Killed two females in Florida, one in 1962 and one in 1981, stabbing his victims to death.

ROBERT OVERSTREET: Killed between two and three males in Iowa between 1955 and 1970, shooting and stabbing his victims to death.

FREDDIE EUGENE OWENS: Killed one Black male and one Black female in South Carolina, one in 1997 and one in 1999, shooting and stabbing his victims to death. While incarcerated, he killed a fellow inmate in 1999.

JOHN F. OWENS: Killed two White females in New York in 1999, raping and bludgeoning his victims to death.

SIR MARIO OWENS: Killed two males and one female in Colorado in 2004 and 2005, shooting his victims to death. His two victims in 2005 included a person who was going to testify against him, and his fiancé.

LYNDON FITZGERALD PACE: Killed four to five females in Georgia in 1988 and 1989, raping and strangling his mostly Black victims to death. He has been cordial but has refused to speak to me because of his pending appeals. He targeted elderly females, and one of his burglary victims was Coretta Scott King, Martin Luther King's widow. His victims were mostly in their seventies and eighties.

IVAN LEE PAGE: Killed three Black female prostitutes in Michigan between 1998 and 2001, raping and strangling his victims to death. He was cordial and wrote me back but proclaimed his innocence, stating that he didn't murder anyone.

GENO PAGET: Killed two males in Illinois, one in 2000 and one in 2014, robbing and shooting his victims to death. He was released to kill again.

ALBERTO PRECE PALMER: Killed one White and one Black female prostitute in Minnesota in 2013, raping, strangling, and bludgeoning his victims to death. His weapon of choice was a hammer, and he is suspected of more murders.

GERALD PARKER: The "Bedroom Basher" killed six to eight White females in California in 1978 and 1979, raping and bludgeoning his victims to death. He was arrested because of DNA evidence.

NORMAN PARKER: Killed one victim in 1966, was sent to prison and escaped in 1976, killing two more victims.

ROBERT LEE PARKER: Killed three White females and one White male in Washington and Georgia in 1995, robbing, raping, stabbing, strangling, and setting his victims on fire. His victims were found bound, gagged, and stabbed to death.

CARROLL JOE PARR: Killed two males in Texas between 2001 and 2003, robbing and shooting his victims to death.

DANTE L. PARRISH: Killed two Black males in Maryland, one in 1999 and one in 2009, shooting and stabbing his victims to death. He was released to kill again, resulting in the murder of a fifteen-year-old.

HAROLD PATTERSON: Killed three males in Connecticut in 2008, shooting his victims to death.

ALFRED BONNET PAYNE: Killed three victims in Virginia and New Jersey in 1947 and 1948.

EDJUAN PAYNE: Killed one Black male and one Black female in Illinois, one in 1987 and one in 2010, shooting and stabbing his victims to death. He killed an adult female and severely injured her eight-month-old granddaughter, leaving them in a rain-soaked alley. The adult female was beaten, strangled, cut, and stabbed, and the baby had skull fractures.

FLENOY PAYNE: Killed two males in Maryland, one in 1933 and one in 1953, shooting his victims to death.

RUSSELL PEELER: Killed two Black males and one Black female in Connecticut in 1998 and 1999, shooting his victims to death. His 1999 case was the murder of a mother and her eight-year-old son.

DOMINIC L. PEREZ: Killed one male and one female in Connecticut, one in 1993 and one in 2010, shooting his victims to death.

EDWIN BERNARD PERKINS: Killed three male victims in Texas in 1994, stabbing his gay White and Hispanic victims to death.

REGINALD WENDELL PERKINS: Killed six Black females in Ohio and Texas between 1980 and 2000, robbing, raping, bludgeoning, and strangling his victims to death. One of his victims was only twelve years old, and his 2000 murder victim was his stepmother.

BJ PERRY: Killed three victims in Georgia between 1960 and 1991.

CALVIN PERRY: Killed five victims in Indiana in 1983, and while awaiting trial, he committed suicide in 1984.

GEORGE LO PERRY: Killed two White females in Massachusetts in 1902, raping and bludgeoning his victims to death.

CHRISTOPHER DWAYNE PETERSON: "The Shotgun Killer" killed five males and two females in Indiana in 1990, robbing and shooting his mostly White victims to death.

NATHANIEL MAURICE PETGRAVE: Killed three male victims in Florida in 2017, shooting and stabbing his victims to death. One of his victims survived the shooting, and one victim was killed with a machete. He wrote a message to the police on the ground with the victim's blood.

DEMOND & MICHAEL PHILLIPS: Killed thirteen Black males and one Black female in Louisiana between 1994 and 2007, robbing and shooting their victims to death. They were both shot dead before their trials.

ANTHONY LEROY PIERCE: Killed two Black males in Texas, one in 1977 and one in 1979, shooting and stabbing his victims to death. While on death row for his first murder, he killed a fellow inmate in 1979, stabbing him to death.

SONNY L. PIERCE: Killed one Black male and three Black females in Illinois in 2009 and 2010, raping and strangling his victims to death. His murder and rape victims were teenage girls. He has been cordial and willing to help me with my project.

ANTWAN MAURICE PITTMAN: Killed six to ten Black females in North Carolina between the years of 2005 and 2009, raping, stabbing, strangling, and dismembering his victims. He is suspected of more murders, but he is claiming innocence. He explained, "I do wanna let you know that first, I'm 100% innocent of the crime I have been convicted of and only one count of first-degree murder."

MICHAEL PLAYER: Shot to death ten homeless males in California in 1986. He then killed himself in 1987.

WALLACE PLEAS: Killed two Black males and three Black females in Florida between 1917 and 1964, shooting and stabbing his victims to death.

ANGELO DENNY PLEASANT: Killed two White males in Washington in 1975, shooting his victims to death.

HENRY POCZYNEK: Killed three White females in Nevada and Florida in 1973, robbing, shooting, and stabbing his victims to death.

WILLIE PORTER: Killed two Black females in Texas between 1924 and 1949, stabbing his victims to death.

JAMES EDWARD POUGH: Killed four males and eight females in Florida between 1971 and 1990, shooting his White and Black victims to death.

ALFRED POWELL: Killed three females in California in 1982 and 1983, bludgeoning his victims to death.

DESHAWN POWELL: Killed three Black males in South Carolina and New York between 1999 and 2010, shooting and stabbing his victims to death.

REGINALD D POWELL: Killed two White victims in New York, one in 1982 and one in 2010, robbing, shooting, and stabbing his male and female victims to death.

SYVASKY LAFAYETTE POYNER: Killed four White females and one Black female during a twelve-day crime spree in Virginia in 1984. The victims were killed in the middle of the day and ranged in age from seventeen to seventy-two years old.

STEVEN PRATT: Killed one Black male and one Black female in New Jersey, one in 1984 and one in 2014, bludgeoning and shooting his victims to death. He killed his first victims when he was just fifteen years old and was sent to prison. He was released to kill again, and when he was released, his family had a welcome home party for him. Two days later, he bludgeoned his own mother to death.

DALTON PREJEAN: Killed two males in Louisiana, one in 1974 and one in 1977, shooting his victims to death. His 1977 murder was a police officer, when he was only seventeen years old. He is one of the few juveniles in history to be convicted of his crimes as a juvenile, sentenced to death, and executed by the electric chair in 1990, at the age of thirty.

AEMAN LOVEL PRESLEY: Killed three males and one female in Georgia in 2014, shooting his Black and White victims to death. His victims included three homeless men and a female walking downtown. Presley is a former actor in Los Angeles and Atlanta with real acting gigs in movies and commercials. I have never heard it explained better than when he described his thought process. He said that he had watched the film *300*, and that the clanging of the swords inspired him to kill. He finished eating his fast food burger, loaded his gun, and went hunting for victims.

ELROY PRESTON: Killed two to three victims in Missouri in 1980, stabbing his victims to death. After killing one of his victims, he dipped some fried chicken in their blood and ate it. The bodies were dumped in an alley behind his house.

SHERMAN PRESTON: Killed two Black females in Ohio, one in 1981 and one in 1983, raping and strangling his victims to death.

CRAIG CHANDLER PRICE: "The Warwick Slasher" killed four White females in Warwick, Rhode Island between 1987 and 1989, stabbing and mutilating his victims to death. The youngest modern-day serial killer in US history, he killed his first victim when he was thirteen years old. The last three victims were a triple murder that included two female children, ages eight and ten. He has been very cordial with me, and he is willing to help me with my project. I have visited Price several times.

JOHN PRICE: Killed two Black females in New York in 1998, raping and strangling his victims to death.

LARME PRICE: Killed four males in New York in 2003, shooting his victims to death. His crimes were racially motivated and he targeted victims of Arab descent.

MOSES PRICE JR.: Killed one male and one female in Wisconsin, one in 1984 and one in 1991, bludgeoning and stabbing his victims to death.

VERON PRIMUS: Killed two females in New York, one in 2006 and one in 2015, raping, stabbing, and strangling his victims to death. One of his victims was sixteen years old, and the other was a female real estate agent.

CLEOPHUS PRINCE JR.: "The Clairemont Killer" murdered six White females in California in 1990, raping, strangling, and stabbing his victims to death. He also posed their bodies after he killed them, and three of his victims were teens.

MARK ANTONIO PROFIT: Suspected as "The Theodore Wirth Park Killer," he killed one male and three females in Minnesota in 1996, raping, bludgeoning, and strangling victims to death. He committed suicide in 2001.

BRAYNARD PURNELL: Killed two Black males in New Jersey, one in 1975 and one in 1988, stabbing and strangling his victims to death.

DERRICK GORDON RAGAN: Killed two Black males in Pennsylvania in 1990, shooting his victims to death.

YUSEF ABDULLAH RAHMAN: Killed four males in New York and Missouri in 1987 and 1988, shooting his White and Black victims to death.

RASHAD ARTHUR RALEIGH: Killed two males and two females in Minnesota in 2007, robbing, bludgeoning, and shooting his White and Black victims to death. One of his victims was former NBA player Howard Porter.

ALFRED CASANOVA RAVENELL: Killed three males in New Jersey and Pennsylvania between 1962 and 1972, shooting his victims to death.

CLIFTON L. RAY: Killed three to nine Black females in Missouri between 1987 and 1994, strangling his victims to death. He is suspected in more murders.

QUAN JOHN RAY: Killed three Black males in Illinois between 1974 and 1995, shooting his victims to death. Ray was a gang member who killed in his duties as a leader of the Gangster Disciples.

ROBERT K. RAY: Killed two Black males and one Black female in Colorado in 2004 and 2005, shooting his victims to death.

WILLIAM EARL RAYFORD: Killed two Black females in Texas, one in 1986 and one in 1999, beating, stabbing, and strangling his victims to death. He killed his estranged wife in 1986 and was sent to prison, only to be released to kill again.

CHARLES HENRY RECTOR: Killed two females in Texas, one in 1974 and one in 1981, robbing and shooting his victims to death. He killed a victim in 1974, was sent to prison, and released to kill again. This time he abducted, raped, shot in the head, and dumped a female victim in a lake.

JOHN REED: Killed ten White males and four White females in Alabama between 1919 and 1923, robbing and bludgeoning his victims to death with an axe.

LEONARD REED: Killed three Black males in Pennsylvania in 1973, shooting, stabbing, and strangling his victims to death.

WALTER D. REED: Killed two victims in Florida, one in 1970 and one in 1982.

BILLY EDWIN REID: Killed between three and twenty-one Black females in Colorado between 1975 and 1995, strangling his victims to death. He would also pose the bodies in humiliating positions.

ROBERT G. REMBERT JR.: Killed two males and three females in Ohio between 1997 and 2015, raping, shooting, bludgeoning, and strangling his White and Black victims to death. He was sent to prison for his first murder and later released to kill again. He used his job as a long haul truck driver to hunt for victims and is suspected of many more murders.

ASBURY RESPUS: Killed two males and six females in North Carolina between 1912 and 1931, bludgeoning, shooting, and drowning his White and Black victims.

BRICE JAMAR RHODES: Killed three Black males in Kentucky in 2016, shooting, beating, and stabbing his victims to death.

BRANDON SEBASTIAN RICE: Killed two Black males in North Carolina in 2007, robbing and shooting his victims to death.

ANTONIO RICHARDS: Killed eleven victims in Louisiana between 1884 and 1898.

DARRELL WAYNE RICHARDS: Killed one Black male and one Black female in Washington, one in 1987 and one in 1991, shooting his victims to death.

CARL SEWANTI RICHARDSON: Killed three males in Maryland in 1987, shooting his victims to death. He committed his crimes as a juvenile, at the age of seventeen.

FREDERICK ALVIN RICHEY: Killed two White females in Oregon in 1984, stabbing and strangling his victims to death.

EARL J. RICHMOND JR.: Killed one male and three females in North Carolina and New Jersey in 1991, raping and strangling his White and Black victims to death. One of his victims was an eight-year-old boy who was stabbed forty times, and a seven-year-old girl whom he strangled to death. He also raped a twelve-year-old female and is responsible for numerous rapes. He was a former drill sergeant at Fort Dix.

WILLIE LEE RICHMOND: Killed two males and one female in Arizona in 1973, robbing and shooting his victims to death, and running over one of his male victims with a vehicle.

MARLON D. RICKS: Killed one Black male and one Black female in Ohio, one in 1990 and one in 2012, shooting and stabbing his victims to death. He killed his stepfather in 1990 and was sent to prison. Released to kill again, he then stabbed his girlfriend to death.

REGINALD REONARD RIGGINS: Killed one White female and one Black female in Florida, one in 2009 and one in 2011. His victims were raped, bludgeoned, and strangled to death. One of his victims had a shirt jammed down her throat with a stick. Another victim was killed with a knife, a hammer, and a kitchen pot.

BENJAMIN JESSE RILEY: Killed three White females in Washington in 1975 and 1976, robbing and stabbing his victims to death. He stabbed two sisters, killing one.

RAYMONDEZE LAMON RIVERA: Killed two Black females in South Carolina in 2006, smothering and strangling his victims to death.

STEVEN J. ROBBINS: Killed four Black victims in Illinois and Indiana between 1968 to 2001, shooting them to death. He killed again after being released from prison. He has been cordial and willing to correspond with me, even asking me to market his paintings. But he claims he is innocent and is shocked that the public thinks he is guilty.

DAVID JAMES ROBERTS: Killed four White victims in Indiana in 1974, raping, strangling, and setting his male and female victims on fire. Three of the victims were a family of three, including a female infant, who died of smoke inhalation.

ALEXANDER ROBINSON: Killed three victims in Florida between 1974 and 2007, robbing and shooting his victims to death. He killed again after being released from prison.

ALFRED LEE ROBINSON: Killed four to five Black females in Florida in 1991, raping and strangling his victims to death. He has been cordial and willing to help me with my project.

ALONZO ROBINSON: Killed six White victims in Ohio, Mississippi, Michigan, and Massachusetts between the years of 1926 and 1934. His victims were raped, shot, and bludgeoned with an axe. He killed mostly women, decapitating one victim, and was also a grave robber.

ANTHONY EUGENE ROBINSON: Known as "The Shopping Cart Killer," he killed six women in Virginia and Washington, DC after meeting them on dating apps like Plenty of Fish and Tagged. After killing them, he transported their dead bodies in a shopping cart before dumping their remains in vacant lots.

LINNELL ROBINSON: Killed one Black male and one Black female in Alabama between 1951 and 1955, stabbing his victims to death.

QUINCY LEE ROBINSON: Killed nine to twenty victims in Michigan between the years of 1974 and 1978, shooting his victims to death. He was killed in prison in 1982.

WILLIAM ALFRED ROBINSON: Killed one White male and one Black male in Texas in 1985, robbing and shooting his victims to death.

THEODORE RODGERS: Killed two Black females in Florida, one in 1978 and one in 2001, shooting his victims to death. He was sent to prison for the first murder and released to kill again, this time killing his wife. After he killed his wife, he shot himself in the head but survived.

ANTONIO RODRIGUEZ: "The Kensington Strangler" killed three White females in Pennsylvania in 2010, raping and strangling his victims to death. He is suspected in more murders and has been cordial in exchanged letters with me.

IRVIN CORNELL ROGERS: Killed one Black male and one Black female in Florida, one in 1987 and one in 1991, bludgeoning his victims to death.

KEVIN ANDRE ROGERS: Shot to death two Black males and two Black females in Colorado in 2009.

LEEROY WILBERT ROGERS: Killed two White females in Ohio in 2015, raping and shooting his victims to death.

PAUL E. ROLLEN: Killed two victims in Missouri and Tennessee in 2000, robbing and shooting his victims to death.

TRENINO F. ROLLINS: Killed two Black males and one Black female in Washington in 1990 and 1991, shooting and stabbing his victims to death. One of his victims was stabbed thirty times with a pair of scissors.

CRAIG ANTHONY ROSS: Killed four Black males in California in 1980, robbing and shooting his victims to death.

SETH JOSEPH ROUZAN: Killed two males in Georgia, one in 2006 and one in 2012, robbing, shooting, and stabbing his victims to death. He is suspected in more murders, and has been cordial in our conversations, willing to help me with my project.

MARCUS ANTONIO ROYAL: Killed one White male and two White females in Florida between 2011 and 2013, robbing, bludgeoning, stabbing, and strangling his victims to death. He was released to kill again and is suspected of more murders.

NORMAN ROYE: Killed three Black females in New York in 1954, raping and strangling his victims to death.

ROBERT EARNEST ROZIER: Killed six to seven White males in Florida and New Jersey between 1984 and 1986, shooting and stabbing his victims to death. He was a member of the Yahweh Cult, played for the NFL's St. Louis Cardinals, and his crimes were racially motivated.

JOSHUA. RUDIGER: "The Vampire Slasher" assaulted and killed homeless people in California, stabbing them to death and drinking their blood. He is by definition not a serial killer, but he operates like one. He killed at least one victim and attempted to kill three others. He considered himself a real vampire and has been cordial in exchanging letters with me. He has also sent me some of his artwork, and he seems to be struggling with mental illness.

ANTONIO WELLINGTON RUFFIN: Killed three Black males in Georgia between 1991 and 2009, bludgeoning, shooting, and stabbing his victims to death. One of his victims was a fellow inmate who was stabbed to death in the prison yard.

GEORGE WATERFIELD RUSSELL JR.: Known as "The Charmer," "The East Side Serial Killer," and "The Bellevue Killer," he killed three White victims in Washington in 1990. His victims were raped, bludgeoned, tortured, strangled, and stabbed to death. After he killed his victims, he posed them in provocative poses, one having a rifle inserted into her vagina, and another a sex toy inserted into her mouth.

MARTIN RUTRELL, LINZIE LEE THOMPSON & BEN A. CHANEY JR.: "The Black Male Hit Squad" had a goal of killing as many White people as possible. They shot and killed seven White male and female victims in Florida and South Carolina in 1970.

STEPHEN SAKAI: Killed four males in New York in 2005 and 2006, shooting and stabbing his victims to death. He was killing New York City bouncers and ended his crime spree with a mass shooting at a nightclub.

ARTHUR LEE SANFORD: Killed two Black females in Virginia, one in 1983 and one in 2003, stabbing his victims to death.

DEMETREOUS SANTIAGO: Killed one Black female and three Black males in Tennessee in 2011 and 2012, robbing and shooting his victims to death.

MARC VINCENT SAPPINGTON: "The Kansas City Vampire" killed four male victims in Kansas in 2001, shooting and stabbing his Black and White victims to death. Under the influence of PCP, he drank his victims' blood and consumed some of their body parts. He has been cordial and has exchanged several letters with me.

FREDERICK K. SATERFIELD: Killed one Black male and two Black females in California between 1950 and 1965, shooting his victims to death.

VERNON LAMAR SATTIEWHITE: Killed two victims in Texas, one in 1976 and one in 1986, shooting his victims to death. His 1986 victim was an ex-girlfriend, whom he shot twice in the head.

CHRISTOPHER J. SCARVER: Killed three White males in Wisconsin between 1990 and 1994, shooting and bludgeoning his victims to death. His last two murders were fellow inmates, including Jeffrey Dahmer, whom he beat to death with a metal bar in the weight room. He has been difficult to work with, demanding thousands of dollars and asking me to sign a contract.

DALE DEVON SCHEANETTE: "The Bathtub Killer" killed a Black female and a Hispanic female in Texas in 1996, raping and strangling his victims to death. He bound his victims' hands and drowned them in their bathtubs, and he is suspected of multiple rapes.

CHRIS SCOTT: Killed one White male and one Black male in Massachusetts and Arizona, one in 1975 and one in 1985, bludgeoning and stabbing his victims to death.

FREDERICK DEMOND SCOTT: "The Indian Creek Trail Killer" killed five White males and one White female in Missouri in 2016 and 2017, shooting his victims to death as they walked their dogs on a trail. His crimes were racially motivated, and he claimed it was revenge for his brother's murder.

JASON THOMAS SCOTT: Killed five Black females in Maryland in 2009 and 2010, robbing and shooting his victims to death. He used his job at UPS to stalk his victims. He killed two mother-daughter pairs, and one of his victims was only sixteen years old. He began as a peeping Tom at ten years old.

CHARLES ANTHONY SEARS: Killed one White male and one Black male in New York in 1981, raping, stabbing, and slicing the throats of his victims. He also attempted to kill thirteen others.

WILLIAM SEWELL: Killed three to four Black males in Maryland and California between 1966 and 1973, shooting his victims to death.

DEMERIUS SHAW: Killed one Black male and one Black female in Indiana, one in 2011 and one in 2012, shooting his victims to death.

MARK ARLO SHEPPARD: Killed one White male and two White females in Virginia in 1993, robbing and shooting his victims to death. Two of his victims were a married couple, and he was suspected of ten more murders. He began his life of crime at the age of nine.

BEORIA ABRAHAM SIMMONS III: Killed three White females in Kentucky between 1981 and 1983, kidnapping, raping, and shooting his victims to death. One of his victims was only fifteen years old.

WILLIE SIMMONS: Killed two Black females in Missouri in 1987, robbing and strangling his victims to death.

RAY DELL SIMMS: Killed five teenage girls in California between 1974 and 1977, raping, stabbing, and strangling his White and Hispanic victims to death. Two of his victims were ages fifteen and seventeen, and one was abducted delivering newspapers on her paper route. He is suspected of more murders.

JCX SIMON: Known as "The Zebra Murders," he killed fifteen White victims in California in 1973 and 1974, shooting and stabbing his male and female victims to death. His murders were racially motivated, and he was part of a group of four killers that called themselves the "Death Angels." They are suspected in possibly seventy-three or more murders, and his co-defendants were Manuel Moore, Jessie Lee Cooks, and Larry Green.

RICHARD NATHAN SIMON: Killed two males and one female in California in 1995 and 1996, kidnapping, raping, and shooting his victims to death.

ZENO EUGENE SIMS: Killed one male and one female in Missouri, one in 1983 and one in 2000, shooting his victims to death.

GARY SINEGAL: Killed between three and six elderly White females in Texas in 2005, robbing, raping, and bludgeoning his victims to death. He is suspected in more murders, and he raped at least two additional victims. Three of his victims were ages eighty-one, eighty-two, and eighty-six.

JOHNNY EUGENE SINGLETARY: Killed one male and one female in Texas in 1997, raping and bludgeoning his White and Black victims to death.

ANTHONY SKINNER: Killed two Black victims in New York, one in 2009 and one in 2010, shooting his victims to death. He also attempted to kill five others and was involved in a street gang.

FRANK SLATER: Killed one Black male and one Black female in Michigan, one in 1949 and one in 1958, bludgeoning and smothering his victims to death.

WARREN HERMAN SLOAN: Killed one male and one female in California in 2012, shooting and stabbing his victims to death.

ROBERT FRANKLIN SMALLWOOD JR.: Killed three Black females in Kentucky between 1999 and 2006. His victims were robbed, raped, sodomized, bludgeoned, and strangled to death.

ALVIN SMITH: Killed one White and three Black victims in Georgia in 1994 and 1995, robbing and shooting his victims to death.

ANDREW SMITH: Killed two Black males in Illinois, one in 2001 and one in 2010, shooting his victims to death.

ANDREW LAVERN SMITH: Killed three males and one female in South Carolina between 1981 and 1983, robbing, shooting, and stabbing his victims to death. Two of his victims were an elderly couple who were stabbed to death for not allowing Smith to borrow their car.

ANTHONY WAYNE SMITH: Killed between four and eight Black males in California between the years of 1999 and 2008, robbing, shooting, and stabbing his victims to death. He is a former NFL football player.

CLYDE SMITH JR.: Killed two White males in Texas in 1992, robbing and shooting his victims to death.

DANNY C. SMITH: Killed one male and one female in Missouri, one in 1986 and one in 2009, robbing, bludgeoning, and shooting his victims to death.

FRANK LEE SMITH: Killed two Black males in Florida between 1960 and 1965, shooting and stabbing his victims to death.

HOWARD L SMITH: Killed two males in Washington, DC and Virginia, one in 1987 and one in 1996, shooting and stabbing his victims to death.

JAMES RANDOLPH SMITH: Killed one White and one Black female in New York and Virginia in 1959, raping and strangling his victims to death.

JIMMY LEE SMITH: Killed three to four Black victims in Missouri between 1970 and 1981, shooting his male and female victims to death.

JUAN SMITH: Killed six Black males and two Black females in Louisiana in 1995, robbing and shooting victims to death.

LEMUEL WARREN SMITH III: Killed one White male and five White females in New York between the years of 1958 and 1977, raping, bludgeoning, stabbing, and strangling his victims to death. He is the only serial killer to continue his lust murders in prison, kidnapping, raping, and killing a female corrections officer. He has been tough to deal with but has exchanged several letters with me. He has stated, "I have been given a few labels, and yes I have killed, and wish I knew why. I don't fit the prototype."

NATHANIEL J. SMITH: Known as "Yorkie," he killed three to four victims in Kansas between the years of 1973 and 1982, raping, bludgeoning, sodomizing, shooting, and stabbing his victims to death. One female victim was stabbed 156 times, and he was released from prison to kill again.

REGINALD SMITH: Killed three elderly White females in Florida in 1994, bludgeoning and stabbing his victims to death. His victims were ages seventy-nine, seventy-nine, and eighty-one. He attacked other women and is suspected in more murders.

ROY GENE SMITH: Killed two males in Texas in 1988, shooting his victims to death. One murder netted him four dollars, which he used to buy a hot dog for his girlfriend.

SAMUEL D. SMITH: Killed one Black male and one Black female in Missouri, one in 1978 and one in 1987, raping and stabbing his victims to death.

STEVEN SMITH: Killed three victims in Illinois between 1964 and 1985.

EVAN DAVID SMYTH: Killed five Black males and one Black female in Maryland in 2003, raping, bludgeoning, shooting, stabbing, strangling, and setting his victims on fire. One of his victims was only seventeen years old, and two of the bodies were discovered in his house.

EMMETT L. SNOW: Killed two males in Massachusetts in 1987 and 1988, stabbing his victims to death.

LEROY SNYDER: Killed seven Black victims in New Jersey in 1969, robbing, raping, beating, and stabbing his victims to death.

LEROY SNYDER: Killed one male and six females in New Jersey in 1969, robbing, bludgeoning, and stabbing his victims to death.

MORRIS SOLOMON JR.: Known as "The Sacramento Slayer," he killed seven female prostitutes in California in 1986 and 1987, raping his mostly Black victims before killing them. While in prison, he raped a female corrections officer, and he is suspected in more murders.

ERNO SOTO: "Charlie Chop-Off" killed five Black children in New York between the years of 1972 and 1974, stabbing and mutilating his victims' genitals.

ANTHONY SOWELL: "The Cleveland Strangler" killed eleven Black females in Ohio between 2007 and 2009, raping, torturing, and strangling his victims to death. He enjoyed having sex with their corpses, and he kept their decomposing bodies in his living room, basement, and back yard. We spoke several times, but I could never get him to work with me.

RICHARD ALLON SPANKS: Killed one White male and two White females in Colorado in 2016, shooting his victims to death. One victim survived but remains paralyzed. The murders could be considered a spree killing, but Spanks operated like a serial killer. His co-defendant was Haywood Eugene Miller Jr.

LONNIE VICTOR SPELLS: Known as "The Trucker Murderer," he killed twelve to seventeen victims in Ohio, Tennessee, Indiana, and Pennsylvania while he worked as a long-haul truck driver. He may have killed victims in nine states, and his victims were raped and strangled to death. He would transport them in the sleeper cab of his semi-truck and dump their bodies several states away from where they were abducted.

ANTIIONY SPENCER: Killed two White females in New York in 1963 and 1964, raping and stabbing his victims to death. He is also suspected of fourteen rapes.

HERSCHEL SPENCER: Killed one male and one female in Indiana, one in 1993 and one in 1995, shooting and strangling his White and Black victims to death. One of his victims was his girlfriend.

TIMOTHY WILSON SPENCER: Known as "The Southside Strangler," "The Southside Slayer," and "The Southside Rapist," he killed five White females in Virginia between 1984 and 1987. His victims were raped and strangled to death.

TRACY LENARD SPENCER: Killed one Black female and one White female in Colorado in 1986, raping and strangling his victims to death, then posing their bodies. Spencer was a US Army specialist, and both victims were killed in the same apartment complex.

JERRY JEROME SPRAGGINS: Killed three White females in New Jersey between 1981 and 1983, raping, robbing, shooting, and strangling his victims to death.

EUGENE SPRUILL: Killed five Black males and one Black female in Pennsylvania between 1972 and 1975, shooting, stabbing, strangling, and setting his victims on fire. He escaped custody and killed four more victims, including a decapitation murder. He is suspected in more murders and has been involved in many prison attacks.

DARRELL LAMONT STALLINGS: Killed three Black males and four Black females in Kansas between 1988 and 2002, shooting his victims to death.

SAM STEENBURGH: Killed eleven victims in New York between 1847 and 1877, robbing and bludgeoning his victims to death.

JASON D. STEPHENS: Killed one Black male and one White male in Florida, one in 1996 and one in 1997. His victims were shot and strangled to death. He has been cordial and is willing to help me with my project, but he insists he isn't a serial killer.

LEE EDWARD STEPHENS: Killed two males in Maryland, one in 1997 and one in 2006. He was sent to prison for a stabbing murder, and while incarcerated, he stabbed corrections officer David McGuinn to death.

GARY LYNN STERLING: Killed three males and one female in Texas in 1988, robbing, shooting, and bludgeoning his White and Black victims to death. His victims were beaten to death with a car jack.

CHARLES ARNETT STEVENS: Killed two males and three females in California in 1989, shooting and stabbing his victims to death. He has been cordial in his communications with me.

ADRIAN LAMONT STEWART: Killed two males in Alabama, one in 2002 and one in 2009, robbing and shooting his victims to death.

TOMMY LEE STEWART: Killed seven females in Texas between 1971 and 1986, raping, robbing, bludgeoning, and strangling his victims to death. He was released from prison to kill again.

RAYMOND LEE STEWART: Killed six people in Illinois and Wisconsin in 1981. He was executed by lethal injection in 1996.

WINFORD LAVERN STOKES: Killed one male and two females in Missouri and Arkansas between 1969 and 1978. His victims were raped, shot, stabbed, and strangled to death.

WILLIE STRICKLAND JR.: Killed four Black males in Washington, DC in 1973, shooting and stabbing his victims to death.

JAMES WILLIAM STUARD: "The Senior Citizen Killer" killed three elderly White females in Arizona in

1989, raping, bludgeoning, stabbing, and strangling his victims to death.

SEAN DANTE SULLIVAN: Killed two males in Pennsylvania, one in 2009 and one in 2011, shooting and stabbing his victims to death.

MICHAEL SUMPTER: Killed three White females in Massachusetts between 1969 and 1973, raping and strangling his victims to death.

EDWARD ARTHUR SURRATT: Known as "The Shotgun Killer," he killed eleven White males and eight White females in Florida, Ohio, Pennsylvania, and South Carolina in 1977 and 1978. His victims were raped, bludgeoned, shot, and stabbed to death. I have exchanged several letters with him, and he explained, "I have mixed feelings about what your intentions are, and I am skeptical about talking to the media."

PAUL LAWRENCE SUTTON: Killed two Black males in Washington, one in 1990 and one in 1993, shooting his victims to death.

JAMES EDWARD SWANN JR.: "The Shotgun Stalker" killed two Black males and two Black females in Washington, DC in 1993, shooting his victims to death with a shotgun. He also wounded five others in fourteen attacks, and he claimed he was driven to kill by disembodied screaming voices, as well as the ghost of activist Malcolm X.

WILLIAM EARL SWEET: Killed two victims in Florida in 1990, shooting his victims to death. One of them was only thirteen years old.

ALEXANDER WINSTON SYLVESTER: Killed one male and one female in New York, one in 1983 and one in 2000. He also killed additional victims in Canada.

JAMES TANNER: Killed one male and one female in Illinois, one in 1986 and one in 1989, stabbing his victims to death.

DANGELO D. TATE: Killed two Black victims in Missouri, one in 2008 and one in 2009, shooting his male and female victims to death.

ALVIN TAYLOR: Killed four White males in Wisconsin between 1985 and 1987, shooting and stabbing his victims to death.

ELKIE LEE TAYLOR: Killed two males in Texas in 1993, robbing and strangling his Black and Hispanic victims to death.

ELMER R. TAYLOR JR.: Killed three Black males in Pennsylvania in 1973, shooting and burning his victims to death.

JAMES TAYLOR JR.: Killed three males and one female in Pennsylvania between 1973 and 1977, bludgeoning, stabbing, and burning his White and Black victims to death.

KEVIN TAYLOR: This Cheesecake Factory cook killed four Black females in Chicago in 2001, raping and strangling his victims to death. He was working as a cook while killing his victims and claimed that he had a very dysfunctional childhood.

LARRY JO TAYLOR: Killed a male and a female in Indiana in 2015, robbing and shooting his White and Hispanic victims to death.

MICHAEL D. TAYLOR: Killed one male and one female in Missouri, one in 1994 and one in 1999, bludgeoning and strangling his White and Black victims to death.

NORRIS CARLTON TAYLOR: Killed three to four females in North Carolina and Virginia between 1975 and 1978, robbing, raping, shooting, and stabbing his White and Black victims to death.

RONALD T. TAYLOR: Shot to death three Black males in Missouri between 2003 and 2011.

TYREESE TAYLOR: Killed two males in Indiana, one in 1980 and one in 2004, shooting his White and Black victims to death.

QUINTON VERDELL TELLIS: Killed one White female and one Asian in Louisiana and Mississippi, one in 2014 and one in 2015, stabbing his victims and setting them on fire.

BENJAMIN TERRY: Killed one male and three females in Pennsylvania between 1971 and 1979, bludgeoning his White and Black victims to death, and then setting them on fire.

MICHAEL DEVERN TERRY: Killed six Black males in Georgia in 1985 and 1986, raping, shooting, and stabbing his victims to death. He worked as a gay prostitute and targeted gay men. He has been cordial and has exchanged a few letters with me, but he claims that he is innocent of his crimes.

BRANDON THOLMER: Killed between twelve and thirty-four Black victims in California between 1981 and 1983, raping, robbing, sodomizing, bludgeoning, stabbing, and strangling his victims to death. He has been cordial, sending me letters and Christmas cards.

ALEX DALE THOMAS: Killed two to three White victims in California between 1978 and 1997, raping, bludgeoning, shooting, stabbing, and strangling his victims to death.

He killed his first victim as a teen, and while in prison, he killed a fellow inmate, slitting his throat. He was released from prison to kill again, and he did so while working as a custodian at a school. He brutally raped and murdered an eighteen-year-old student, beating her with a crowbar and slicing her throat. He has been cordial but has said he can't work with us as he is working on his appeal.

ANDRE THOMAS: Killed three Black males in Ohio in 2002, shooting his victims to death.

DANIEL G. THOMAS: Killed two victims in Florida between 1955 and 1969.

DANIEL MORRIS THOMAS: Killed two White males in Florida in 1975 and 1976, raping and shooting his victims to death.

DANNY LAMONT THOMAS: Killed four Black males and one Black female in North Carolina in 2005, robbing and shooting his victims to death. One of his crimes was a triple homicide.

JOHN FLOYD THOMAS: Known as "The Westside Rapist" and "The Southland Strangler," he killed between seven and thirty-nine White females in California between 1972 and 1986. His victims were raped, shot, and strangled to death.

REGIS DEON THOMAS: Killed three males in California in 1992 and 1993, shooting his Black and White victims to death. Two of his victims were police officers.

RENARD CARLOS THOMAS: Killed three Black victims in Georgia between 1981 and 1998. His victims were kidnapped, stabbed, and shot to death.

RICHARD FRANK THOMAS: Killed one White male and one Black male in Michigan, one in 1971 and one in 1974, shooting his victims to death.

RONALD PERCEL THOMAS: Killed one White female and one Black female in Washington, one in 1985 and one in 1986, raping and strangling his victims to death.

TROY TYRONE THOMAS III: Killed two Black males in California, one in 1981 and one in 2008, shooting and strangling his victims to death. His committed his first murder as a teen, and he was sent to prison and then released to kill again. He has been cordial, exchanging letters with me and sending me pictures. He explained his life to me: "I grew up poor and rejected as a child. I've been sexually abused so many times I've lost count. I've been lost from the very beginning."

EARL A. THOMPSON: Killed two victims in Florida, one in 1979 and one in 1992.

JESSE N. THOMPSON: Killed three victims in Kentucky and Ohio in 1935, shooting his victims to death.

LINZIE LEE THOMPSON: Killed two White males and two White females in Florida and South Carolina in 1970, shooting his victims to death. His crimes were racially motivated.

SCOTTIE L. THOMPSON: Killed one male and one female in Illinois, one in 1989 and one in 2013, bludgeoning and stabbing his victims to death. After being sent to prison for his first murder, he was released to kill again.

DAVID THORNTON: Killed three Black males in Maryland between 2004 and 2014, shooting and stabbing his victims to death.

FREDDIE TILLER: Killed five victims in Illinois, and with co-defendant Andre Jones went on a spree killing, killing three victims.

JAMES WILLIAM TOLBERT: Killed one White female and one Black female in Utah, one in 1987 and one in 2007. His first victim was his wife, whom he strangled to death. He was released to kill again, and he strangled his second wife to death.

ANTHONY TOWNSER: Killed three elderly White victims in Illinois and Missouri in 1993 and 1994, raping and strangling his victims to death. He killed his first victim when he was nineteen years old, and his victims include an eighty-seven-year-old and a seventy-year-old. He has been cordial and wants to help me, and he informed me that he is only guilty of one murder and one attempted murder.

MAURY TROY TRAVIS: Killed between ten and seventeen female prostitutes in Missouri and Illinois between the years of 2000 and 2002. He kidnapped, tortured, raped, sodomized, and strangled his mostly Black victims to death, as he filmed them. Police discovered a torture chamber in his basement, complete with a stun gun, newspaper clippings of his crimes, and videotapes of him raping, torturing, sodomizing, and killing his victims while they were chained up in his basement. He hung himself in the jail the night he was arrested.

JOHN THOMAS TREVILLION: Killed two victims in Missouri, one in 1998 and one in 2014, shooting his victims to death. He killed again after being released from prison and is suspected in more murders.

CLARENCE TROTTER: Killed one White female and one Black female in Illinois, one in 1981 and one in 1986, raping, shooting, and drowning his victims. One of his victims was found in her bathtub with her arms and legs bound and a sock stuffed into her mouth. He has been cordial but not super easy to work with. He is very suspicious about what facts we know regarding his case.

GARY U. TROUTMAN: Killed two Black females in Florida in 1986, raping and bludgeoning his victims to death.

EMERSON TUCKER: Killed three Black females in New Jersey, New York, and Illinois between 1990 and 2007, stabbing and strangling his victims to death. One of his victims was found mutilated in a basement apartment, stabbed sixty-two times. He was released from prison to kill again and is suspected of more murders.

RICHARD TUCKER: Killed one White female and one Black female in Georgia, one in 1964 and one in 1978, raping, bludgeoning, and stabbing his victims to death. He was released from prison to kill again, and his last victim was a nurse who was kidnapped from the hospital parking lot.

RUSSELL WILLIAM TUCKER: Killed one White male and one Black male in North Carolina in 1994, robbing and shooting his victims to death. One of his victims was found stuffed into a suitcase, and he shot two police officers.

CHESTER DEWAYNE TURNER: "The Southside Slayer" killed between sixteen and twenty-four victims in California between 1987 and 1998. His mostly Black female victims were raped and strangled to death, and some were pregnant. He is suspected in as many as 100 murders, yet he has been very cordial with me in his letters and phone calls.

DARRYL DONNELL TURNER: Killed nine Black females in Washington, DC between 1994 and 1997, raping and strangling his victims to death.

JEROME UPSHAW: Killed one Black male and one Black female in Georgia, one in 1996 and one in 2007, robbing, bludgeoning, and shooting his victims to death.

DARREN DEON VANN: "The Gary Strangler" killed at least seven Black females in Indiana in 2013 and 2014, raping and strangling his victims to death. He then dumped their bodies in abandoned buildings. He is suspected of up to 100 murders and has been cordial in our conversations.

EDDIE G. VAUGHN: Killed one White female and one Black female in Ohio, one in 1984 and one in 1990, stabbing and burning his victims to death. While serving his life sentence in an Ohio prison, he followed a female teacher into a prison bathroom and slashed her throat, killing her.

JAMES HOWARD VAUGHN: Killed two Black females in New Jersey, one in 1980 and one in 2003, shooting his victims to death.

CLARENCE VICTOR: Killed three females in Nebraska between 1964 and 1987, stabbing and strangling his victims to death. He was released from prison to kill again, and he did so, killing two more victims.

JAVIER WILLIAM VICTORIANNE: Killed three White females in California in 1999 and 2000, raping, strangling, and setting his victims on fire. Two of his victims were hanged, and one of them was only sixteen years old.

DIONE ANDRE WADE: Killed three to four males in Michigan and Ohio in 2008 and 2009, robbing and shooting his Arab-looking victims to death. He is suspected of more murders, and he told me he has killed more victims than anyone I am talking to, and he is able to prove it. He has also been one of the most interesting people I communicate with, as he explains how he tried to hang himself, fell and knocked his tooth out, and now is asking us to help him with his needed dental work. He boasts, "I don't have a problem discussing details about the people I've killed. I've been killing since I was fourteen years old. I didn't give a fuck about who I killed, and I really didn't need a reason to kill. If I wanted you dead, you were going to die. I've killed dozens of people, thirty-two, to be exact."

ANTHONY LAMAR WADSWORTH: Killed two Black males in Ohio in 2012, shooting his victims to death.

ANTHONY GUY WALKER: Killed two males and four females in Michigan, shooting his mostly White victims to death and setting them on fire.

CLARENCE WALKER: Killed fourteen to nineteen females in Tennessee, Illinois, Indiana, Ohio, and Michigan between the years of 1945 and 1966. His victims were raped, shot, beaten, and stabbed to death.

DARICK DEMORRIS WALKER: Killed two Black males in Virginia, one in 1996 and one in 1997, shooting his victims to death. The victims were killed in front of their families. He was executed in 2023.

TONY LEE WALKER: Killed three victims in Texas between 1977 and 1992, raping, robbing, and bludgeoning his male and female victims to death. He was sent to prison for his first murder and later released to kill again. He then murdered an elderly couple, beating and bludgeoning them to death. He raped the female and tried to rape her corpse.

TYRONE WALKER: Killed two Black females in Kansas, one in 1989 and one in 2011, strangling his victims to death. He killed again after being released from prison.

TYRONE WALKER: Killed two White males and one White female in New York between 1987 and 1993, robbing and shooting his victims to death.

HENRY LOUIS WALLACE: "The Charlotte Strangler," also known as "The Taco Bell Strangler," killed eleven Black females in North Carolina and South Carolina between 1990 and 1994. His victims were raped, bludgeoned, drowned, stabbed, and strangled to death. He was the Taco Bell manager, hence the nickname.

EDWARD WALTON: Killed two males and three females in multiple states including Illinois, Pennsylvania, and Ohio between 1896 and 1908, shooting his Black and Hispanic victims to death.

PERCY LEVAR WALTON: Killed two males and one female in Virginia in 1996, robbing and shooting his White and Black victims to death. He killed his first victim as a teen, and two of his victims were ages eighty and eighty-one.

CARMEN LEE WARD: Killed two Black males in California, one in 1987 and one in 1988, shooting his victims to death.

LUCKY WARD: Killed one gay male and four gay females in Texas between 1985 and 2010, strangling his Black and Hispanic victims to death.

PHILIP WARD: Killed two Black females in New York, one in 1989 and one in 1994, shooting and stabbing his victims to death. His last victim was his wife, and after he shot her six times, he raped her eleven-year-old daughter. His first victim was the mother of his children, who was stabbed and beaten to death with a metal pipe.

PAUL D. WARE: Killed three White males and one White female in Pennsylvania in 1962 and 1963, robbing and bludgeoning his victims to death.

PEARISON WARE: Killed two victims in Florida between 1966 and 1990, stabbing his victims to death.

ALANDUS O. WARREN: Killed two Black males in Nebraska, one in 1997 and one in 2015, shooting his victims to death.

BRIAN WARREN: Killed two males and one female in Missouri in 2001, robbing and shooting his victims to death.

CHARLES EDWARD WASHINGTON: Killed three victims in Florida between 1977 and 1985. He was sent to prison for his first murder and was released to kill again.

DAVID LEROY WASHINGTON: Killed two males and one female in Florida in 1976, stabbing his victims to death. His victims included a pastor, a student, and an elderly female.

STEVEN WASHINGTON JR.: Killed three to five elderly White females in Florida in 1963, raping and strangling his victims to death. He is suspected of more murders.

WILLIE WASHINGTON: Killed one Black male and two Black females in Ohio and Michigan between 1977 and 2008, bludgeoning, shooting, and stabbing his victims to death.

PATRICK WATKINS: Known as "The Western Bandit," he killed one White male and one White female in California, one in 2011 and one in 2014, robbing and shooting his victims to death. He also committed many other crimes, including dozens of cases of attempted murder.

ALEXANDER WAYNE WATSON JR.: Killed four females in Maryland between 1986 and 1994, raping and stabbing his White and Black victims to death. One of his victims was only fourteen years old.

CARL "CORAL" EUGENE WATTS: "The Sunday Morning Slasher" killed at least forty-four and as many as 120 mostly White females in Texas, Michigan, and all across the Midwest between 1972 and 1982. His victims were raped, shot, stabbed, drowned, bludgeoned, tortured, and strangled to death. He confessed to 100 murders before he died, but the authorities suspect him of 120 murders.

ROBERT AUSTIN WATTS: Killed five White females in Indiana between 1943 and 1947, raping, bludgeoning, shooting, and stabbing his victims to death. He stalked his victims while he worked as a delivery truck driver.

EMANUEL LOVELL WEBB: Killed five females in Connecticut and Georgia between 1990 and 1994, raping and strangling his White and Black victims to death. He may have killed up to eight more victims, working construction by day and killing at night. He has been very cordial and explained his motivation: "I don't like to talk about my past. I am very ashamed of where I allowed drugs and alcohol to take me."

WILLIE WEBB: Killed four Black victims in Mississippi between 1911 and 1913, shooting his male and female victims to death.

RONALD L. WELLS: Killed three Black males in Illinois between 1997 and 2001, bludgeoning his victims to death. One of them was buried in his back yard.

DAMEON LAREESE WESLEY: Killed two to three Black victims in Ohio between 1994 and 2013, shooting his male and female victims to death. He was released from prison to kill again. This time, he raped and murdered his girlfriend's thirteen-year-old cousin. He also shot two young females in the head, his girlfriend's cousins, killing one. He was found dead in his prison cell in 2013.

KENNETH WEST: Killed one male and one female in New York, one in 1983 and one in 1987, shooting and strangling his victims to death. He is suspected of more murders. He has been cordial and explained that he is only guilty of killing one person, a male victim named Allen Edwards.

TODD KENYAN WEST: Killed six males and one female in New Jersey and Pennsylvania in 2015, shooting his victims to death. He had two co-defendants, and his crimes could be considered a spree killing.

DARYL KEITH WHEATFALL: Killed three Black victims in Texas in 1990, shooting his male and female victims to death. His first murder was a double homicide.

KHALIL WHEELER-WEAVER: Killed four Black females in New Jersey in 2016, strangling his victims to death. He used social media pages to lure his victims to their death. One of his victims was only fifteen years old. Victim Sarah Butler texted him before they met a haunting text that read: "You're not a serial killer, right?"

JOHN LAURENCE WHITAKER: Killed two females in California, one in 1975 and one in 1983, raping and strangling his victims to death.

CAREY WHITE: Killed one male and one female in Ohio, one in 1969 and one in 1991, robbing and shooting his Black and White victims to death.

DONTESE ROLLMELL WHITE: Shot to death one male and one female in Washington, one in 1989 and one in 1992.

GARCIA GLEN WHITE: Killed one male and four females in Texas between 1989 and 1995, raping, stabbing, and strangling his mostly Black victims to death. Some of his victims were children, when he stabbed to death a mother and her twin sixteen-year-old daughters.

JOHN WHITE: Killed five females in New York in 1991 and 1992, stabbing and strangling his victims to death.

JUSTIN MATTHEW WHITE: Killed two females in Alabama in 2006, raping and strangling his victims to death. One of his victims was a seventeen-year-old female.

LARRY LAMONT WHITE: Killed three Black females in Kentucky in 1983, raping and shooting his victims to death.

NATHANIEL WHITE: Killed six females in New York in 1991 and 1992, raping, bludgeoning, and stabbing his White and Black victims to death. He was released from prison to kill again. He claimed he was influenced by the movie *Robocop*.

WILLIE ODELL WHITEHEAD JR.: Killed four males and one female in North Carolina in 2012, robbing and shooting his White and Black victims to death. Three of his murders occurred in a triple homicide at a convenience store, and he was also charged with plotting to kill the sheriff, the sheriff's wife, and the prosecutor's child.

J.B. WHITELOW: Killed three Black males in Indiana between 2006 and 2008, shooting his victims to death.

DANA SYLVESTER WHITLEY: Killed four males and one female in Maryland between 1993 and 1995, robbing, shooting, and suffocating his White and Black victims to death.

GEORGE WHITMORE: Killed three White victims in New York in 1964, raping and stabbing his victims to death.

NICHOLAS LEE WILEY: Killed between three and seven White females in New York in 2004, raping, strangling, and stabbing his victims to death. He claimed he was a Ninja as he slit each of the women's throats.

PATRICK DONET WILKES: Killed three Black males in Maryland in 2007, robbing and shooting his victims to death.

EDWARD CHARLES WILKINS JR.: Killed one Black male and two Black females in Georgia in 1999 and 2000, raping and shooting his victims to death. He targeted prostitutes, left used condoms at the scenes, and was arrested due to his DNA.

MAURICE ADRIAN WILKINS & MICHAEL ALLEN WILKINS: They killed two males and one female in Pennsylvania in 2012, kidnapping, shooting, torturing, and setting his victims on fire. The co-defendants were brothers.

ANTHONY LOUIS WILLIAMS: Killed two to four White victims in Florida and New Jersey between 1995 and 2000, bludgeoning his victims to death. He was arrested after he called police about a body wrapped in plastic near his home. He also killed a fellow inmate in prison and is suspected of more murders. He explained that he had a drug problem, heard voices in his head, and the reason why he killed an inmate in prison was because the inmate was a child molester.

BRUCE WILLIAMS: Killed three Black females in Virginia between 1990 and 2011, stabbing and strangling his victims to death.

CHARLES HENRY WILLIAMS: Killed two Black females in Florida, one in 1980 and one in 1988, raping and strangling his victims to death.

CLARENCE WILLIAMS: Killed two White females in Washington in 1978, raping and stabbing his victims to death.

CONNIE J. WILLIAMS: Killed one male and one female in Pennsylvania, one in 1974 and one in 1999, stabbing his victims to death. He was released from prison to kill again. His first murder was his landlord, whose body was found under his bed. After being released, he killed his wife and dismembered her body.

DARNELL LEE WILLIAMS JR.: Killed one Black male and one Black female in California in 2013, shooting his victims to death. His youngest victim was only eight years old, and he is suspected of more murders.

DAVID RAY WILLIAMS: Killed two females in Texas in 2009, raping and bludgeoning his victims to death.

DONALD WILLIAMS: Killed one male and one female in Pennsylvania, one in 1994 and one in 2013, shooting and stabbing his victims to death. He was released to kill again, this time stabbing his girlfriend to death with a screwdriver and setting her on fire.

FRANK CHARLES WILLIAMS: Killed two White females in Louisiana, one in 1961 and one in 1964, raping, shooting, strangling, and stabbing his victims to death.

HARRY WILLIAMS: Killed one male and one female in Illinois, one in 1950 and one in 1951, bludgeoning and shooting his White and Black victims to death.

JERRY LEE WILLIAMS: Killed two to three females in Florida between 2004 and 2007, raping and strangling his victims to death. He has been cordial and is willing to help me with my project, stating, "I regret very much the things I have done in my past."

JOHN WILLIAMS JR.: Killed four to six Black females in North Carolina in 1996, raping, bludgeoning, and strangling his victims to death.

JOSEPH WILLIAMS: Killed four males in Georgia between 1999 and 2003, shooting, stabbing, and strangling his White and Black victims to death. His last victim was a fellow inmate. He has been cordial and willing to help me, and mused, "I once had a narrow perspective, but it is the darkness which has led me to the light."

KENNETH WILLIAMS: Killed one White male and one White female in Florida in 2000, robbing and strangling his victims to death.

KENNETH D. WILLIAMS: Killed two males and one female in Arkansas in 1998 and 1999, robbing and shooting his White and Black victims to death.

LARON RONALD WILLIAMS: Killed two males and one female in Tennessee between 1977 and 1981, shooting and strangling his victims to death.

LARRY LESTER WILLIAMS: Killed two victims in Florida, one in 1980 and one in 2004.

MICHAEL JEROME WILLIAMS: Killed two Black victims in Georgia and Florida, one in 1998 and one in 1999, raping and strangling his White and Black victims to death.

RAYMOND WILLIAMS: Killed one male and one female in Pennsylvania, one in 1989 and one in 1992, shooting and strangling his victims to death.

ROBERT E. WILLIAMS JR.: Killed three White females in Nebraska and Iowa in 1977, raping and shooting his victims to death.

RONNIE KEITH WILLIAMS: Killed two Black females in Florida, one in 1984 and one in 1993, raping and stabbing his victims to death. He was released from prison to kill again.

ROY L. WILLIAMS: Killed a White male and a Black male in Massachusetts and Pennsylvania in 1988, shooting his victims to death.

SIDNEY WILLIAMS: Killed three males in Louisiana in 1989, shooting his victims to death.

TERRANCE WILLIAMS: Killed two Black males in Pennsylvania in 1984, bludgeoning and stabbing his victims to death.

TOM WILLIAMS: Killed four White victims in Georgia between 1940 and 1954, robbing, shooting, and stabbing his male and female victims to death.

WAYNE BERTRAM WILLIAMS: Responsible for "The Atlanta Child Murders," he killed thirty young Black victims in Atlanta, Georgia between 1979 and 1981. His victims were children and young men whom he bludgeoned, shot, stabbed, smothered, and strangled to death. He killed twenty-eight males and two females. There was plenty of physical evidence to convict him, but he has maintained his innocence.

STEVE L. WILLIAMSON: Killed one male and one female in New York and Florida, one in 1991 and one in 1997, bludgeoning his Black and Asian victims to death.

CHARLES WILLIAM WILLIS: Killed two males in North Carolina, one in 2016 and one in 2017.

FRED WILLIS: Killed two females in Nevada and California, one in 1984 and one in 1997, raping and strangling his victims to death.

HERBERT TITUS WILSON: Killed two victims in Florida, one in 2000 and one in 2003.

RICHARD WILSON: Killed four Black victims in Georgia between 1991 and 2014, shooting his male and female victims to death.

ANTHONY RENE WIMBERLEY: Killed three females in California in 1984 and 1985, robbing and shooting his victims to death.

JEREMY CURTARUS WINTERS: Killed two Black males in Alabama, one in 2004 and one in 2005, robbing and shooting his victims to death.

JESSE LEE WISE: Killed two White victims in Missouri, one in 1971 and one in 1988, robbing, bludgeoning, and shooting his male and female victims to death.

OTTO WITHERS: Killed two Black females in North Carolina, one in 1966 and one in 1982, shooting his victims to death.

JAMES WOODRIDGE: Killed one male and one female in Texas, one in 1961 and one in 1976, smothering his victims to death.

FREDERICK WOOTEN JR.: Killed two females in New York, one in 1993 and one in 1994, raping and strangling his victims to death.

DWAYNE ALLEN WRIGHT: Killed three Black victims in Virginia, Maryland and Washington, DC in 1989 at the age of seventeen, shooting his male and female victims to death.

MICHAEL WRIGHT: Killed two Black victims in New York, one in 2012 and one in 2013, raping and shooting his victims to death. One of his victims was held captive for a month.

MICHAEL WRIGHT: Killed one Black male and one Black female in Mississippi, one in 2012 and one in 2013, shooting and strangling his victims to death.

SAMUEL CARLTON WRIGHT: Killed two Black victims in Florida, one in 1991 and one in 2012, shooting his male and female victims to death. He was sent to prison for his first murder and was released to kill again. His second victim was his girlfriend, whom he shot three times in the head.

FELIPE WYATT: Killed five victims in Georgia in 1994, shooting his victims to death.

GREGORY WYNDER: Killed two Black females in New York, one in 1997 and one in 2001, stabbing and strangling his victims to death.

MOSES YORK: Killed two males in Mississippi and Arkansas in 1900.

HERBERT YOUNGBLOOD: Killed two victims in Michigan and Indiana, one in 1933 and one in 1934, shooting his victims to death.

DONALD EUGENE YOUNGE JR.: Responsible for "The Garbage Bag Murders," he killed between four and six females in Illinois and Utah in 1999 and 2000, raping, stabbing, and strangling his White and Black victims to death. He began his crime spree as a rapist, and three of his murders were Illinois sex workers. His fourth murder was a Utah home invasion. He has since been exonerated for these crimes, although some still believe he is responsible for some of these murders.

WANT MORE PHIL CHALMERS?

I want to thank you for reading this first serial killer book of mine, and I hope you weren't only entertained, but you learned something valuable that might help you keep you and your family safe. If you want to continue to explore my content, the first step I recommend is to check out my website, www.philchalmers.com. You will find everything you are looking for on my website, including links to my socials, podcast, tour dates, and SWAG.

After exploring my website, I would suggest you follow my Instagram account, send me a Facebook friend request or follow, and subscribe to my YouTube channel. There you can continue to view my research and interviews and keep up with crime on a daily basis. I post almost daily about serial killers, mass murderers, violent crime, and school shootings. You can find direct links to all of my social media pages on my website.

Another great resource would be my podcast, which is owned by actor Dennis Quaid. I did twenty episodes on that podcast, recording two seasons. The podcast is called "Where The Bodies Are Buried," and as of this writing, it is still up. The other place to watch my interviews would be my YouTube channel, which I think you will really enjoy.

For a real up close and personal experience, I would recommend you come to one of my live appearances. I tour constantly, doing both professional trainings for law enforcement and school employees, as well as some more relaxed appearances at places like wineries, breweries, and country clubs. My "Serial Killers: The Experience" tour is lit, and attendees are going crazy over the content. Check out my tour schedule on my website, grab a few tickets, and bring some friends to an unforgettable evening show. This is about as close as you can get to a serial killer without being their cellie.

I also have more books on Amazon, my first two major releases dealing with juvenile killers and school shooters. Those titles are *Inside the Mind of a Teen Killer* and *The Teen Killer Whisperer.* And lastly, you can represent the Phil Chalmers nation by wearing some of my SWAG. I have an online merchandise store that you can access on my website, and you can sport my latest true crime designs, my "Serial Killers: The Experience" tour logo, my Punisher speaking logo, and grab a T-shirt, a hoodie, or a wine tumbler.

In the spring of 2026, I will be opening a true crime museum in Mount Airy, North Carolina, the hometown of Andy Griffith. The museum will be called "Serial Killers: The Experience," and it will be a one-of-a-kind immersive serial killer experience. You will be entertained, educated, and have your mind blown. Watch my website and socials for details.

I want to thank you so much for your interest and support, and please let me know if you ever need anything from me. You can reach me on my website, message me on my socials, or just send me an email at BookPhilChalmers@ gmail.com. My wife Wendi and I appreciate and love you all. Please be safe out there!

ABOUT THE AUTHOR

Phil Chalmers is an American profiler with a forty-year career of interviewing serial killers, as well as school shooters, mass murderers, and other dangerous killers. He is also a true crime writer with numerous titles under his belt, including the landmark book *Inside the Mind of a Teen Killer*, where he shared the valuable information about why today's teens are committing murder. He also hosted the Dennis Quaid-owned podcast "Where The Bodies Are Buried," which hit the Top 50 podcast charts in the world, and had over one million downloads in the first season. Phil has appeared on many television shows, including *Killer Kids* on A&E, *Killer Teens* on Bio, and *Crime Watch Daily* on Fox.

Phil's law enforcement profiling trainings are legendary in the US, as he trains law enforcement and the FBI all across America. His new live evening show, "Serial Killers: The Experience," is gaining a lot of fans as he allows civilians to attend and get the same training law enforcement gets at his professional trainings, with a little bit of entertainment and fun.

Phil is married to his beautiful wife Wendi and they have two deaf dogs, a Boxer named Daisy and a Pitbull named

Lily. Phil and Wendi are opening a true crime museum in Mount Airy, North Carolina in the Spring of 2026, called "Serial Killers: The Experience," and they will retire in that town. In their spare time when not touring, Phil and Wendi love music, travel, fitness, cruise ships, Disney, wineries, and watching movies.

One of Phil's mottos in life, which is also his favorite Bible verse, is tattooed on his chest. The verse is Philippians 4:13, and it reads: "You can do all things through Christ who gives you strength."

*For More News About Phil Chalmers,
Signup For Our Newsletter:*

http://wbp.bz/newsletter

Word-of-mouth is critical to an author's long-term success. If you appreciated this book please leave a review on the Amazon sales page:

https://wbp.bz/stter

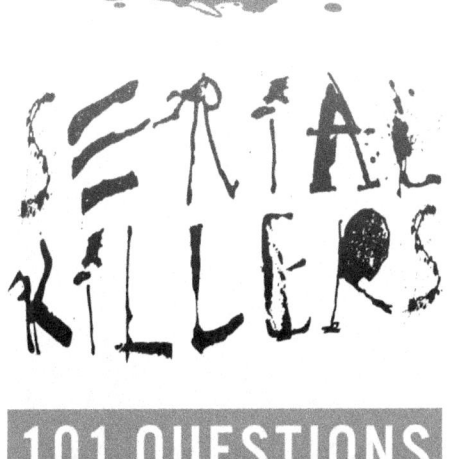

www.ingramcontent.com/pod-product-compliance
Lightning Source LLC
Chambersburg PA
CBHW061138120626
46546CB00005B/1839